The Color of
Atmosphere

The Color of Atmosphere

One Doctor's Journey
In and Out of Medicine

MAGGIE KOZEL, MD

Chelsea Green Publishing
White River Junction, Vermont

Project Manager: Patricia Stone
Editorial Contact: Susan Warner
Developmental Editor: Jonathan Cobb
Copy Editor: Laura Jorstad
Proofreader: Eileen M. Clawson
Designer: Peter Holm, Sterling Hill Productions

Printed in the United States of America
First printing January, 2011
10 9 8 7 6 5 4 3 2 1   11 12 13 14 15

Our Commitment to Green Publishing

Library of Congress Cataloging-in-Publication Data
Kozel, Maggie, 1955-
  The color of atmosphere : one doctor's journey in and out of medicine /
Maggie Kozel.
     p. cm.
  Includes bibliographical references.
  ISBN 978-1-60358-297-1
  1. Kozel, Maggie, 1955- 2. Pediatricians--Rhode Island--Biography. 3.
Chemistry teachers--Rhode Island--Biography. 4. Medical care--United
States. I. Title.
  RJ43.K69A3 2011
  618.9200092--dc22
  [B]
                              2010040750

Chelsea Green Publishing
Post Office Box 428
White River Junction, VT 05001
(802) 295-6300
www.chelseagreen.com

DEDICATION

For Randy, of course

CONTENTS

AUTHOR'S NOTE

All the events and patient encounters I present in this book are real, and I accurately describe them to the best of my memory. The names of all patients and their families have been changed to respect patient confidentiality, and I have altered a few students' names as well. In a few instances when I describe a typical encounter in general terms, such as the well-baby visit with "Matthew," I use compilation characters for purposes of illustration. On the few occasions when I portrayed a health professional in a potentially compromising light, I have changed that professional's name, out of respect to her own doctor–patient relationships. Most of the health care professionals I have come to know over the past two decades have my deep respect and admiration, and I have used their actual names with pride and affection.

INTRODUCTION

Back in 1980, as a fourth-year medical student at Georgetown University, I attended a panel discussion chaired by Senator Edward Kennedy on the cost of health care. The premise of the discussion was that soon our nation would not be able to sustain traditional fee-for-service health care, in which the doctor sets the fee, and the patient or health insurance company pays it. There was little question that the United States was home to some of the most advanced and remarkable medical resources on the planet. The problem, as Senator Kennedy saw it, was that we were not going to be able to afford to deliver these medical miracles to our citizens much longer if we didn't change the way we paid for health care. Payments for doctors' fees and other medical services were going to have to be regulated and, in some instances, limited. Most of us sitting in that auditorium, medical students and doctors-in-training, listened with skepticism. We were aware of some of the trends in medical economics, but we were also products of our society. And our society, back in the 1970s and '80s, was in denial.

It seemed unbelievable to me back then, sitting in that sea of white lab coats, that the time-honored, traditional doctor–patient relationship could be tampered with. I was not alone in thinking that employers, insurance companies, and legislators had no business interfering with how a doctor practiced medicine. Nourished by a blend of naïveté, idealism, and self-importance, most of us in the hospital auditorium that morning felt secure that our traditional role in determining the allocation of medical resources for our patients was inviolable. The idea that these resources would not be limitless, and that the clinical choices offered to our patients would often be out of the physician's control, was too unsettling to be embraced. The notion that these clinical decisions would be made by nonphysicians seemed absurd.

As the health care drama unfolded over the next few decades, I viewed it from a different vantage point from most of the doctors I sat with in the auditorium that day. I went through medical school on a navy scholarship and spent my first, formative decade as a pediatrician in the US military, with its universal, single-payer health coverage. Every family I treated, no matter their financial circumstances, had the same ready access to state-of-the-art health care, and no money ever changed hands. My only job was to practice good medicine. Meanwhile, in the civilian world, skyrocketing health costs and societal trends were turning patients into consumers, changing the doctor–patient relationship in profound ways. Health care insurers, otherwise known as third-party payers, were putting a stranglehold on the way doctors practiced. Malpractice lawyers carved out a lucrative niche from the inherently risky business of medicine, driving up the cost of malpractice insurance, at the same time that health insurers were siphoning off a huge portion of our precious health care dollars to support bloated administrative costs. Primary care doctors—internists, family practitioners, pediatricians—were spending more and more of their time as gatekeepers, paper pushers, and customer service representatives, watching their own incomes erode, squeezing more and more patients into harried schedules, and rarely speaking a word or making a chart entry that was not, at its core, defensive. Their patients, meanwhile, struggled to afford the care offered. Health care was looking more and more like an industry, and less like a human service.

These changes may have seemed gradual, if unrelenting, to most of my colleagues, but they were sudden and seismic for me the moment I left the navy. I resigned from active duty in 1988, and so was already a seasoned pediatrician by the time I was dropped into this churning sea of civilian health care that was practiced for profit. In the years that followed, I would find to my dismay that these swirling currents of change carried me farther and farther away from the doctor I had been.

My journey through medicine is in many ways a very personal story. Like any other doctor on the planet, my attitudes and perspectives were shaped to a significant degree by where I came from, and who influenced me. But my personal journey plays out against the backdrop of our changing health care system and is intertwined with it. As the story of my career moves from the bubble of academia, through the military system, and on into managed care and private practice, this book becomes not just about me, but also about how our method of paying for health care, with its complicated array of incentives and disincentives, profoundly influences the way medicine is practiced and the quality of care that is delivered.

We all need to understand the way that our reimbursement methods have shaped the way medicine is practiced. Otherwise, our attempts to improve the quality and accessibility of health care, as well as its cost-effectiveness, are likely to miss the mark. In our "health-industrial complex," standards of medical practice and public health policy are set in the boardrooms of insurance companies as much as they are in the halls of academia. Now, more than ever, clinical decisions are based on who gets paid for what. Pediatricians are managing serious psychiatric conditions, diagnosing learning disorders, and valiantly fighting against childhood obesity not because we are the most expert or cost-effective professionals to do this, but because too often we are the professionals whom insurers are more likely to pay. We take on things we probably shouldn't because, if we don't, who will? At the same time, pharmaceutical companies cast a wide net of influence with massive marketing, profit-driven research, and powerful lobbyists shaping the therapies we choose. As a result, health-for-profit, as it now exists, is often at odds with the best that modern medical science has to offer.

These trends, and the tethering of health insurance to employment, as well as the growing out-of-pocket expenses patients incur, have fueled a sense of consumerism among patients, and too often this translates into a "more is better" expectation, where every cold deserves an expensive antibiotic, every sore back warrants an MRI, and elective surgery should be scheduled as promptly as a haircut.

As patient's attitudes change, physician behavior changes as well. Like most pediatricians, I did my part to put a scientific spin on our approach to learning disorders, trying to convince myself as well as my patients that my office was the most appropriate place for this to happen. I patiently played along with obsessive discussions on toilet training, trying to rationalize the toll such indulgence took on precious health care dollars. I tried to meet parents' expectations—to get the child to sleep through the night, or get back to day care, or not be sick on Thanksgiving—as if these things, and not the dangers of over-intervention, were the more serious health concerns. In short, I, like my colleagues, helped put the *dys* in what had become a dysfunctional relationship. In the process, I moved farther and farther away from what I was trained to do, to the point that I almost couldn't recognize the doctor I had become.

This growing sense of alienation and disillusionment is widespread among doctors. A survey of physicians by the Massachusetts Medical Society back in 2003[1] revealed that less than 50 percent of physicians under the age of sixty, if given the chance to do it all again, would choose a career in medicine. Follow-up surveys since then have shown no change in that level of physician dissatisfaction.[2] Workplace satisfaction is not the only issue, not even the biggest one. A national survey conducted in 2010 by Sermo,[3] a large online physician network, documented physicians' anger and frustration in greater depth. One startling result start was that only one-fifth of doctors felt they could make clinical decisions based on what was best for the patient, rather than what insurance paid for. This feedback matters to all of us, because the reason that so many doctors, especially primary caregivers, are unhappy is closely related to the complicated ills of our current health care system. To understand one is to go a long way toward understanding the other.

This book says a lot about medical education and the daily routine of pediatric practice, pointing out the ever-widening gap between how pediatricians are trained and what they are expected and paid to do. It is also about the expectations of the public, and the powerful pressures those expectations exert on doctors. It is about the economics of health care, and the degree to which medical practice is shaped by health insurance reimbursements and pharmaceutical marketing rather than by science. In the end, my agonizing decision to leave medical practice parallels the disconnect between the incredible possibilities of modern medicine and the ways our health care system falls short of delivering them.

How can we best utilize our considerable medical resources in a way that we can afford? Who should decide how health care dollars are spent? Just how well does our system of private health insurance serve us? What are the moral and economic imperatives of universal health coverage? Can we even agree on what it means to be healthy? These are complex questions, but we have to face them, for the sake of our own health and that of our economy. It is my hope that understanding one doctor's experience in a variety of health care settings over a span of two decades and her ultimate decision to leave the profession she loved may offer some insight into the ways our current health care system defines medical practice—for doctors and patients—and what implications that has for reform.

ONE

Big Dreams in a Small Place

I remember the exact moment I knew I wanted to be a doctor. I was a sophomore in high school, staring out beyond the rattling windowpane of a cramped, overheated school bus, when my future suddenly reached in through the window and grabbed me.

There was nothing exceptional about the morning until that moment. As usual, I had awakened to kitchen noises, riddled with tension, making their way through my bedroom wall.

"Oh, for Christ's sake, Helen. The coffee's weak."

The sound of the metal coffeepot striking the stovetop was as effective as an alarm clock. Leaving my huddle of blankets and dog, I dressed for school like I did every weekday, hiking up the blue uniform skirt of Maria Regina High School, picking out socks from the flotsam and jetsam of laundry that seemed to cover every horizontal surface in the house. When the endless arguing that functioned as atmosphere in our home wasn't too close or vicious to ignore, I grabbed a bowl of cereal. At the last minute, I always ducked into the grimy bathroom to sneak on some makeup before bolting out the back door.

There was usually time for a cigarette at the corner before the bus came. Once the bus hit the highway on its hour-long, nauseating drive toward the Blessed Virgin Mary, I craned and shifted in my seat for a bit of conversation. Then I started my homework. And for long moments I stared out the window, dreaming up a future.

At one time I had considered being a nurse, but that memory doesn't really distinguish itself from my other dreams to be an actress or a teacher. The closest thing I had to a medical role model was a TV heartthrob, young Dr. Kildare, and in truth I really just wanted to marry him. The only doctor I knew growing up was Dr. Malinski, the town's scary general practitioner. His tiny waiting room held little but a few plastic chairs, some outdated issues of *Life* magazine, and the warning smell of antiseptic. A louvered door separated the waiting area from the exam room; confidentiality slipped through those wooden slats as easily as the doctor's thick Polish accent.

When I was eight years old, I was brought before Dr. Malinski for an infected cut on my arm. He shouted at my mother for not bringing me in sooner. "You're lucky she doesn't need an amputation!" I left his office ashamed for the hundredth time of our family's dereliction, and in a panic over the offending limb. For days I obsessively checked under the bandage, sure that my arm was going to rot off at the elbow. It didn't, and my relief at retaining all my body parts was followed closely by the relief of not having to face the wrath of medicine again for a while.

My early education hardly fostered a career in science. In Catholic elementary school in the 1960s, I was using my emerging cognitive skills to memorize the Baltimore Catechism.

> Is God all-wise, all-holy, all-merciful, and all-just?
> Yes, God is all-wise, all-holy, all-merciful, and all-just.

Science was discussed on a smaller scale. Mrs. Haffey, the elementary school's sole science teacher, pushed her rolling cart of observable facts into each classroom for one period a week. I vaguely remember one discussion of how water turns to ice, but I entered high school still largely shielded from the distractions of scientific thought.

Then I found myself in Mr. McCormick's sophomore biology class. It was love at first sight—not for Mr. McCormick, though he actually was kind of cute, but for the revelations that emerged from under the microscope and in the dissecting pans. Biology class in Maria Regina High School was where I discovered the divine, watching my teacher turn chalk and slate into the intricate wonder of a dividing cell. In biology lab, mesmerized by planarians swimming around on a glass slide, I became fervently interested in just what begat what. I traced the exquisite nervous system of an earthworm with reverence, and as I probed the evolutionary miracle of a frog's three-chambered heart, I felt connected with an existence much larger than myself. The more I learned, the hungrier I was to know more. I had found my passion.

At fifteen, the worried child of an alcoholic family, I was hardly on the fast track for a brilliant career. By the time I had my school bus epiphany, I had been smoking on and off for five years, included alcohol in most social events, and had done more than my fair share of experimenting with drugs and boys. But there I sat on the bus that morning, staring out that window, hoping for a future. In defiance of my lifestyle, my gender, even my shaky history with the healing profession, I connected the dots. I could be a doctor. At a focal point somewhere just beyond that pane of glass, every ray of confidence and hope I could generate converged to form a marvelous image—an attractive, grown-up me in a white coat, handily diagnosing illnesses, ordering tests, writing prescriptions. Happy. Successful. Respected. In the span of a few electrifying moments, a daydream had turned into a life plan. I didn't worry if I was smart enough. I never considered that I might not get into medical school or bothered to count the years it would take before I could step out into practice. I knew where I was going, and that was all that mattered. I had a life somewhere else waiting for me.

I just had to survive the next few years.

The key to survival in my childhood home was flying below the radar. My three older siblings never chose this strategy, preferring to engage the enemy head-on in never-ending battles in a hopeless war. Helen Marie, the oldest, and named for my mother, was a bright and beautiful target who had already endured ten years of parental viciousness by the time I arrived on the scene.

"You're not happy unless you're destroying things for everybody!" my mother would shriek when Helen Marie revealed her evil nature by leaving the milk out on the counter or lingering in front of the bathroom mirror too long. "What the hell did I ever do to deserve this?"

Helen Marie was not one to turn the other cheek. "Maybe you're unhappy because you drink all day," she spat out defiantly.

"I have to drink just to keep my sanity in this goddamn house!"

My mother's voice grew shriller with each challenge, her face more florid.

"You just have to get her started, don't you, Helen?" my father would hiss at her. There was no confusion about which Helen he was attacking. He never challenged my mother like that.

"I wish the whole goddamn lot of you had never been born!" my mother wept as she retreated upstairs, a can of beer in one hand, her transistor radio in the other. She never missed Billy Graham's inspirational message.

I had no heart for the fight. It became family legend that as a baby, long before I should have been expected to talk, I would stand up in my crib at the first signs of an argument and implore, "Everybody love everybody!" My parents told and retold this story as if the essential truth in it was how precocious and sweet I was. They never felt the shame in it. By fifteen, I knew they would never figure out the point of that story. I wished I could figure out how to make them happy. But mostly, I just wanted to get away.

The New York town where I grew up, Point Lookout, is the easternmost tip of a sliver of beachfront that hangs off the South Shore of Long Island. Its beach cottages had been winterized in the 1940s and '50s by my parents' generation, many of whom, like my parents, were Irish Americans from the boroughs of New York City. The isolated town, only eleven blocks long and three blocks wide, was home to only a few hundred year-round families at that time, but supported four bars, a liquor store, two restaurants with bars, and a grocery store and deli that each sold beer—except on Sunday mornings.

By the late 1960s and early 1970s, teenagers were spilling out of the cramped houses, many driven to the streets not only by lack of space but also by the misery that filled their homes. We congregated on the street corner outside the luncheonette—me and Jane Fay and Terise Ianfola, Margaret Platt and Nancy Murphy, with all the longhaired, bell-bottomed boys—tugging on cigarettes and exhaling laughter at an endless stream of inside jokes. We paired off, played politics, shared secrets, mocked everything—and planned parties. Alcohol, the very thing that was sucking the life out of so many of our families, was part of the glue that held our young group together. It was what we had been taught.

One afternoon, not long after I had set my optimistic sights on a medical career, I was huddled with my friends outside the luncheonette when I saw my mother staggering out of Merola's grocery store, her limp hair the same ugly tan as her trench coat, a six-pack of beer under her arm. She was single-handedly carrying on some argument that must have started inside the store.

"You're all full of crap," she hollered in disgust at the storefront. "All you care about is your lousy money. Go to hell, all of you!"

Acute embarrassment at this public display led me to abandon my instincts and leave the safety of the herd to go to her, hoping to quiet her somehow, hoping to control the damage. I saw my mistake too late. Those blue eyes, *my* blue eyes, met me with hate and fury. There, in the middle of the boulevard, she turned on me with the same venom she usually reserved for my siblings and father.

"What the hell are you looking at, with that stupid look on your face?" She punctuated this by slapping my stupid face, hard. "I'll tell you what you look like," she went on hysterically, "like some kind of trollop, hanging out on a corner with your useless friends. I thought I raised you better than this, Maggie. You're no better than the rest of them." Cars slowed down to gawk and my friends tried to look away. Burning with shame, I turned back to the corner, where the herd swallowed me back up and offered their support the only way they knew how, by trying to act as if nothing had happened.

I approached my father after dinner to demand that he do something, say something, to Mom. Already mellowed by half a bottle of wine, his bushy eyebrows raised in resignation over a blank stare, Dad fell back on his tried-and-true advice: "We can't feel sorry for ourselves, Maggie. Keep your chin up." Fortunately for me, I had a more substantial plan.

Which is not to say that I cleaned up my act—at least not completely. But I took charge. I signed up for every science and math course I could schedule and was able to precisely calculate the minimum amount of work needed in each course to get straight A's. Even the sneering chemistry teacher, Mr. Chalmers, disdainful of my eye shadow and crowd of friends, didn't deter me. If my mother was passed out on the sofa when I got home from school, I headed for my room, popped in an eight-track, and did as much trigonometry or French as I could before the ticking bomb outside my door exploded, as it always would.

"Oh God, I wish I were dead," she'd moan—her usual ten-second warning. Then—*Kaboom!*

"I hate you, I hate every damn one of you."

As she ranted at my brother Brian, or me, or the TV, or God, I would grab a book and run, slamming the broken screen door behind me in recrimination.

"Oh no, Maggie, not you. Come back!" she'd wail through the open window. "You're the only decent thing in this house!" Three scapegoats had apparently been enough for my mother. With my eagerness to please, to keep the peace, to hold our shattered family together, I was the trophy child that would vindicate her. She couldn't have me running off.

Turnabout was sad play. Half a dozen years earlier, when I was a little girl who believed that Helen Marie really was the reason that Mom drank, and Johnny really was a disappointment, and Brian really couldn't help being a "pain in the ass," I would run sobbing down the block after her, pleading with her not to leave us again.

"Mom," I begged, "come back. They didn't mean it. We'll be better." But she always kept storming on. My pleading only served to heighten her dramatic moment. She would stay away just long enough to punish us for her misery.

Now, in my teenage years, I was on the run, and the sound of her shrieked soliloquy mercifully receded as I hurried down the street, past the neighbors closing their front windows, past the kids looking up uneasily at me from their game of stickball. Even as I escaped out of earshot I knew what she would be saying; Mom always stuck to the script. She would be up to the part about my father:

"If he were any kind of real man"—most of the neighbors, a seasoned audience at the town's own *Rocky Horror Picture Show,* could have filled in the blanks by now—"he wouldn't allow me to live in this hellhole!"

As a younger girl, I would have ducked into the sanctuary of Aunt Dorothy's house at this point. She lived down the street from us in a sweet, doll-like home where the floors were always swept clean. I knew I could find refuge there and not have to answer any questions, taking unspoken comfort in the Nabisco cookies she served me on flowered antique china. No matter how badly my parents treated her, nothing would weaken her loyalty to my siblings and me. It was Aunt Dorothy, my father's sister, who kept offering me lifesaving examples of what a loving relationship could be.

But now, the wounded teenager seeking escape more than comfort, I pressed on, my unruly mutt Chip trotting close behind. By the time Chip and I were stamping our footprints onto the empty beach, Mom would have popped open another Ballantine, her anger diffused to a low rumble. As for me, sinking into the warmth of the leeward side of a sand dune, I would get back to work. I could study almost anywhere, even propped up against a KEEP OFF THE DUNES sign, with Chip darting around me, kicking sand all over my papers and shaking the Atlantic Ocean at me from his coat.

By my senior year of high school, I put my faith in the Jesuits to get me into medical school: I applied to the premed program at Fairfield University in Connecticut. I kept pushing. I worked after school at the library and all summer at the beach to earn money. I babysat every chance I got for the family of a prominent Manhattan physician. Dr. Cahill, a product of Ivy League academia, talked to me about my future in medicine as if I were the most likely candidate in the world. "You're different, Maggie," he said to me one time, his intellectual drawl reminding me of Mr. Howell on *Gilligan's Island*. "When I look at you I see your strength." I couldn't always tell what he was getting at, and if he thought I was strongly constructed, then that was just further proof of what could slip by the notice of adults. But I was relieved that I could fool him, and pleased that he approved of me and my plans.

One night when Dr. Cahill was walking me home, he began to tell me about his upbringing in a large Irish Catholic family; he understood how difficult it was to grow up with an alcoholic parent. We both knew what he was referring to, but I was too stunned and embarrassed to respond. Never in all my sixteen years had any adult who had witnessed my parents' mean brand of drunkenness—not aunts, uncles, grandparents, the priests who lived across the street, teachers, or neighbors—never before had any of them made even the most oblique acknowledgment to me of the daily horror show I called my home.

Dr. Cahill must have wondered, as we walked on in silence, if his surprising story had fallen on deaf ears. It hadn't, but it took a while to appreciate fully what had happened on that summer stroll. Without benefit of lab coat or beeper, Dr. Cahill had shown me what a real doctor could do. He wasn't so easily fooled after all. He could look straight at pain without averting his eyes. He saw what needed healing without being told, and he said what needed to be said. The Medical Barbie of my school bus vision, no longer up to the task, stepped aside. I was beginning to flesh out my own image. I wanted to be able to do what Dr. Cahill could do.

Fairfield accepted me. I was getting closer. I kept up my grades, worked two or three jobs at a time, and went home only to sleep. I secretly white-knuckled my way through horrifying panic attacks, not understanding what they were. I didn't get pregnant. I saved my money. I packed. And on a hot September day in my seventeenth year, with little but my frayed jeans and a crate full of record albums for comfort, I stepped off the edge of a precarious world, into my own life.

TWO

Safe Landing

When my parents dropped me off at Fairfield University, its rolling campus nestled in the handsome landscape of suburban Connecticut, I was overcome with terror. It was like landing on strange shores after a harrowing sea voyage. I had become so accustomed to the boat's pitch and roll that I didn't recognize solid ground when I first felt it under my feet. But terra firma it proved to be, a land inhabited for the most part by reasonable, predictable people, a safe harbor.

I met Nancy Ryan's wardrobe before I met the girl. My new roommate had arrived for freshman orientation some hours earlier, and the Ryan clan already had her unpacked and had taken off for a tour of campus. The plaid kilts hanging in her closet and the fuzzy pink slippers tucked under her bed suggested an alien being I would have little in common with. Over the next four years, as we moved together from the freshman dorm to an upperclassman room to a tiny beachfront apartment where she baked bread and tended plants, I never stopped teasing Nancy about her wholesome ways. That didn't keep me, though, from devouring the quiches and breads that emerged from our miniature oven, or from proudly wearing the dusky blue raglan sweater she knit for my birthday, or from being captivated by her remarkable ability to tell a good story.

Characters, unvarnished and irresistible, crammed our little dorm room—Father McInerney, the contemptuous English professor who held court in Canisius Hall, speaking in affected tongues, eating freshmen for breakfast, and Kenny, the handsome, cynical, skinny sophomore boy who came by every night to tell Nancy how he wasn't interested in a relationship, and Sue, her high school friend who now lived in New York City and kept getting lost on the subways. It was too generous to be gossip, too rich to be chat.

Nancy was insatiably curious about people, always asking them about themselves. Where I stood by and observed human activity, judging the emotional content by the feeling on the back of my neck, Nancy just dove in. She had lots of questions about John, my boyfriend back in Point Lookout who worked for a lobster company.

"Maggie," she'd ask out of the blue, looking at me intently, probing me with her eyes, "what if John stays a lobsterman? Would he stay home and raise the kids while you went to medical school?" She wanted to know what John was thinking, how I felt, where was it all going. I didn't even ask myself those questions.

I was slow to figure out why Nancy had stories. It wasn't that so many unusual things happened to her. It was that she saw the drama in things I barely even noticed. She paid attention, felt what was happening. She welcomed the little events of life for what they were, didn't try to put a lid on them the way I did. And once those moments were hers, she could artfully summon them back to life, coloring them with her humor and insight.

To Nancy, I must have seemed full of myself at times—too self-important in the way I talked about my studies, too uptight to go out for a beer with her during exam week. "Nancy," I would say with exasperation, "I have six chapters of organic chemistry I have to cover tonight." But Nancy, who preferred to sit around a smoky dorm room all evening in deep conversation and then stay up all night to turn out an A paper on Sylvia Plath, seemed to like me just fine the way I was, didn't criticize me or try to change me. She seemed content to watch my story unfold.

At the end of freshman year, Nancy decided she was going to switch to Fairfield's nursing program. I was surprised. She could analyze a poem or produce an insightful term paper as easily as I could solve a calculus problem. I was sure she was a natural English major. I don't know why I was surprised that someone who was so creative and intensely interested in other people would be drawn to the healing arts.

Unlike most of my friends, I settled down in college. I lugged chemistry and biology books down the steep path to the library every evening while most of my friends entertained themselves back at the dorm, halfheartedly reading assignments they couldn't put off any longer, stopping to chat at the slightest excuse. Once the library closed and I packed up my books and papers for the night, I would seek out whatever overcrowded room they were in, slide into a comfy corner, and allow myself to briefly reenter their world.

Academic life suited me. I rarely skipped class; I studied like a fiend. While my friends were pulling all-nighters, often with chemical assistance, I was meeting deadlines with time to spare for a good night's sleep and a nutritious breakfast. I was uptight to be sure, but very satisfied with my successes. At the end of freshman year, Dr. Boggio called me into his office to tell me how pleased he was with my work.

"Do not tell me you got the highest grade in your chemistry class!" laughed Nancy, waving me away with mock exasperation, shaking her head, smiling at my good fortune.

"I'm so proud of you," gushed Eileen.

"Way to go, girl," exhaled Mary through a puff of smoke. "I definitely see med school in your future."

Draped across my unmade bed, I soaked in the teasing and the affection. Such news flashes seldom made their way to my family, though. I hated telling my parents good news; it felt like I was patting them on the back. And I couldn't bear the thought of how they would use it as a weapon to belittle whichever of my siblings were still talking to them at the time. As for being in contact with my brothers or sister directly, I don't think that ever crossed any of our minds. Once we each escaped the orbit of our parents' home, we kept to our own paths.

Mary was right, of course. I did get into med school. In August 1976, I entered Georgetown University School of Medicine as one of forty women in a class of two hundred. Amid the blur of new faces and confusing schedules, I was completely aware that a dream had come true.

THREE

The Color of Atmosphere

A natomy lab was the only class we had aboveground the first year of medical school. For most of that year, we were sequestered in a windowless basement auditorium, straining to understand professors with exotic accents as they described how amino acids lined up to make DNA, or squinting in the dark at slides filled with complicated diagrams of how glucose is metabolized in the liver. This auditorium was our cocoon, where we sat untouched by the messy questions of human illness, fed only by a steady stream of facts.

But to get to anatomy lab, we had to climb the basement stairs, pass the medical library that was built into the ground like a bomb shelter, and take an elevator up to the sunny fourth floor. We were assigned to our cadavers alphabetically, so it was no coincidence that the most lasting friendships I formed in medical school were with a group of five guys whose last names started with *K* or *L*. We nicknamed our cadaver Pickles, and as we carried out the slow and often tedious work of dissection those first few months, the six of us got to know one another pretty well. As we bent over Pickles, teasing out cellophane-like layers of tissue, tracing fragile webs of nerves and blood vessels, we heard all about Chris's dog Bob, and how Kevin, shy and sweet, was tuning up his Datsun 240Z. Joe, who spoke only mumbling Brooklynese, kept us howling with laughter. And Steve flirted with Pickles in a style we would see him use with all the nurses in his future. We learned that Randy played football in college and meditated twice a day. He planned on going into psychiatry. I liked it when he talked; it gave me the perfect excuse to look at him. Sometimes I would just watch his hands, his long beautiful fingers bent gracefully, as still and perfect as a sculpture as they rested on his crossed legs. I liked him a lot.

I entertained the boys with stories of my odd assortment of roommates up on Wisconsin Avenue. They couldn't wait to meet Kathy, the daughter of a dairy farmer, who sported a forty-inch chest on her five-foot frame and never kept less than six dozen eggs in the refrigerator, pointedly labeled with her name in case one of us should get hungry for an omelet.

The guys were funny and irreverent and teased me mercilessly. I spent more time laughing with them than I would have thought possible in the company of a dead person. But that was just background. A semester in anatomy lab meant painfully slow dissections and endless memorization. We needed to have the bones of the hand on the tips of our tongues. We needed to know every blood vessel that fed into the intestinal tract, and what unpronounceable branches sprouted off the vagus nerve. Black humor gave us just enough distance to get the job done, but the reality of what we were doing with this foul-smelling, leathery form was inescapable. Pickles had been a real person, with a real life—like us. Anatomy lab made for a fitting passage into the study of medicine. There, amid the nerve tracing and the heart probing and the stench of departed soul, extraordinary knowledge was humbled by unflinching, naked mortality.

The bridge between the first two preclinical classroom years of medical school and the next two hospital-based years was a course the second year known as Physical Diagnosis, in which we were finally allowed to talk to—and even touch—living patients. I had taken it on faith up to this point that my course work would eventually turn me into a physician in a long white coat, saving lives and stamping out disease, but I hadn't quite grasped the pain and mess of translating all those bits of information into useful clinical skills. As in all lessons of life, the most important ones I learned in medical school were not those I was force-fed, but those I could accept with humility.

I was assigned to DC General Hospital for this Physical Diagnosis course and was paired with Randy once again. We read all about how to perform a thorough history and physical—which is like reading all about how to sail a boat while sitting safely on shore. Sitting in Randy's living room as we shared a pizza, we made a list of all the questions we should ask.

- Have you ever had double vision?
- Do you have ringing in your ears?
- Lumps in your neck? Burning in your feet?

Then we wrote down all the steps of a complete physical exam, starting at the top.

- Is there any unusual shape to the head?
- Does the hair appear brittle?

And so on. Completeness was our watchword.

The next day we donned our hospital name tags, bolstered by the thought that only the most astute patients would notice the MS (medical student) after our name instead of MD. We gathered our expensive new doctor toys—ophthalmoscope, otoscope, stethoscope, penlight—and packed them in our stiff new black bags, the kind used only by medical students and actors who play doctors on TV. We drove across town to DC General and wound our way through a maze of soiled hallways and slow-moving elevators to the internal medicine ward, clutching those little black bags as if they were life-support systems.

DC General was as far from Georgetown as you could get without a passport. For one thing, the nurses, all women of color, seemed exceedingly kind. They handled us like little lost lambs that were under no circumstances going to get slaughtered on their shift. This was a foreign practice to us, worlds away from the I-could-squash-you-like-a-bug receptions we had experienced from nurses on our brief forays into the healing halls at Georgetown. But "the General's" healing halls had problems, too. The floors weren't going to lose that grayish brown hue no matter how often they were scrubbed, and the walls wept for a new coat of paint. More important, the most highly trained person in the room was, too often, the one with MS on her coat.

Dr. Razi was the ward resident, an Iranian doctor who had come to the United States to do his internal medicine training. His last name wasn't Razi, but in Georgetown's orbit back in 1977, if your ethnic name was too hard to pronounce, you either got a nickname, like Razi, or were called by your first one. It did not occur to me to question such a workable arrangement.

Dr. Razi was nervous and skinny, with a wild look in his eye. He immediately began interrogating us about our role, as US citizens, in propping up the shah of Iran. He became agitated when he realized we had only a vague idea of what he was talking about. I guess I hadn't questioned US foreign policy too much, either. I couldn't wait till he found out how little we knew about heart murmurs.

Dr. Razi handed us a metal chart thick with handwritten pages. The first unsuspecting victim of our medical careers was an aging gentleman with alcoholic liver disease. Our job was simply to check him over from head to toe, to get the feel of what it was like to talk to and examine an actual patient. Randy and I sat down in a cluttered corner of the nurses' station and combed through that chart like it was the Dead Sea Scrolls, searching for the information that was going to make us feel like we knew what we were doing. That avenue had been pretty much exhausted by the time the revolutionary reappeared to get our sorry imperialistic butts in gear.

"Haven't you two started yet?" Dr. Razi demanded.

A few doors down, in a room with rows of beds separated by drapes that were hung like shower curtains, Mr. Williams was lying on his freshly made bed, waiting for us. He had dressed for company, with crisp blue pajamas and a seersucker bathrobe tied neatly at the waist. He had white hair and white teeth; his brown face was a little raw, as if he had just shaved. He looked pleased that we dropped by. If answers were what I craved back then, poised as I was on the threshold of my medical career, then Mr. Williams was just what the doctor ordered.

We all want answers that fit, that reassure us of our rightness, our competence. Nowhere is this truer than in medicine. We the initiates as well as the experienced, the doctors as well as the patients, tend to harvest our answers as selectively—and sometimes as foolishly—as we plant our questions.

Randy and I introduced ourselves, then produced the clipboard that held our list of questions and our physical exam cheat sheet. Mr. Williams, as calm and patient as a snow-covered garden, answered every one of our questions, the relevant ones and all the others, too. He assured us that he did not have facial pain, or droopy lids or fruity-smelling breath, or unusual rashes on his palms or soles. As I stood there perspiring in that stifling room, our patient relieved us of any concern that his heart skipped beats or that pain radiated down his legs. With unwavering dignity, he denied any troublesome penile discharges or scrotal swelling. And when he finished answering all those questions, Mr. Williams endured an equally exhaustive inquiry into his family history, straining for our sake to recall what he could about his grandparents' health at the turn of the previous century. He never asked for a glass of water, much less an attorney.

Talking was just the warm-up. After an hour or so of interrogation, which had probably violated several articles of the Geneva Conventions as well as the Hippocratic Oath, it came time for the physical. Randy and I double-teamed it, each of us causing the poor man temporary blindness, first in one eye and then the other, while doggedly looking for the optic nerve with our spiffy new halogen lights. We worked our way down the dusty surface of his body, looking for congenital malformations of the ear lobes, and farther down, concentrating on his heart sounds at great length so that we could correlate the lubs, dubs, and swishes we heard to the unseen machinations under his chest wall. We checked him for hernias and noted every brown spot that had come to grace this man's surface over the previous six or seven decades. To our credit, caught up as we were in mole counting and toenail inspection, we managed not to miss the yellow tinge of his eyes or the fact that the rubbery edge of Mr. Williams's liver, which we tried so insistently to locate at the bottom of the rib cage, actually extended several inches below it.

A diagnosis of alcoholic hepatitis. Enlarged liver. Got it.

Then, as now, nothing in this world seemed as satisfying as having the puzzle pieces fit together.

The formal mental status exam came last. Randy and I had finished our four-week psychiatry course and felt we knew a thing or two. We had conspired in advance to check our patient for alcohol-related brain damage. His unfaltering performance up to this point had somehow not settled the question for us. A supervising doctor had taught us a "trick" in assessing cortical function: Pretend to hold up a string, and ask the patient what color it is. The patient should of course respond that there is no string there. If he says it's pink or orange, he is confabulating, meaning his brain cortex isn't working so well. He is sure that there is a right answer, so he makes up an answer that he hopes will fit. So, with thumbs and forefingers pinched together, Randy held up an invisible string and asked this saintly man what color it was. It was our turn to be patient. After some time, Mr. Williams gave us his considered answer:

"It is the cullah of atmosphere."

A self-satisfied grin broke across Mr. Williams's face. Confused, I looked over at Randy. He was frowning at the string himself, as if wondering if he'd missed something. I scanned my clipboard uselessly. We were both startled into the sudden realization that all the factual information in the world couldn't protect you from uncertainty. Sometimes, it could even distract you from the truth. After all, it was the color of atmosphere. Except, of course, for the fact that there was no string.

Of all the pearls that Mr. Williams offered us that day, this was the one I would carry with me throughout my career as a pediatrician. Even as the practice of pediatrics evolved, the lesson never lost its relevance. We all have to be careful about how much we idealize, or even mystify, medical knowledge. It is a science and an art, not a belief. Doctors, like anyone, can get so comfortable with a practice that they neglect to question it, and we can all be misled as a result. There was, for example, pediatricians' relentless use of antibiotics to treat the middle ear fluid that was ubiquitous in our patients as we waged war, through the 1980s and '90s, against an imaginary epidemic of language delay that was supposed to occur if we didn't act. We had plenty of scientific studies to refer to, telling us which antibiotics did the best job of clearing microbes from the middle ear. There was plenty of supportive data from big-name ENT surgeons documenting that fluid in the ears could temporarily alter a child's ability to hear. All that information somehow obscured the fact that our goal was invisible. No one had ever shown that common middle ear fluid produced long-term language delay. And it would still be decades before most of us realized that overuse of antibiotics caused huge problems by promoting the growth of resistant strains of bacteria, while offering little benefit to our patients. We had devoured answers without asking the right questions.

There would be plenty of other examples in my future—outnumbered, but also camouflaged, by our true accomplishments. In the years that followed my visit with Mr. Williams, pediatricians would be handed the task of diagnosing ADHD, and it would be assumed that they could use their powers of persuasion to stem the tide of childhood obesity. We would all respond with dedication and commitment, stepping up to the plate in a game for which we didn't make the rules, but I for one have learned to pay attention to that elusive feeling that a strategy doesn't make sense, or that the goal has grown blurry. I learned, over decades of caring for patients, that when we really can't see the string clearly, we need to say so.

But back then, an initiate at Mr. Williams's bedside, I couldn't discern much beyond that hospital room. All I could see was the discomfort of uncertainty, and the seduction of an answer that fit. I slowly repacked my bag, neatly wedging my reflex hammer between the penlight and the coiled measuring tape, comforted by the way they all fit together. Randy and I said our thanks and good-byes as we backed out of the room and turned to face the dizzying traffic of the corridor, hoping to make our getaway without running into the difficult medical resident whose name I had already forgotten, hoping for a chance to regain our footing. We had just tripped over an unsettling reality that I was starting to sense more than see: It would not always be a simple matter to distinguish a satisfying answer from the truth.

FOUR

The Heart of the Matter

Iwill always remember the third year of medical school as the year I fell in love. I don't mean with Randy, who indeed remained my partner well beyond our Physical Diagnosis course—that love story took a little longer to unfold. No, what I fell head-over-heels in love with, to have and to hold from that day forward, was the beautiful mystery of the human body, and the exquisite art of healing it. It is hard to name what it is that makes a good doctor, just as it is to define a good teacher, or a good mother, even though we all know one when we see her. I believe the defining factor is this: At one point or another, they fell in love with their work. Back then, I assumed it was till-death-do-us-part love, and I was going to let nothing get in the way of my pursuit.

In our third year at Georgetown, we began working in the hospitals full-time. We were assigned to a team that worked with an "attending physician"—the specialist in charge—and directly supervised by the most senior doctor-in-training on the team, the chief resident. The short white jackets that medical students were required to wear made us stand out among the real doctors like dislocated thumbs.

My first assignment was with the surgery service, my first attending physician was Dr. Conrad, a famous but intimidating cardiothoracic surgeon, and my first day was spent in the operating room. Mrs. Babson, a woman I had met briefly the night before, was having the mitral valve in her heart replaced.

It was barely dawn when I passed through the automatic doors marked OR Personnel Only and into an inner sanctum where no initiate felt welcome. Every green-clad person bustling around in there was busy. The woman I first asked directions of didn't even stop as she pointed me to the nurses' locker room. The rest of my team, all male, were changing on the other side of the hall, just off the doctors' lounge, so I was on my own as I surveyed the tall stacks of folded green scrubs next to the lockers. It was like being at the Gap, but with only one style and color to choose from. I changed quickly, found the door that led into the "clean" side of the OR suite, and took a few steps inside.

A huge board covered the wall behind the nurses' desk, like the arrival/departure board at a train station, listing what patient/ surgeon/procedure was in what operating room. My train was leaving from OR 10. Leery of asking for any more help, I wandered down the hall past big picture windows that looked into each room. It was hard to recognize people in their surgical garb.

"Are you lost?" asked another masked face.

"I'm looking for room ten," I said.

"C'mon." She sighed, as if I was the twelfth lost med student she'd had to rescue that morning. "This is really the chief resident's job."

We stopped at a room that looked identical to all the rest, and she stuck her head through a crack in the door. "I've got one of yours," she directed to the chief. "You might want to keep track of your students." I was causing trouble already. "Scrub up," she said to me in parting, and I turned to face the deep sinks against the wall.

The spray of water from the long, curved faucets completely doused me, and by the time I pushed my way through swinging doors into the OR, hands held up, elbows dripping, the front of my scrubs was soaked. The scrub nurse, already passing out instruments to the team, was delighted to interrupt what she was doing to hand me sterile towels. In a world inhabited by masked people, I was learning eye language very quickly. I methodically dried each finger, each hand, each arm, just as I had seen in the instructional video the day before, and then held out my arms to receive my sterile gown. For a moment, I was like Cinderella being gowned for the ball by a swirl of birds, as a team of anonymous hands pulled the gown back against my shoulders, wrapped it around me, tied it at my neck. My fingers waited, outstretched, as the scrub nurse took another break from her life-sustaining tasks to snap sterile gloves on my hands.

Except my ungloved hand brushed against her sterile arm.

"I'm contaminated," she announced to the room, and called for a clean gown. Dr. Conrad sighed deeply, and the chief resident shook his head. The anesthesiologist peeked out over his curtain at me, then went back to maintaining his patient in deep sedation while we made wardrobe changes. Once the scrub nurse regowned, she returned to the instrument table and the surgeons continued their work. I stood there gloveless, holding my inept hands up in the air where they couldn't get into trouble. An eternity later, a second nurse came around with a fresh package of gloves.

By the time I stepped up to the table, directly across from the newly decontaminated nurse, I was dehydrated from sweating and light-headed from hyperventilating. Dr. Conrad was the first to acknowledge me: "You're late." And then to the chief resident, "Does your medical student know the causes of mitral valve insufficiency?"

"I'm sure she does," he returned in the same third-person style. "Dr. Keavey, tell me three causes of mitral valve insufficiency in an adult, starting with the most common."

We were off and running. "Mitral valve prolapse, myocardial infarction, rheumatic heart disease." My gloved hands lay uselessly on the sterile field as I parried the questions they thrust at me while they worked. Classical music played in the background, softening the steady pulse of electronic beeps. Finally, an hour or so into the procedure, the team having worked their way through the chest cavity and down to the pulsing red heart lying pillowed in the lungs, I was handed a retractor—a small rake-like structure that holds back tissue so the surgeon can better visualize the field. My hand cramped as I doggedly kept the instrument in place, and my mouth parched as I answered the endless questions.

Gradually, I was given a little more to do. Dr. Conrad handed me the suction catheter. "Keep the tip there!" he instructed. My job was to keep the site from filling up with blood but, despite my best efforts, a small pool formed just where Dr. Conrad was about to make an incision. He grabbed the catheter away in disgust and handed it to the chief.

Finally, the patient was ready to go on cardiopulmonary bypass. Her blood flow would be redirected so that it was pumped out of

her body, oxygenated in a machine, and pumped back in, bypass-
ing the heart so that it could be stopped and operated on. While
the surgeons busied themselves with the bypass apparatus, I stood
mesmerized by the steady pumping of the fist-sized heart, blood still
surging through its chambers. I gingerly laid my fingers across the
heaving muscle. Everything else in the room slipped away as I felt it
pulsating to an ancient rhythm under my touch, connecting me to
the power and beauty of life itself.

I knew I would go through anything for this. I could handle the
old-boy, survival-of-the-fittest teaching style, the humiliation of feeling like the most ignorant one in the room, the long hours, the
inevitable failures and criticisms. It would all be worth it. I really
was in love.

The pace of events shifted rapidly as the heart was stopped and
bypass was established: Tubes were inserted into spurting vessels,
bleeding was controlled, rapid-fire commands passed back and
forth. My main role was to stay out of the way.

Things went poorly over the next several hours. The surgeons
struggled in vain to attach the artificial valve to the weakened heart
chamber, but everywhere they went, the tissue gave way, and the
bleeding eventually was unstoppable. Six hours after I had dripped
my way into that room, Mrs. Babson was pronounced dead. Her
defeated heart lay still and useless in its bed.

A calm came over the room as Dr. Conrad left to talk to the
family. A fresh shift of nurses came on duty, and the anesthesiologist began disconnecting all the tubes and lines that just moments
before had been so necessary. The chief resident and I remained at
the table to close up the remains of Mrs. Babson. He handed me
tweezer-like forceps and suturing thread connected to a crescent-
shaped needle. There was a lot of space that needed closing, and I
worked slowly with the unfamiliar instruments. The chief seemed
in no rush. There were no more interrogations, just quiet instruc-
tion as I reunited layer after layer of tissue. I had to pee really badly,
and my muscles were sore, but I was totally engrossed in the task,
as detached from my own human needs as I was from the human
drama of a passing life.

Still feeling the electricity that had surged through me at the touch of a beating heart, it seemed like I had stepped into a sacred circle, no longer an initiate. By the time I was running nylon thread through the skin, my wrist was carving smoothly through the air, laying down stitches in neat little slants.

There I am, a tireless and idealistic twenty-three-year-old, my gloved hand for the first time holding a surgical instrument aloft, my head swirling with obscure anatomical facts, lists of differential diagnoses on the tip of my tongue, and the wonders of modern medicine quite literally open before me. While I try to put aside, for that moment, the humbling fact of Mrs. Babson's passing, my twenty-three-year-old self is trying to concentrate on what can still be accomplished as I master the art of suturing. At this glorious if tragic moment, modern medicine and health care are one and the same for me. What I can learn, I can do. It will be many years and several practice models later, in a career that takes me through a variety of military and civilian settings, before I realize how disconnected medical science can get from health care delivery. For now, at least, I am on the right path. I will be the good doctor.

FIVE

The Facts of Life

My journey through the health care landscape involved several quantum leaps, the first of which occurred the day I graduated from medical school. I would not ease from academia into the gathering currents of third-party payers by way of a civilian training program, like most of my colleagues. Instead, my path took a sudden turn into the most socialized system of medical care in the world: that of the US military. It was a turn that would shape my perspective on health care for the rest of my career.

Internship placement is determined senior year by a computer-dating service known as The Match. In this system, graduating medical students from all over the country list their preferences as to where they would most like to do their specialty training, and training programs list the students that they would most like to have in their internships and residencies. The matches are made based on the preferences of both parties and are announced on one dramatic April day. By senior year of medical school, I hoped to stay at Georgetown for an internal medicine internship. Randy had set his sights on a psychiatry internship in Denver.

The tuition at Georgetown's medical school had jumped by magnitudes to the highest in the country between our first and second years and continued to climb after that. Almost three-quarters of the med students that year, sons and daughters of the middle class, survived the jump by enlisting in one of the uniformed services. On Match Day, the reality of that decision hit home, and many of us found out that we were going not to the programs of our choice, but to military hospitals. Despite our well-laid plans to be in opposite parts of the country doing civilian internships, Randy and I were both headed for the National Naval Medical Center in Bethesda, Maryland.

The two of us had dated on and off during our years at Georgetown. Our time together in med school was more like a tug-of-war with a bungee cord than it was a romance—neither of us ever desiring the same amount of entanglement at the same time, one day feeling close, the next day acting detached. Medical school was the perfect backdrop for avoiding intimacy; as long as fat glob-ules were floating around in human arteries, there would be more urgent matters of the heart demanding our attention. Whatever we were to each other, it appeared to have an expiration date. That changed on Match Day.

The shock of finding out that we were both assigned navy intern-ships united Randy and me in a common cause. In a few short weeks we had to buy uniforms, unravel the mysteries of rank, and learn how to salute. There was no time for officer training, but Randy had watched the old TV series *Combat* as a boy and was able to draw on that wealth of experience. We were a team. I moved into an apart-ment with a med school classmate close to where Randy set up house with his old college roommates.

When I stepped onto Ward 5-D, the all-male internal medicine ward of the National Naval Medical Center, on July 1, 1980, the title *Doctor* was not my only new accessory. There were lieutenant stripes on my shoulders and medical corps insignias on my collar. I had stepped into a brand-new culture, compounding the strangeness of my new responsibilities.

After four years of medical school, I thought I understood the pain and suffering that illness brings. I thought I understood a lot of things, and I was mostly wrong. A medical student's job is to learn information. There is such rapid turnover of patients and doctors that you hardly get to know any of them, and you are not really responsible, at the end of the day, for anything that happens. Detachment carried a high premium when I was in med school. Compassion that extended beyond lip service distracted you from the serious business of being a doctor and could come off as danger-ously girlie for a woman trying to prove herself in a man's world. So participation in "my" patients' heartache and grief could feel real, but it was a little like watching a sentimental movie where the

Julia Roberts character is struck down in her prime by an incurable illness. The tears we shed are mostly self-indulgent, and by the time we are squinting outside the theater, our eyes are no longer even puffy.

No, the real understanding of patients' suffering comes during internship, when the patients are your patients, day in and day out; when you connect with them and feel responsible for them. Internship is where you struggle with your own limitations, and face the horror of your own mistakes. It is where the privilege of being a doctor meets the cost. This understanding is at the heart of becoming a doctor. If we do not grasp the many ways our patients suffer, or our own complicated responses to their suffering, we can never really understand what it is we are supposed to be doing, and why. If gaining such understanding is the measure of an internship, I had a great one.

I began my internship on Ward 5-D, an old-style open hospital ward that featured a remarkable blend of communal living with orderliness. The old linoleum floors were immaculate; tall windows glistened from all the attention they received. Two long rows of beds lined the walls, each bed separated by a flimsy beige curtain that bulged with the contours of doctor and nurse bodies during rounds. As we ambled our way up the rows of beds, flipping through charts, absorbed in our conversations, two dozen sets of eyes followed us with varying interest.

The male patients all wore blue cotton pajamas and bathrobes stamped with the hospital logo, and they spoke politely in accents that had been formed all over the country. The sailors' cumulative medical charts traveled with them every step of the way, and their records were the most complete I would ever see as a doctor. These patients were sent here from military bases throughout the world, bringing us their cancers and exotic infections, common ailments and rare metabolic disorders. Cost was not an issue—for them or for us. It all blurred into the defense-spending tab that the American taxpayer picked up.

Chief Moseley, a retired chief petty officer, had been a trombone player in the navy band for thirty years. He came to the emergency room one night because he had started to cough up blood. What he found waiting there for him was a sleepy-eyed, brand-spanking-new, twenty-five-year-old intern by the name of Dr. Maggie Keavey.

An X-ray showed a scatter of lesions across his lungs. His tiny wife sat nervously clutching her pocketbook in a folding chair next to his bed as the chief told me in his lovely baritone voice how he had been coughing for months. He had a sad, soulful look in his eyes, as if he already knew bad news was in store. Mrs. Moseley had a thousand frightened questions in her eyes but hardly uttered a word.

These were very sweet people. Their eyes would light up when I approached them, and a slow broad smile would curve around the chief's face. They asked me questions about myself as if I were a granddaughter they just didn't see often enough. They filled me with colorful stories about the places they had traveled to with the band, presidents the chief had performed for, famous people he had met. I sat on the edge of his bed on quiet evenings, enjoying the fuss they made over me, giving in to the kindness and warmth.

I had bad news for them. It turned out Chief Moseley had advanced prostate cancer, and he was exhausted by the aggressive workup even before we started any treatment. He grew quieter and paler as the weeks went by. Both he and his wife lost weight. When I came by to suggest lab work or an IV, the neighboring patients would convene to suggest to me that maybe this wasn't such a good day for that. (This was long before the introduction of HIPAA laws, which protect patients' privacy, but sometimes at the expense of human warmth.) Mrs. M looked to me every day for some reassuring word, and I would try to find something. "His red blood cell count is up a little today," or "He didn't have any fever spikes last night." She clutched these talismans with desperation as she watched her beloved husband sink into the pillows.

It was all going badly, and I was powerless to help. By the time I left 5-D for my next rotation a few weeks later, the chief had grown very quiet and hollow-eyed, withdrawing to a place where stories sat silently in the shadows. I was finding it harder and harder to face them. I hadn't realized that I had gradually become as concerned with not disappointing this lovely couple as I was with treating the chief. When they needed me most, I was floundering, shortening my visits, assuming they expected more of me than I could give. Detachment was the least of my problems.

Internship year did not lend itself to self-reflection. I was caught in a constant swirl of emotions that were always being shoved aside so I could admit the next patient, or start the next IV. The doctors who supervised me were not much farther along on the road of life than I was, and they had been trained in the same school of repression. It was a school I felt comfortable attending. By the time I began to sort out what my patients really needed from me, and what I could really do to help, Chief Moseley had long passed, and Mrs. M had cried a gallon of tears at his loss. What I learned a little too slowly was that truth and compassion work best hand in hand and that these, not detachment, were the measure of a doctor. This is the lesson I would carry forward, that would serve me decades later in private practice: Speak the truth, whether it is a seismic matter or a trivial one, whether it relieves or frightens or angers your patients. It is not yours to play with. And speak it with compassion, because that is what gives truth its healing powers.

A navy internship, unlike a typical civilian program, not only trains interns in a specialty but also prepares them for the possibility that they might be practicing medicine in very remote locations, where they would need broad competencies. So my training, unlike a typical internal medicine internship, included rotations on orthopedics, on ear, nose, and throat surgery, and on other specialties. Much to my chagrin, this plan also included a monthlong rotation on pediatrics. After a year of serious, academic patient care, the last thing I wanted to do was spend my time locked in mortal combat with screaming kids, digging wax out of their ears while their deranged parents hovered over me, wringing their hands.

I had hated pediatrics in medical school. That student rotation took place in the polished halls of the university hospital, land of crisp white lab coats and no-nonsense nurses. I had been assigned to Dr. Assan, a specialist in rare metabolic disorders, and I spent more time with a biochemistry book that month than I did with patients, trying to figure out the difference between phenyl-some-thing-or-other and phenyl-something-else. What little contact I had with patients mostly involved sweaty wrestling matches as I tried to coax sample after sample of bodily fluids for the lab from terrified children before their distraught mothers insisted I leave. I knew somebody needed to be interested in rare conditions like dihydro-lipoyl dehydrogenase deficiency, but I couldn't wait to get back to a world where you could talk reasonably to patients, use normal-sized stethoscopes to examine them, pronounce their diagnoses correctly on the first attempt, and know that their mothers were safely retired somewhere in Florida. Now I dreaded the prospect of wrapping up my long year of internship with a similar experience.

The waiting room for the pediatric clinic at Bethesda was always standing-room-only, largely because hyperactive toddlers were jumping all over any furniture not already occupied by car seats and diaper bags. In the center of the room, clusters of small chil-dren played with slimed plastic toys, which, if cultured, would surely demonstrate every organism known to humankind. There were tugs-of-war and temper tantrums, strewn baby bottles and stomped-on pacifiers, tired moms in oversized T-shirts rolling strollers back and forth to soothe irritable babies. This was the minefield I crossed on the first day of my last month as an intern.

Behind the reception desk, inexplicably pleasant nurses answered phones that never stopped ringing and checked in screeching chil-dren with a calmness that suggested they were all heavily medicated. One sweet, gray-haired nurse directed me to a side door, and as I passed through, I collided with a furious red-faced little girl trying frantically to squirm out of her mother's arms. She was well heeled in sturdy white leather sandals, one of which kicked me in the face as she was hurried out the door. I checked for bleeding, regained my balance, and made a beeline for the office of the chief of pediatrics.

Dr. MacHurley was a clean-cut, middle-aged man with regulation navy glasses who was known simply as Dr. Mac. He eagerly came around his desk to greet me with a hearty handshake. While I tried to keep my eyes off the fuzzy little koala bear attached to his collar, we chatted about how my year had been going. He caught sight of the pediatric chief resident walking by and interrupted himself mid-chuckle. "Hey, John, come in here a minute. I want you to meet the visiting intern."

John Nadeau's coiled, wiry look, suggesting he was ready at any moment to spring into action, made his slow, polite drawl a surprise. "Nice to have you aboard, Dr. Keavey. We're just about to start morning report if you want to follow me to the conference room." But our exit from Dr. Mac's office was blocked by two attendings in a heated discussion. Dr. Casamassima, a fireplug in a commander's uniform, was arguing with the dark, willowy child psychiatrist, Dr. Gemelli, in an Italian American dialect that sounded like it was pulled from the set of *The Godfather*—except that what they appeared to be discussing was the size of some poor child's penis. Joe Loprieato, who, unlike me, was a bona-fide pediatric intern, arrived on the scene disheveled and sleepy and was immediately drawn into the debate.

"What'sa matter with you guys?" He turned to John and me. "Whaddya want? A geneticist and a shrink. If they're not talking about somebody's schlong they're not happy."

"Now, now," the chief resident interjected with a smile, "let's keep it professional."

At that moment, another nurse with a blissful countenance led a mother and her two children past us to an exam room down the hall. The little boy was screaming, "Nooo . . . I don't want to see the doctor," and struggled in vain to yank his arm out of his mother's grip. The baby Mom carried in her other arm was watching this with concern, and her face shriveled into a two-second warning before she let off an earsplitting cry just as she passed our group.

"Good morning, Doctors," said the nurse cheerfully as she ushered her charges-from-hell to what I could only assume was a torture chamber down the hall.

I tripped over the legs of a dozing senior resident as I located a seat in the conference room. John began morning report with a sense of decorum that seemed wasted on the chattering, chair-shuffling crowd, but the group settled down as another intern, Mary, sporting a bunny on her stethoscope, began a polished presentation of her first case from the night before, a young infant with unexplained fever. There were a few clarifying questions—"What was the highest temperature here in the hospital?" and "Do you have a follow-up blood count this morning?" Mary's answers were crisp and no-nonsense as she elaborated on her decision process.

"So what are the most likely causative organisms?" asked an infectious disease specialist from the back of the room. The mild-mannered intern answered directly, obviously prepared for the line of questioning. A debate ensued about using the trendy antibiotic of the day, as opposed to an old standard. Somewhere in the discussion of blood cell lines, French hematologist Dr. Duval-Arnold poked fun at the nephrologist's Canadian accent, and he could hardly finish his sentence from giggling. I feared we were going back down the road to chaos, but John managed to regain control from up front, and we moved on to the next case.

After morning report, I was directed to the outpatient clinic where, along with one of the attendings, I was to see children who had come in for "sick" visits—those with acute illness or complaints. On that first morning, I was with Joel Labow, a clinical professor who had a special interest in pediatric intensive care. I assumed that his turn in "snotty nose clinic" would be torture for him, but he actually seemed quite content with his morning duty. If not as happy-go-lucky as the rest of his merry band, Joel seemed comfortable as long as he was teaching, whether it be interns, students, parents, or patients. He eschewed dangling fuzzy animals, possibly because he vaguely resembled a Berenstain bear himself. I opted to shadow him for the first few patients instead of jumping in myself. I was in no hurry to be left alone with a sick child and its mother.

Our first patient was a four-year-old Filipino girl with a rash. Her mother worried it was ringworm. Before we stepped into the room, Joel gave me a short discourse on eczema, fairly certain already that this is what it would be. He began working the room as soon as we opened the door, his ear bent toward the mom even as he was smiling at the child, and he gradually moved his rolling stool closer to the exam table to tickle her toes. I watched with admiration as he took ordinary speech and body language and raised it to an art form that spun apprehension into relief. The rash was, in fact, eczema. Our little patient did crumple into tears eventually, but the visit didn't end until Joel had helped her button up her sweater and dabbed softly at her wet cheeks with a tissue.

Much of my time that month was spent in the subspecialty clinics. I saw children with end-stage renal disease, their cheeks puffed into cherubic form by steroids, and meticulously recorded the results of their latest kidney function tests in their thick charts. I worked with Dr. Duval-Arnold in oncology clinic, examining bald-headed grade school children in baseball caps, taking care to palpate every chain of lymph nodes, thoroughly test the cranial nerves, carefully inspect the ears and mouth. Children won't necessarily complain that their visual field has changed, or that one of their legs feels funny. We had to be vigilant for them.

"It is better to be conscientious than smart," Dr. D-A constantly reminded me.

Pediatric patients, unlike many internal medicine patients at the other end of life's spectrum, never came in with self-inflicted illness. They didn't smoke too much, or drink too much, and they only ate what the grown-ups in their lives made available. It was in their nature to be well. There was a hopefulness to them that defied the pain of youthful suffering.

The hopefulness was well justified. Given half a chance, most of these children who had been ambushed by illness would get well. Even the vast majority of leukemia patients were being cured with new chemotherapy protocols. I was in awe of how rapidly a small child in extreme respiratory distress from asthma could respond to our medications, how quickly his oxygen-starved tissues would restore themselves, and how soon we had to implore his mother to keep him from running around so much.

"Come over here, you crazy kid," Dr. Poth would laugh, pulling a whirling dervish onto her lap. Lee Poth was widely respected for her research in pediatric endocrinology, but this month she was taking her turn as inpatient attending. "We think you need to get out of here before you drive us all crazy. What do you think?" The giggling, wriggling child squirmed out of her lap, and both Dr. Poth and the conversation abruptly turned to me. "Dr. Keavey, you come from the land of big people. What would they say over in the ICU about the ventilation/perfusion mismatch on this little guy's first arterial blood sample?"

And so it went over those first few days, and into the following weeks. Serious doctors with Daffy Duck windup toys in their pockets discussed their research on infant intestinal disease one minute and rocked a colicky baby the next; neonatologists resuscitated premature infants and changed diapers. This blurring of boundaries, this melting of traditional barriers, made sense to me. By the end of that rotation, having learned more ways than a cop to restrain another human being, and having acquired an army of puppets and toys for my own amusement and that of my patients, I came to realize that I felt more at home in my doctor skin than I ever had. I notified the chief of medicine (he had a nickname, too—The Shark) that I would not be coming back for an internal medicine residency. I was going to be a pediatrician.

Casper and Friends

I began my pediatric residency in the summer of 1982, the same summer in which Randy and I were married. We may have set out on our internship as loyal friends determined to help each other navigate a strange new world, but over the course of that year, which proved to be a long, intense roller-coaster ride to maturity, we figured things out. I cannot say at what point between Pickles and pediatrics we actually fell in love. Randy insists it was at first sight, but in my mind that gives him a lot of explaining to do about the ensuing five years. What I do know is that by the time we were choosing our residency programs, we had agreed to have and to hold a thirty-year mortgage on a little white house in Bethesda, and we were very, very happy being together.

We had planned a small wedding up in Point Lookout, but the church of my childhood overflowed with uninvited as well as invited guests. I was pleased to see Dr. Cahill in the crowd. I had completely lost touch with my sister Helen Marie by then; even my parents had no idea how to contact her, so she wasn't there. But Brian and Johnny returned, bravely tackling household grime as well as the grime of their childhoods in order to prepare the nicest setting for me they could. My parents maintained alcohol levels that kept them, for the most part, cordial, and Randy's family treated mine as if they were perfectly normal. It was not just a union, but a reunion as well. Nancy, my college roommate who was now eight months' pregnant with her first baby, drove down from Vermont with her husband, Rob. And as we toasted with champagne later that day at the local restaurant, a familiar circle of *K* through *L*'s surrounded us, most of them married by now, too.

Five days later, we were back at work. The wall of hot, humid air that hit us as we reentered the Washington, DC, Beltway was of but passing concern; I would breathe little but climate-controlled hospital air for the next three years.

The National Naval Medical Center is a large referral center, and most of my patients were seriously ill. We had a busy cancer service, and we saw a wide variety of metabolic and infectious illnesses as well. On a typical day, I might take care of two or three cancer patients, a diabetic, a child with meningitis, and a number of children undergoing diagnostic tests for complex disorders of every sort. I was constantly reading journals and studying to keep up with my teaching responsibilities. Pediatric residency training was a staircase to be climbed in three years—teaching, interrogating, and watching the trainees on the steps below us, increasingly accountable to the attending physicians at the top.

I spent a great deal of my residency caring for sick and premature infants in the neonatal intensive care unit. The NICU was a pressure cooker where technical skills were paramount. It had the feel of a Las Vegas casino with its bright lights and constant frenzy of activity, no matter the hour, and the stakes were always high. All the brains in the world were no help at all if you couldn't get an IV started in a baby whose blood pressure was dropping. The tasks were as difficult as they were urgent; the IV catheters that we threaded into the infants' fragile veins were the size of fishing line.

One night, my intern John and I were called to a delivery because of "fetal distress." Minor variations in the expected heart rate were a common occurrence, and our presence was usually precautionary. The OB doctors were there primarily for the mother. Peds was called if there was any likelihood the baby would need extra attention, and in this case some fluctuations in the fetal heart rate were a warning sign.

The delivery was to be by cesarean section. John and I strolled over to labor and delivery, chatting about what days off we each had coming. Scrubbed and gowned, we headed over to the infant warmer in the operating room and began checking our instruments and oxygen supply while the obstetricians hovered over the mother's open belly. It was all very routine, until a sudden urgency in the obstetrician's voice reverberated through the room. "We've got an abruption," she called to us. The placenta had separated from the uterus; the baby was hemorrhaging. I went immediately to out-of-body emergency mode, shouting orders without seeming to think, acting on a level that bypassed book learning and lectures. I called for blood from the blood bank just before the OB doc handed me the whitest, limpest human form I had ever seen. I didn't know that a human being could actually be that paper-white.

The baby looked dead. We could detect no heart rate or breathing. John, his eyes bugging out, started two-finger chest compressions while the nurse squeezed oxygen into the baby's lungs through a mask, but I knew that there was not enough blood volume pushing through the heart for either of these things to work. Oxygen needs to be attached to red blood cells, which in turn need to be swimming in fluid that the heart can pump. I sliced open the umbilical cord, threaded a catheter through one of its spiraling veins, and started pushing fluids into the limp form, timing myself by the wall clock to resist the urge to push it in too quickly; a surge of fluid through a vein that size could blow out the vessels in an infant's brain. It seemed like a million years had passed, and still no blood had arrived from the blood bank. I handed the syringe of fluid to John so I could pass a breathing tube into the infant's airway, sending a flood of oxygen directly into his lungs.

"I think I feel a pulse," John said. I reached over and gently pushed down on the gelatinous cord. It took a few seconds before I felt the thready beat pushing up at my fingertips, too fast to have originated in my own pounding heart. It was a definite, glorious pulse. The baby, still disturbingly white, slowly came alive in front of us—an eye flutter, a grimace, a feeble punch at the air. I looked over to the OR table to see both the surgeons and the anesthesiologist standing motionless by the mother, watching us. "We have a pulse," I said, and only then did I begin to tremble. A few hours later in the NICU, after benefit of transfusion and with his breathing tube removed, our patient looked like a very pale but otherwise healthy newborn. The card on his isolette listed only his last name. We nicknamed him Casper, after the friendly ghost.

Saving Casper was a remarkable event, a defining moment. Most of the time, doctors take it on faith that they are doing some good. When I started the hundredth IV on a leukemia patient, treated pneumonia with antibiotics, or adjusted an asthmatic's meds, I assumed that I was helping, that in one way or another the patient was better off for my action. If I started a treatment at night, and the patient was doing better by morning, I felt pretty confident about my role in it. But this rescue in the delivery room was different. The whole sequence—illness, intervention, restoration—was compressed into a few miraculous moments. It was all that doctoring could be, in capsule form.

By the time the sun came up, Casper was curled up in a ball in his isolette box, belly moving up and down to the rhythm of his peaceful breaths. His mother, who had only heard of the drama after emerging from the groggy mist of anesthesia, sat on a stool next to him, gazing through the Plexiglas at his sleeping face, holding her sore belly with one hand, stroking the isolette with the other. I left the nursery early; I was starting a new rotation in radiology that morning and had a long day ahead of me. Driving home later that night, I fell asleep at a red light, awakened finally by a long line of honking down Rock Creek Parkway.

My schedule during residency was as insane and unrelenting as that of my internship. The hospital, once again a way of life for Randy and me, became the backdrop to our marriage. Randy had decided on a neurology residency, which was also a three-year program. We met for dinner in the cafeteria when we could; we might otherwise not see each other for days. When one of us had been on call the night before, coming off a thirty-six-hour shift, we would try to stay awake through dinner and maybe even a TV show when we got home, just to be sociable. After one of us stood an ER shift, we often met on the street—Randy drooping home in the dawn hour, stubbled and disoriented, me moving briskly toward a day of work, my hair still wet from the shower. We'd kiss good morning on a street corner.

"We need cereal," I'd remind him.

"Did you feed Elwood?" he'd ask. Elwood was our dog—a long

black nose driving a hundred pounds of Labrador retriever—and Randy fussed over him like a baby.

We did way too much on too little sleep. Almost every day at lunch hour, there was a lecture we were expected to attend, and staying awake through it was always a challenge, especially after being on call the night before. Occasionally, the lectures paid some academic attention to "the new morbidities" of pediatrics, topics like obesity and learning impairments. We all tended to fall asleep during these, even if we hadn't been on call. Like any young doctors, we were drawn to the drama and intellectual challenge of medicine—the calcium metabolism of a sick newborn, or the controversies around the treatment of meningitis—and these were what demanded all our energy. Parents might obsess about toilet training and how to get their baby to sleep through the night; we had bigger fish to fry. Those of us going into general, community-based pediatrics had no way of knowing that the fuzzy science of discipline techniques, or the developmental controversies around potty training, would come to represent the lion's share of our future practice, while the challenging work that consumed us day and night for years of residency would fade into memory, largely irrelevant to our daily tasks, rekindled for us over the years mostly in the form of interesting journal articles or academic conferences.

Baby Casper's glorious resurrection in the delivery room at Bethesda, on that long-ago night, looms large in my memory still, but in real time it was the smallest of moments in a long and intense pediatric residency. The challenging work of residency, diagnosing and treating serious illness, day in and day out, was seldom filled with that level of drama. But it required my complete focus and almost all of my energy. It also required resiliency—especially in pediatrics, where children do not sit still for X-rays, and IVs often need to be placed in moving, screaming targets. It required toughness, as everyone from parent to attending physician to the third-year medical student would second-guess a resident's decisions. And it required the cultivation of communication skills well beyond a young doctor's years—the skills it takes to get past a parent's terror and earn her trust.

Several months after Casper and I spent that night together, back on the general pediatric ward, I was having a rough afternoon and was about to get grilled by our hematologist-oncologist, Dr. Duval-Arnold.

Dr. D-A was upset that our five-year-old leukemia patient Danny still hadn't had his afternoon labs drawn. He needed the results in order to make a decision about more chemotherapy. It was getting increasingly difficult to draw blood samples from Danny, and his mother, who had acquired the frightened look of a wounded animal, was narrowing her list of whom she would let near him. She had turned away the medical student before he could uncap his needle and allowed the intern, Paul, three attempts, by which point Danny was screaming hysterically and the nurse who was holding him down was soaked in sweat—Danny's and hers. "No one else is touching him!" cried Danny's mom. "I want to see Dr. D-A!" Paul, disgraced, came looking for me.

Meanwhile, down the hall, I was trying to convince another anxious mom that we really did need to draw a second blood gas sample on her daughter. The little girl had come in with an asthma attack, and I had obtained an arterial blood sample to check her oxygen and carbon dioxide levels. An arterial stick really hurts, and children shriek when they have it done to them—the kind of shriek that stabs at parents' chests, makes them forget how frightened they were just minutes before when their child couldn't breathe, makes them want to grab their coughing, gasping kid and run from the building. The results of this child's initial blood gas weren't great, and I needed to repeat the test to make sure things had improved with treatment. I was speaking in my calm-and-reasonable voice.

"I know how upsetting this is, and I know it is painful, but it is just for a moment and it gives us very important information."

Mom wasn't buying it. Paul walked sheepishly into the room and interrupted me to tell me about Danny. "You're not gonna like this," he started, but then there was Dr. D-A, lips pursed, brow furrowed, beckoning me out to the hallway.

Frustration was clamping my chest as I looked from the asthmatic child to her mother to Dr. D-A out in the hall. On tough days like this, parents could look like roadblocks. Why hadn't Danny's mother let us place more permanent IV access when we had recommended it, so that we wouldn't have to keep sticking him? Why couldn't this mother understand that respiratory failure was a lot more dangerous than the pain of a needle stick? I wondered cynically if we should put all parents under anesthesia while we carried out our unpleasant tasks.

I stepped into the hall to face Dr. D-A's music, but my pager went off just as he was warming up. I was hardly being saved by the bell; pages never brought news that made your life easier. Sure enough, it was the nurse from the well-baby clinic calling with a message from Joe Stegman, a fellow resident. He needed me to come down "right away" and look at a baby. Dr. D-A sputtered something unpleasant in French as I threw up my hands and said I had to leave.

How am I supposed to get anything done around here? I fumed to myself as I waited for the elevator.

And what's up with Joe? Whatever the problem is, can't he handle it?

I huffed along the clinic corridor and, with what must have been an imperious I'm-too-busy-for-this expression on my face, pushed into the exam room.

The scene I encountered didn't immediately clear things up. A fat, bald, robust baby, snugly dressed in spotless blue terry cloth, was happily drooling all over the sheet of paper that covered the exam table. His legs were energetically kicking the air and his hands reached and grabbed at unseen treasures. He looked like he needed an urgent second opinion about as much as he needed a barber. On either side of him, beaming parents stood facing me, each with one hand on the table, as if they were presenting me with a Thanksgiving Butterball Turkey. I stammered a moment, trying to orient myself, when in rushed Joe Stegman behind me. "Oh good! This is Dr. Kozel," he announced to the butterball's parents. "She was the doctor there that night." And to me, he said, "This is Casper."

I was still smiling a few minutes later as I waited for the elevator to bring me back up to the ward, where battles would continue to be waged slowly and painfully, where IV lines leaked and blood samples clotted before they could get to the lab, where parents begged God to cut their child a break and railed at the doctors when He didn't.

I can do this, I said to myself. *I can calm the patients, answer the desperate questions, get the tests run, help make them better,* I thought, partly believing it, partly praying for it to be true. Never was it clearer to me that parents and pediatricians were on the same side, with the same goals, the same hopes.

I returned to the din of the pediatric ward, and the image of Casper (I would always call him that, even when I learned his real name) was still with me as I joined Dr. D-A in Danny's room. Danny and his mother had both dried their tears, calmed their breathing. This hospital room was Danny's home-away-from-home. Stuffed animals watched us from every corner and surface. Mylar balloons registered our every movement as they bounced around his bed.

"Can't you draw the blood, Dr. D-A?" Danny's mother pleaded, as if he alone held the secret to success. She had been handed this horrible choice—to stand by and watch her child suffer the pains of medical treatment, or to watch him die. The fact that the choice was obvious made it no less excruciating. Dr. D-A knew as well as I did that the blood had to be drawn and that the interns and residents tended to be better at it than the attendings. But he wasn't frustrated—that was his secret. He just knew what he knew. He walked Danny and his mom through the plan again, talked about the results he was hoping for, and when Danny might go home. He respected their suffering as much as he respected fever and abnormal lab results.

"Danny, what is your favorite ice cream?"

"Chocolate," he answered weakly.

"After we are finished here, your mother is going to go to Swenson's. Have you been to Swenson's? She is going to get you chocolate ice cream, because you are a very good boy."

Dr. D-A wasn't bribing or apologizing, simply giving Danny a hope for good things and easing his mother's helplessness. Truth and compassion. I watched this with the same mix of awe and inspiration that I had felt when Dr. Cahill, long ago in Point Lookout, first showed me what a doctor could do. With Dr. D-A holding Danny's arm, I drew the blood, and Mom gathered her sweater and car keys. Blood tubes labeled and delivered, I moved down the hall to the asthmatic's room, ready to try again.

We all thrive on having our work appreciated. It seems less than mature, professionally speaking, for doctors to require patient (or parental) gratitude. But we are as human as everyone else. I had already known that my night with Casper had been a success, but seeing the proof of that, in the form of a healthy child and joyous, grateful parents, was something I could draw strength from for a very long time. It was strength I would rely on to face the long hours, the uncertain outcomes, my own doubts. It was the strength that reminded me to be patient with a frightened parent, to focus on the therapeutic goals, just as Dr. D-A had done, even as we were distracted by the more immediate pains and heartaches of treatment.

I took that appreciation and gratification for granted back then. It was icing on the cake. I didn't fully realize how much this give-and-take between doctor and patient keeps a doctor going—or how I would feel its absence in the future. For a pediatrician who loves what she is doing, a trusting, respectful doctor–patient relationship will sustain her through the corrosive effects of long hours, arbitrary reimbursements, senseless paperwork, and, yes, even malpractice lawyers.

SEVEN

Nature and Other Mothers

My pediatric residency at Bethesda was dominated by nursery and inpatient rotations, but in between these duties I cared for my own clinic outpatients. It was a chance to become skilled in bread-and-butter pediatrics—state-of-the-art well-child checks and treatment of minor illness. It was also the chance to provide primary care for children with chronic medical conditions. In theory at least, this was where sound, evidence-based clinical practice met the commonplace ailments and concerns of childhood. What this task lacked in drama, it more than made up in the satisfaction of doing something well, and in opportunities to touch children's lives on more levels than would be chronicled in their health record.

It was in outpatient clinic that I became involved in the primary care of some children with hemophilia—children who from birth lacked certain clotting factors and were at risk for dangerous bleeding. During a visit for a school physical, one mother, Mrs. D, told me how difficult it was for her school-aged boys to have a summer camp experience because of the risk from even mild trauma and the level of medical support they required. With the help of Dr. D-A and some contacts I had made at the hematology clinic at the children's hospital, I organized a one-week camp experience for area hemophiliacs. My department chairman arranged time off not only for me, but for Randy as well, arguing that head trauma was one of the most serious risks with hemophilia, and having a neurology resident along would be invaluable. Loaded down with clotting factor and all the medical equipment that went along with it, the two of us and nine eager boys headed off to Virginia for a week, to join a YMCA camp in progress.

For the first time in most of their lives, the boys were freed from the umbilical cords of parents and hospitals. There were lots of bumps and bruises, a fair amount of clotting factor infusions, and a few phone calls to the hematologists back home. But we all made it through just fine.

What fearless souls those boys were, racing through the woods that summer, jumping off docks, playing ball with the rest of the campers. No one asked to go home early, even though staying meant receiving IV infusions in dirt-floor cabins, without benefit of parents to hold their hands. They would cheerfully accept whatever it was we had to do to stop the bleeding in their knee or their muscle or their nose, as I doused every visible surface with alcohol to try to maintain some semblance of clean technique. Randy held the bags of clotting factor over his head, a human IV pole that told funny stories instead of beeping.

The memory is bittersweet. It would not be the dirt on the cabin floor or topples from bunk beds that would ultimately defeat these boys. They had all received hundreds of infusions of clotting factor over the course of their short lives. In the few years surrounding the earliest recognition of what was to be known as AIDS, doctors did not realize that the causative virus could be transmitted through such blood products. In a cruel irony, most of these boys contracted HIV from the very treatment that was meant to sustain their lives.

This was the nature of the healing arts being handed down to me. To "do no harm" seemed sadly unrealistic to a doctor finishing her training. If I lived by that dictum, I would never dispense a dose of chemotherapy or suppress an asthmatic's immune system with steroids. I could claim "no harm" with Casper, but that was only because babies don't talk, and his mother was out cold while I pushed plastic tubes into her son's belly. But every puncture of the skin caused pain, and often terror. Every aggressive treatment required loving parents to make the heartbreaking decision to become complicit with the tormenters. Every medication had its side effects; sometimes it even killed. Suffering was part of the package.

To do no harm would be to call it quits, go home, and pull down the shades. What I had learned during residency was to square off with Mother Nature while trying to do the least amount of harm possible. Sometimes I'd win, sometimes I wouldn't. Sometimes, as with those brave campers, or with the news of Danny's cure, I wouldn't know until years had gone by which way the scales had ultimately tipped. Either way, I knew this was what I wanted to do.

I also chose pediatrics as my specialty because I wanted to keep healthy children healthy. I wanted to make a difference in their lives that required artistry beyond the use of a prescription pad, and as part of a health team, I wanted to partner with their parents to keep my patients strong and safe, able to learn and supported through crises. After three years of residency training, I felt ready.

What I didn't see coming was that Nature was not the only mother with whom I might need to square off. Still young and idealistic, not to mention childless, I was unprepared for the fact that many parents I would encounter would have a different version of "do no harm." An antibiotic that was likely to be ineffective, and increase the risk of antibiotic resistance, would be viewed by an anxious parent as less harmful than risking a sleepless night with an ear infection. Useless cold medicines with awful side effects might seem to them a better option than not having a remedy to offer. As health insurance extracted its pound of flesh from families, the expectation for a doctor to "do something" would eclipse the role of observation and reassurance. If I was going to be any good at this, I would have to try to reconcile scientific evidence and clinical detachment with the realities of being a loving, worried, stressed-out parent in today's quick-fix, consumer world.

Truth and compassion, I would learn, would be no less challenging to blend into my encounters with the worried well than they were with the seriously ill.

EIGHT

The Front Line

I finished my pediatric residency in the summer of 1985. I was thirty years old. I still had to take oral and written boards, but the hard part was over. Randy and I were eager to travel, and there was a US Navy Hospital in Yokosuka, Japan, just outside Tokyo, that needed both a neurologist and a pediatrician. Bob Frenck, a pediatrician I had worked with at Bethesda, was already there and urged us to come.

Before we left, Randy and I went back up to Point Lookout to see my parents, now in their seventies. My mother was acting stranger than usual. I took her to breakfast one morning at the same luncheonette where I had loitered as a teenager. Still sober at that early hour, she surprised and embarrassed me with a typical drunken harangue, complete with racist and religious epithets—loud enough for the elderly waitress and nearby tables to hear.

"Mom, keep it down," I begged. That only annoyed her more, and the pinched-faced waitress and I colluded to get us out of there as quickly as possible.

"I can't believe she's getting nastier than she already was!" I complained to Randy.

Randy's mouth formed into a no-nonsense flat line, but his eyes were sad and sympathetic. "She's getting demented, Maggie. Somebody needs to talk to your dad. It's only going to get worse—especially if she keeps drinking."

Dad didn't want to hear it. He certainly wasn't going to try to get my mother to stop drinking. He'd had his own way of coping since retirement: a nightly bacon cheeseburger, a cigar, and a bottle of red wine. They were both picking up speed on a downward slide that started long before I was born. We begged them to see their doctors and for Mom to see a neurologist. They resented our intrusion.

"We were doing just fine without you," they accused.

So I left, confused and guilty, feeling as if I was abandoning them, yet knowing I was leaving them to their chosen fates—the final acknowledgment that I could not make their lives better, that I'd never get everybody to love everybody. Back in Bethesda, we sold our little house, crated our enormous dog, and pushed our way over another horizon.

US Naval Hospital Yokosuka, Japan, is a tiered, five-story building that squats alongside the waters of Yokohama Bay. When Randy, Elwood, and I arrived there in the summer of 1985, Old Glory flapped out front in the same breeze that carried strains of the Japanese national anthem over to us from a nearby park. Pediatrics Department head Seiji Kitagawa was born and raised not far from the hospital, but almost all the other doctors were American-born, including, of course, our good friend from Bethesda, the tall, redheaded Valley Boy named Bob Frenck. Most of the non-health-care employees—the secretaries and receptionists, housekeepers and drivers—were Japanese, making for an ongoing drama in the hallways and dining halls of half bows and awkward handshakes, shy attempts at English from mouths hidden by a hand, and a limited repertoire on our part of "hai!" and "domo arigato."

This was a hospital of specialists—pediatricians, internists, general surgeons, orthopedists. Randy was the sole neurologist. Our mission was to provide medical care to active-duty military personnel and their families. There were no subspecialists for us to turn to, except by phone call back to the States, and no nearby medical centers to which we could easily refer patients. Language was the primary obstacle to tapping into the Japanese health care system, but cultural differences also loomed large. Japanese doctors operated for the most part as masters of their domain. They were never to be questioned. The only relevant standard of care was whatever each individual doctor decided it was. And even though the overall quality of care in Japan was quite high, this lack of accountability was fundamentally at odds with the way American doctors were trained, and we felt uncomfortable relinquishing the care of our own patients into this system.

So Bob, Seiji, and I managed most pediatric emergencies on our own. If a premature or sick baby was born, one of us pediatricians would hover over the baby warmer adjusting the ventilator settings ourselves, watching the minute-by-minute changes until the infant was stable enough to transport. If Seiji was around, and particularly if the mother was Japanese, he could escort an infant on the wild ambulance ride down the Yokohama–Yokosuka road to a large Japanese hospital with a neonatal intensive care unit. But often, Bob and I were left alone with our native tongues, and if neither parent spoke Japanese, a local hospital was not a great option. We needed to communicate with the hospital physicians; we needed to act as liaisons for the worried families. So instead we would try to arrange a medevac flight to Guam or Hawaii, where there were larger navy medical centers with neonatologists.

When children were diagnosed with leukemia, we would do as much of the preliminary work as we could, getting blood, spinal fluid, and even bone marrow samples, then starting transfusions and antibiotics before transporting them stateside. There was no neonatal or pediatric ICU at our small hospital, so a hospital bed became an ICU by virtue of our constant presence. We saw meningitis frequently—these were the days before the *H. influenzae* vaccine—and for as long as the child needed intensive care, Bob, Seiji, and I took turns sitting at the patient's bedside, coordinating respiratory therapy, IV fluids, antibiotics, and laboratory procedures. A newly diagnosed case of diabetes was especially demanding, since one of us would have to personally monitor every sugar and serum electrolyte value, sitting there in the patient's room, obsessively adjusting the insulin pump. We couldn't chance that instructions to adjust insulin, say, would get missed during a change of shifts, potentially depriving the brain of its only fuel, glucose. Until the patient was stable, one of us would keep vigil at the nurses' station or bedside, while the other two covered that pediatrician's clinic patients.

At Yokosuka we saw illnesses we never saw back in the States— typhoid fever, malaria, tuberculosis, and many more. The list of challenging diagnoses went on and on. There were expert subspecialists a phone call and twelve time zones away, but we were the front line, doing what we were trained to do, and being a doctor was wonderful.

It was also exhausting. Young military families are a fertile bunch, and the three of us were charged not only with caring for a large pediatric population, but also with providing round-the-clock support to the newborn nursery. There must have been at least four hundred deliveries per year at Yokosuka. The pediatrician on call attended all C-sections and high-risk deliveries, dropped everything to check any ill-appearing newborn, and did physical exams on every baby.

One of the most distasteful tasks we faced on a daily basis at Yokosuka was performing circumcisions. There are many myths about the benefits of circumcisions. The only medical consideration that is backed by any evidence is a possible decrease in the occurrence of urinary tract infections in circumcised male infants. These studies, however, are not well controlled, especially for method of obtaining urine samples, so it is hard to interpret them. Regardless, the incidence of urinary tract infections in both circumcised and noncircumcised infants is low—less than 1 percent—so routine circumcision of newborns is not recommended on medical grounds.[4] The desire to circumcise our male babies is predominantly culture-driven.

Both Bob Frenck and I hated doing them. There is something fundamentally ungratifying about picking up a sweet, warm, sleeping baby, placing him on a cold plastic board, and hearing his high-pitched scream as you strap his arms and legs down with Velcro. You take it on faith that the shot of lidocaine for his penis is going to alleviate more pain than it just caused. The stainless-steel clamping device looks as if its prototype was devised by a medieval sadist. When we sliced those condemned sleeves of smooth skin off, hastily covering our assaults with Vaseline gauze, had we done no harm?

Bob and I spent a great deal of time and energy on morning rounds trying to subtly dissuade parents from having their child circumcised, sparing them the gory details, but emphasizing the lack of medical necessity. It was usually not too hard to convince Mom, especially if she was Asian. But as soon as Dad from Peoria walked in, the stay of execution would be reversed. We eventually realized what a waste of time our pro-foreskin campaign was. If Dad was circumcised, baby boy was going to be.

Ironically, our Japanese-born colleague Seiji, who came from a culture that did not circumcise, had no problem with it. In fact, he was amazing to behold. Seiji could finish a "slice and dice," as we called it, before I could even get my gloves on. Bob and I would change every poopy, slimy diaper in that nursery just to stall until Seiji finished the circs. We would tease him, grunting our Hollywood idea of martial arts sounds as he wielded his scalpel, calling him the samurai circumciser. Even if we could get him to laugh, it didn't slow him down. He'd just keep chopping away like a chef at Benihana.

The poor Japanese interns were another story. Four were assigned to us every year, and accompanying us on nursery rounds was part of their duties. Circumcisions horrified them. One time I stood fully scrubbed, an audibly worried baby strapped down in front of me, and turned to my intern, Dr. Ishigawa, so that he could hand me the clamp. As I removed the stainless-steel instrument from its wrapper, poor Ishigawa-sensei fell over in a dead faint.

"Oh boy!" I commented, shaking my head at our fallen soldier. The other three interns bent over him, frightened, slipping back into nervous exchanges of Japanese. I was pretty sure it was a harmless faint, but I was scrubbed, and the baby was screaming, so I was counting on the intern's colleagues to go to his rescue. "Hellooo!" I called down through their huddle. "Should somebody maybe check his breathing and pulse?" Their confused stares reminded me for the hundredth time that sarcasm does not cross language barriers. But by that time the nurse had run over, and the good doctor's eyes were fluttering open. Both patients survived the ordeal.

"Why do you do this if the boys are not Jewish?" the interns asked politely, over and over again, unable to comprehend the strange practice. After a while, we gave up trying to explain what we really couldn't understand ourselves. We just smiled, shrugged, and sliced.

Years later, working at a community hospital in Rhode Island, I was delighted to learn that it was the obstetricians at that hospital, not the pediatricians, who did the circumcisions. They hated it as much as we did. I listened to them grumble as I made my rounds in the morning. They'd stand impatiently at the circ table, scrubbed up, waiting until I had done a heart examination on every baby in the nursery before they got started; once they got going, there was no way I was going to be able to detect any heart sounds or murmurs over the indignant cries of the restrained babies. I nodded with sympathy as the OBs complained about having to do the circumcisions and continued on with my physicals. No way were they ever going to find out that I had done hundreds of circs and had even been taught the secrets of a samurai master.

Practicing pediatrics in Asia meant that we had to be especially alert and sensitive to culturally based medical practices—everything from cupping to amulets to herbal remedies. But it also made us aware of our own cultural biases toward health care. If we were ever tempted to look down our noses at such "primitive" practices, we had only to remind ourselves of good old American circumcisions to restore our humility.

Such humility seems needed now more than ever. We have rested for decades on the laurels of being the most medically advanced country on the planet (which we are) but have become so comfortable, even smug, in that knowledge that we have ignored or rationalized away not only the illogic of some of our practices, but the often wasteful utilization of our resources and erosion of our health.

NINE

Universal Appeal

Throughout the ten years I spent in the navy, both in training and in practice, no money ever changed hands between a patient and health care provider. It was called a "benefit," as opposed to an "entitlement," a distinction that makes all the difference in the world to the American psyche. This benefit provided 100 percent coverage to every eligible person. If you were active-duty military, then you and your entire family were eligible for no-cost health care. You just showed your military ID (or your "dependent" ID if you were a family member), and you were in the door. No questions. No forms. No submitting for reimbursement. No co-pay. No prescription cost, even for many over-the-counter medicines. No out-of-pocket expenses of any kind to any patient.

Did it cost "too much"? Possibly. The actual numbers, in the hands of the Department of Defense, were hard to know. Then again, our society seems to have an infinite capacity for defense spending, so, hitched to that wagon, our tolerance for Pentagon health care spending goes way up, too. But whatever the cost, it would have to be considered in the cost-saving context of the better use of manpower, the elimination of the third-party payer as middleman, and the effectiveness of treating small problems long before they became big, expensive problems.

Back home in the States, poor children were being pointed to the back of the health care bus. But in Yokosuka, admirals' sons received the same care as the Filipino stepchildren of a twenty-year-old seaman apprentice. The care they received—the little blond tennis pros with headaches and the dark-skinned Tagalic-speaking urchins with tuberculosis—was state-of-the-art. Doctors were paid well and held to high standards. Dental care and mental health services were part of the package. Social support, like family counseling and addiction services, was as available as it was desperately needed.

What has been demonized by our culture in general, the specter of universal health coverage, had been fully embraced by that bastion of socially progressive thinking, the US military.

The outpatient clinic at Yokosuka brought many challenges, including a stunning diversity of language and culture, but in most ways it was a model of practice that made sense to me. We did lots of well-baby exams and saw plenty of minor acute illness, but visits were structured differently than in a typical private practice back home. The most important parts of the well-baby visit, for instance, are health maintenance, education, and immunizations; this means that most of a well-baby visit—anywhere—is best handled by nursing staff. So this is what happened at Yokosuka. Different nurse managers did it in different ways. One of the most effective approaches was to schedule the visits in small clusters.

The nurse would have six families who had babies scheduled for the same kind of visit—say, the six-month-old check—all come in at 9 AM. He would then sit and talk to them about the common concerns at that age, like sleeping through the night, introducing solid food, bowel patterns, safety, and so on. It was part lecture, part discussion, and would run for about half an hour. During the talk, the nurse would jot down notes in the patients' charts: "This baby started solid food as a newborn!" or "Baby never sleeps more than half an hour." Next, the babies would get all their weights and measures done by corpsmen and only then be sent in to see one of the three doctors. So by the time I saw my patients, they had already had half an hour of expert, unhurried advice, and most of their concerns had been patiently addressed. I would address any lingering issues, whether the parent's or the nurse's.

The beauty of this strategy could be seen on many levels. Primarily, a significant amount of basic information was conveyed in a manner that most parents could digest. We were not force-feeding or glossing over the most useful part of the visit. Almost as important was the efficiency. The pediatricians were able to see more patients, in a much more focused, helpful way, because of this appropriate division of labor. And finally, not only were most patients very satisfied, so were the doctors and nurses, with both groups focusing their energies on what they did well.

I had time to do a careful exam, give cautionary or reassuring advice as needed, and send them off to get their immunizations. If I needed them to come back sooner than their next scheduled visit, no problem. They weren't paying for it. If I prescribed vitamins or diaper rash cream, or any other medicine, they would just go down to the pharmacy and pick it up. No out-of-pocket expense. If the baby had a wry neck from lying too much in the same position, the physical therapists would be happy to see her. Again, no cost. And if I needed more time to deal with something more complicated, it was there. A developmental delay did not have to compete with burping questions for my attention. This wasn't about me only having to do "interesting" things; I actually got a kick out of drooling babies and rambunctious toddlers. This was about rational utilization of expensive, valuable resources.

The US military is not an egalitarian organization. But the beauty of working in the military health care system was that it was egalitarian. The only price of admission was a military ID. We did make some trivial concessions. If a visiting admiral's child needed to be seen, we tended not to keep him waiting too long. And one of the nurses would walk the parents to the pharmacy instead of giving them directions. That celebrity factor operates everywhere. But mostly, we were the professionals and so set the priorities and delivered health care based on our best professional judgment. Such a simple, important concept.

I assumed back then that this is what well-baby visits would be like throughout my career. There would be lots of good, effective interaction between patients and the health team, bringing each child the most up-to-date, highest-quality care available. I personally would have a well-defined role, making sure the child did indeed appear healthy, watching for red flags, and contributing credibility to the process with my medical degree. This would be fine. It didn't carry the excitement of saving lives and stamping out disease, but it was a noble pursuit in which my involvement was appropriate, limited, and effective.

Rational use of medical resources was at the heart of military medicine: setting clear priorities and goals, and then matching skill level to the task at hand. There was, however, another more subtle benefit, one that is sorely needed in civilian pediatric practice today. Once a common problem gets to the level of an MD, it automatically assumes a certain gravity and expectation for a cure—this is my "You go to a muffler shop, you get a muffler" argument. Take spit-up, for example. When baby barf attained the status of "gastro-esophageal reflux," partly due to direct drug marketing, pharmaceutical shareholders in our country became very happy. Once spit-up became hard to pronounce, prescriptions for potentially toxic medications, like metoclopramide, began flying off our pads and into very young infants' mouths, with little data as to what we were trying to prevent or how effective we were being. Parenting magazines carried full-page ads for the name brands, and parents came to expect a medical treatment for it. Doctors got too much of their "scientific data" from smooth-talking pharmaceutical reps over expensive dinners at fancy restaurants. Pharmaceutical giants funded research studies that narrowed their aim to immediate physiologic responses (it stops the reflux!) rather than broader efficacy (will it make any difference to this child six months down the road?), and these studies appeared in our professional journals. More than seven million prescriptions for this anti-reflux drug were dispensed in 2004 alone, and it is estimated that 30 percent of these were for pediatric patients. Once use of metoclopramide came under closer, unbiased scrutiny by pediatricians, we realized there was very little evidence to support its safety or efficacy.[5] The push for using anti-reflux medications in infants is only one in a long list of treatments that continue to be driven much more by marketing than by science.

There are so many examples like this in pediatrics—bed-wetting, constipation, fluid in the ears—where less is often more, where health professionals need to slow the flow of intervention, not ratchet it up. One way to slow it down is to not begin the discussion of common complaints with the person who writes prescriptions. If a highly qualified nurse is evaluating the spit-up, she is likely to provide sensible advice to the majority of patients and refer a small number to the physician, like the baby who is falling off her growth curve or who has unexplained wheezing. Good, basic triage scales down the muffler shop factor, to the benefit of the patient and the pocket.

Blissfully moving through the military's world of universal health coverage, I gave little thought to the obsolete method of health care funding that awaited me back in the States. Third-party payers, private or government-based, reimburse for a short doctor's visit and consider only the short-term results. It's all they know how to do. They will not reimburse for anything that happens outside the doctor's visit, except perhaps a nominal fee for the cost of administering vaccinations. The insurers waiting for me back home were certainly not going to pay for an educational session with a nurse and would often deny a "follow-up" visit if it didn't fall into a narrow list of categories. No, to get a well-child visit paid for in a way that earns income, it would have to be accomplished in twenty minutes, by a person with a very advanced degree, because that is the only paradigm insurance companies understand. The only way to dispense napping advice to a parent would be to dress it up as urgent pathology that warranted a doctor's time. The inefficiency and inappropriateness of it would be beside the point.

TEN

Cradle Wisdom

I left Yokosuka a different pediatrician than when I arrived because of two related experiences. I learned what it was like for a doctor to be a patient, and then, in the blink of an eye—among other bodily contractions—I became a mother. When I gave birth to our first daughter, Caitlin, a new story unfolded that would weave through the rest of my professional career. Parenting changes a pediatrician. For me, it gave me better understanding of my patients' parents. But just as important, it led me to question some of my own practices, and that developed into a healthy habit that stayed with me throughout the rest of my career. And as Caitlin and I basked in the finest medical care the world had to offer, the inequalities of our health care system began to haunt me.

I had a healthy pregnancy and worked through my fortieth week, still jumping up in the middle of the night to run to deliveries, still flying solo on those long weekend stretches on call. It was not until I was a week overdue, and "baby doc" still hadn't made an appearance, that I began to slow down. I awoke one morning to the shock of a strangely bloated face in the mirror. I called Seiji and told him I looked too scary to come to work. A few days later, in an unsettling role reversal, I was admitted to labor and delivery. I felt faintly foolish changing into the hospital gown, emptying my bowels and bladder on command. Even Randy looked uncomfortably out of place as he gathered up my belongings into a little plastic bag.

Having spent so much time working on this ward, I knew the staff well, knew their strengths and shortcomings. When I realized Janice was going to be my nurse, I was not happy. A tall, curvy young woman with gorgeous red hair and dramatic makeup, Janice was nice enough, but it seemed to me she went through life waiting for someone to explain to her what was going on. The pediatricians always groaned when we found out Janice would be the one assisting us with a sick baby. Now she was taking care of me.

I was given medications to start the labor that didn't want to start on its own. The result was long and futile, with lots of pain and no gain. Several hours into the ordeal, Janice settled into a chair next to me to watch the fetal monitor scratch a tracing of the baby's heartbeat across a scrolling sheet of paper, like the cylinder of a player piano. But instead of music being produced, there was the constant *ping, ping* that indicated the baby's pulse. The pinging began to slow down with my contractions, indicating that my baby wasn't tolerating the stress of labor well. Janice stared for a few moments, looking worried. "Dr. Kozel, this tracing doesn't look very good to me. What do you think?"

I was still trying to gather my sanity and my breath after the last tidal wave of pain. "You're kidding me, right?" I wheezed. "You want me to read the tracing?" But I did look at the tracing. I couldn't help it, because she turned the machine toward me. I saw what she saw: The baby's heart rate was plummeting during my contractions and taking too long to bounce back. "Get Dr. Slesinski," I said in my calmest doctor voice; I didn't want Florence Nightingale to freak out on me. She looked relieved to have something to do and darted from the room. Left alone, I couldn't remember where Randy had gone and started to panic. Mike Slesinski came hustling in—with Randy close behind.

We knew Mike from back at Georgetown, a smart, practical guy whose classic Boston mouth never let an *r* escape unflattened. Now those flat *r*'s were telling me something I really didn't want to hear. "We gotta delivah this baby, guys. Right now. I'm gonna do a C-section." This precipitated a sudden flurry of activity as furniture was rolled out of the way, monitors were adjusted, and staff relayed urgent hushed messages into the phone. "Get anesthesia in here," I heard one nurse say. "And call peds stat."

"That idiot nurse just had me read my own tracing, Mike. I swear to God, you better keep her away from me." In another time and place, I might have considered that she was as confused by the role reversal as I was, but I was terrified, beyond soft edges.

Randy thought this was just crazy labor talk, like you hear about on childbirth videos, and he tried to shush me, embarrassed. But Mike understood immediately what a terrible blunder that had been. I desperately needed these people to take care of my baby and me. Janice, in her eagerness to have someone else make a decision for her, hadn't stopped to think what effect it would have on me to diagnose my own baby's peril. Stone-faced, Mike stepped out of the room and reappeared with Sue, one of my favorite nursery nurses. She smiled calmly into my face, brushing the hair from my forehead. Then she turned off the audio on the baby's heart monitor, replacing the cold penetrating beep with her own soothing words. "Your baby will be here in a few minutes, Maggie. This is what you've been waiting for." Relief and gratitude washed over me as I let go of the decisions and sank into the pillows. Gripping Randy's hand, I began hoping and praying for my baby instead of calculating its pulse. I was a woman in labor, and I would never again stand at the foot of a laboring woman's bed without feeling this moment rise up in me.

A few minutes later I was shivering on an OR table, closing my eyes against the bright overhead lights. Paul, a nurse anesthetist, had given me an epidural—anesthesia through the spinal column— which meant I would be awake for the surgery but unable to feel anything below my chest; I was in no pain. I told him with gratitude that I was going to name the baby Paul, even if it was a girl. "That's not the first time I've been told that," he chuckled through his mask. "I've even gotten some better offers."

Bob Frenck tumbled into the room, still tucking in his scrubs. He had been called into this C-section, just as a pediatrician is called to every C-section. In a shaky voice I started to tell him about the heart tracing, slipping back into the role I couldn't quite handle, but he hushed me. "Hey, Mom, you're not the doctor, I am," he said with a smile. I retreated again in relief.

The numbness that mercifully ran along my lower spine left me feeling strangely detached. There was a cacophony of beeps now, but they were indistinguishable: my heart monitor, the baby's, the autoclave, the temperature probe on the baby warmer. I judged when they started the surgery by the tense mumblings and clink of surgical steel. Neither Randy nor I said a word. Time was suspended. I heard a sputtering first, and then the loud, indignant wail of a strong newborn. Randy, bolting up to look over the screen that separated us from the action, preempted any announcements from the surgical team. He brought his face in close to me, his eyes locked in to mine as if this was the most important thing he ever had to tell me. "It's a girl, Maggie. And she's beautiful. She looks just like you."

I was well looked after in the hospital the next few days, although there was a lingering self-consciousness in the air. Nurses had a halting quality to their questions, as if they weren't sure if it was okay to offer a doctor Jell-O. Janice ducked in now and then for a brief task, but we mostly avoided each other's eyes. Even Seiji and Bob joked a little more heartily than usual, teasing me about my ten-pound baby, leaving the topic of breast-feeding to the nursing staff. My days in the hospital sharpened my sense of how vulnerable patients can feel and gave me a new appreciation for the miracles of modern obstetrics available to privileged women. Health professionals are often the first ones to take ourselves, and what we do, for granted. My obstetrician's calm decisiveness, the nurse's soothing manner, the anesthetist's technical expertise, and the firsthand knowledge that Caitlin's pediatrician knew how to care for the sickest of newborns—all seemed newly wondrous to me as I stared down at my safe, healthy baby.

What a contrast with my medical school experience in OB! At the suburban hospitals, where call rooms had TVs and hospital food was better than what we fixed for ourselves at home, women delivered in private rooms with experienced doctors at the foot of the bed. But within the barbed-wire perimeter of DC General, medical students never slept, so it didn't matter that we had no call rooms. We ate out of vending machines, and poor women had no choice but to let us practice on them.

Halfway through my third year at Georgetown I had been sent back to DC General, the hospital where Randy and I had met our first patient, Mr. Williams. This time, however, we were there for an obstetrics/gynecology rotation. At DC General, poor women of color labored in open wards, cursing or praying their way through pain in a multitude of languages. "Ay, ay, ay, ay!" they would cry in Spanish, or "Lordy, Lordy! Take—this—bay—bee—from—me!" in a thick, drawling shriek. There were many more patients than doctors, and we were given the most responsibility we had ever had. Having much less experience than the average grandmother, I was left alone with women on the verge of delivery while the harried obstetrics resident ran around trying to get to the delivery rooms before the babies popped out.

It was the first time I was scared of more than just the attending physician's wrath. So much could go wrong so quickly. It was the nurses who got the mothers and the med students through the terrifying ordeal.

"Why don't you put some gloves on, 'Doctor.' Dr. Sullivan will be here in just a moment."

"There are sterile drapes to your right, 'Doctor.' This might be a good time to use them." And so on.

We were frequently in over our heads with hysterical, drug-addicted mothers, with menacingly crazy partners, with language barriers, and with the sounds and smells of fear everywhere. The students would gather at the end of a day to share their funny stories and outrageous anecdotes, in an attempt to decompress, but even as we tried to detach ourselves from the chaos, we all knew the sad truth of why we were there. The truth was that not all patients were created equal. We were the best option poor women had.

But I had left that two-tiered system far behind as soon as I put on a navy uniform. That world of haves and have-nots seemed dream-like to me as I cuddled my baby in the comfort of Yokosuka Naval Hospital's OB wing—in the same comfort shared by all the mothers up and down the hall, from all walks of life, from lieutenants in the medical corps to illiterate, non-English-speaking wives of young sailors. Debates about whether or not health care is a right confuse me. Would anyone want a doctor who did not feel a moral imperative to treat all patients to the best of his or her ability? Is it possible to feel morally bound to treat insured patients, but not uninsured ones? Maybe the question about health care being a right is phrased poorly, from the wrong perspective. Maybe the question is this: Given all the medical resources that we have, what moral accountability do we have for the way we use them?

My experience during labor, and in the days that followed, led me to ask other questions as well. I slowly came to an awareness that I needed to be more careful about how authoritatively I practiced. I had been getting by pretty well in life operating on a narrow wavelength of light—one sufficient to distinguish black and white. No solid food until six months old. Don't start toilet training until age two at the earliest. Babies should only fall asleep in their own cribs. This is how I had been taught. Now, with motherhood, my vision seemed suddenly broader and blurrier; the concrete rules were softening.

One afternoon, I half dozed in complete bliss, with Caitlin a warm soft sack in the crook of my arm. Joni, a feisty Filipino nurse, jolted me back to reality. "Dr. Kozel, you of all people should know that you shouldn't let the baby sleep in bed with you."

"Randy's coming to take her from me in a minute," I lied, just to get her out of the room, to get back to my reverie. I thought back to all the patients I had chided in the same way. As I settled back into the pillows, reentering what was one of the most perfect moments of my life, I realized with chagrin that pediatricians sometimes speak as if we get our information directly from the mouth of God.

For decades, the prevailing wisdom in the United States was that babies should sleep on their stomachs. It didn't matter that most of the world had a different view and yet had lower rates of SIDS (sudden infant death syndrome) than we did. It made sense to us, in the absence of real scientific evidence, that babies were at less of a choking risk if they were belly-down. Putting babies to sleep on their backs was tantamount to child neglect. When the nurses wheeled Caitlin in to me in her little isolette, she was on her tummy. All the Japanese babies in the nursery were on their tummies, too. But not for long. We knew perfectly well that as soon as they got home they would sleep in their mother's bed (cardinal sin number one) and on their backs (that would be number two). And yet it was our American babies who were dying of SIDS at the greater rate; the incidence of SIDS in Japan was significant lower than in the US.[6]

By the time my daughter Molly was wheeled into my hospital room at Bethesda, three years later, she was on her back. Two well-designed studies, one from New Zealand and the other from the United Kingdom, pulled the rug out from under this common US practice. Placing babies on their backs to sleep dramatically decreased the incidence of SIDS. The data was too compelling to dismiss, and the US medical profession did an about-face overnight. Five years into our "Back to Sleep" campaign, the incidence of SIDS in the United States had fallen by an estimated 20 percent.[7]

It is interesting, and perhaps telling, that this basic, observational data came from abroad. Our medical literature was filled with sophisticated, important research, but we had chosen to pay attention to certain kinds of data while ignoring some plain facts. No matter what our "medical gut" tells us (as in: *Babies will choke if they sleep on their backs*), we should be able to back it up with evidence. Pediatricians are the first to want to pull our hair out when parents argue against immunizations on the basis of faulty or nonexistent science, just because what they read on the Internet "makes sense" to them. Yet pediatricians had to learn the hard way that we must also hold our own advice to scientific standards of evidence. Claiming we knew the best approach to preventing SIDS just didn't make sense in the face of our own disproportionate number of cases, no matter how much sophisticated supporting data we collected on, say, the exhaled CO_2 content of sleeping babies, or whatever other research we conducted. It didn't make sense. So intent were we on explaining why we couldn't see the string that we missed the fact that it wasn't there.

This is not unlike our current insistence that we have the best health care in the world, even as every indicator of health shows us lagging far behind other developed countries.

Breast-feeding was another area where conventional pediatric wisdom began to fall short of reality. The eye-opener was most clearly provided to me by my second daughter, Molly. An incredibly content baby, she sat happily for hours, smiling and drooling—but not eating—while I was at work and went to sleep for Randy still calmly refusing a bottle. The moment I walked in the door at 2 AM, she woke up to nurse, and she continued to nurse every two hours through the rest of the morning.

"You just need to get her on a schedule" was the party line of most pediatricians at that time, as it was for a generation of grandmothers that hadn't breast-fed their own babies—another one of those fuzzy pearls of pediatric wisdom delivered with a tone of certainty but without the evidence to back it up. I tried to make it a point never to argue with grandmothers, but little Molly, fat and happy, was making a mockery of such dictums. She gave new meaning to the term *well nourished* and was easy to comfort. She readily soothed herself to sleep after a long afternoon of chewing on her developmental toys and slept soundly. She simply outsmarted us into getting all her nutrition from breast-feeding. Molly had no scheduling problems; I did. In the office, my conversations with nursing mothers began to take a distinctive "go-with-the-flow" turn.

There are a lot of fuzzy issues out there on which pediatricians are expected to offer definitive wisdom—toilet training, developmental toys, discipline techniques. We have to be constantly on our guard, no matter how hard we are being pressed for "the right answer," or how tempting it is to convey that sense of expertise the parent is hoping for, that our advice is never more authoritative than the supporting evidence allows it to be.

Six weeks after giving birth to Caitlin in Japan, I had used up all my maternity leave and vacation time and had to return to a full schedule of work. The next year and a half was a clumsy juggling act of patient care and family life. I pumped breast milk in between seeing patients and visited Caitlin at lunchtime when I could. We moved on base so that she would be nearby. Randy carried her to the hospital on frigid winter nights, Caitlin curled up in a ball under his down jacket, so that I could nurse her in the on-call room, the three of us squeezed onto the narrow bed, watching American TV.

We hired an elderly Japanese woman, Misako-san, to care for Caitlin while we were at work. When Randy and I were both on call, Misako-san would spend the night. She and Caitlin made a sweet pair—Misako-san, her graying hair pulled back in combs, speaking softly in Japanese, Caitlin's head bent to hers as if she understood. The joke in the neighborhood was that Caitlin was the only child on the block without a bug bite. Misako-san fanned her vigilantly, never allowing a single insect to land on her perfect pink flesh. I was jealous of the way Misako-san mothered Caitlin but comforted that Caitlin seemed to love her in return. It was the best I could do; by the time Caitlin was six months old, Seiji and Bob had left, and I was breaking in a new pediatrician.

I missed Caitlin terribly. Sometimes it was an actual physical ache. But I understood the twisted interpretation that "women's lib" had been given in American society: *Fine. You want to have the same opportunities as a man? Go for it. But don't start whining when you want to have a family life, too. You brought this on yourself.* Bottom line, if you cared about child rearing, you weren't really ready for the important jobs. It didn't feel like liberation so much as running a gauntlet, proving women could take more of a beating than any men we knew, in order to be allowed to contribute our talents to a profession.

When Bob and Seiji transferred back to the States, an energetic ball of fire named Cora Colette was their only replacement, leaving the two of us to do the work of three. I worked an average of eighty hours a week between the outpatient clinic and hospital coverage that last year. When one of us left for vacation or professional development, the other provided all the coverage twenty-four hours a day for a week or more. Eventually, everyone burned out; of all the pediatricians who passed through Yokosuka during my three years there, I was the only one who didn't leave general pediatrics. Practicing pediatrics at Yokosuka demanded everything I was capable of, and in return for that, I watched very sick children get well, and frantic parents be overcome with relief and gratitude. Tired or not, it was the most fun I would ever have being a doctor.

By the time we left Japan, I was a seasoned pediatrician. Caitlin was twenty months old and understood Japanese better than English. And Randy and I were very, very tired. I resigned from the navy, naively imagining that the biggest difference in my future medical practice would be my improved civilian wardrobe. But it was time for me to leave. As much as I loved practicing medicine in the navy,

I was never at home with the authoritarian structures; it just didn't fit my personality. And I wanted to settle down in one place, get to know my patients over the span of years. There was no way to do that in the navy. Randy accepted a neurology position back at the navy hospital at Bethesda, and I planned on finding civilian work nearby while we worked out a more long-range plan. Although I couldn't quite see the shape of my future, I had no intention of leaving pediatrics out of it. We packed our expanding inventory of household items, crated our aging dog, Elwood, back up, and bid our beloved Misako-san a tearful farewell.

ELEVEN

Reality, Civilian Style

There's no better way to get a feel for the fast pace of change in our society than to step out of it for a while. I remember shopping for groceries shortly after our return from three years in Japan. It was the fall of 1988, and Randy and I were now feeling as disoriented back in Bethesda as we had felt when we first landed in Tokyo's Narita Airport three years earlier.

"Paper or plastic?" the cashier at the grocery store asked us. Randy and I stood there dumbly, not sure how this even constituted a question. I was the first to figure it out—and I told her we'd pay cash.

"I mean the bag. Do you want a paper bag or a plastic bag?" she drawled impatiently at us, as if she couldn't believe the stupidity of some people. Off we went with our paper bags; we had officially begun our reentry into America's atmosphere.

Other changes were gathering momentum. The exploding cost of health care and its far-reaching repercussions had grabbed the full attention of both middle-class and corporate America. Now that I was a civilian physician, they were grabbing my attention, too. Health benefits, which for decades had been linked to employment, were less comprehensive for many; patients resented that they were now being told what doctors they could go to, what procedures were allowable. Even worse, a growing percentage of working Americans were no longer offered or could no longer afford health plans. In the scramble for cost containment, alternative ways of delivering health care were springing up. Privately run HMOs—health maintenance organizations—were relatively new on the scene, but gaining a strong foothold. Health care changes were happening at breakneck speed, but it was happening behind the closed doors of corporate offices, out of earshot of the public or the medical community, without the messy interference of public debate.

My career path as a pediatrician, I soon would realize, gave me a front-row seat from which to observe how medical economics was shaping medical practice. What I would learn firsthand along the way was not just how the mechanics of health care delivery were affected by method of payment, but also how the purse strings stretched into the exam room, into the relationship between doctor and patient, shaping the decision making and the outcome. Those purse strings have shaped the face of medicine—how many dermatologists we have, how many geriatricians—as well as the heart of medicine—who sits in an ER waiting room for six hours with asthma and who gets a same-day appointment for diaper rash.

When I entered civilian practice on my return to Bethesda, I unknowingly jumped right into the eye of the storm, into corporate-style medicine. I took a position working for a large HMO in their after-hours clinic. In the vocabulary of my fellow doctors, I was a "doc-in-a-box," a cynical reference to the fast-food/convenience-store nature of after-hours work.

Most of my nights and weekends in the service of the HMO were very uneventful. I worked in any one of a number of Washington, DC, centers from 6 PM until the last patient was seen, usually around 1 AM. I treated lots of ear infections and diagnosed lots of viral syndromes. Usually, the most notable thing about my shift was the amazing number of patients the organization funneled my way night after night. I would see up to forty or fifty children on a "five"-hour shift. With a scheduling policy apparently based on wishful thinking, the phone triage nurses would go back and start double-booking me once my initial 6 to 11 PM schedule was full, so that I would have two patients at 7:10, two at 7:20, and so on. There were even occasions of triple-booking. Of course I couldn't see patients three times faster, so the waiting times grew longer and longer.

Once parents are kept waiting for an hour and a half, they can be extremely annoyed at the diagnosis of viral syndrome.

"So there's nothing wrong with him?"

I turned to grandma-style recommendations for symptomatic relief, my prescription pad lying blank and useless on the desk. "Try running a cool mist vaporizer, give him plenty to drink, and keep the head of his crib elevated."

"I've been here two hours, and you're telling me you're not going to do anything for him?"

"Well . . ." I'd start again, and fall farther, hopelessly behind.

Parents wouldn't get annoyed at their employer for the kind of health benefit they had negotiated. They wouldn't get annoyed at the HMO for the staffing decisions and scheduling policies that kept patients waiting so long. They would get annoyed at the doctor who had kept them waiting.

In this center-based HMO model, patients (or more likely, their employers) paid a fixed sum for membership. Enrollees were assigned a primary care physician (PCP) at a specific center. This physician oversaw all their care and, significantly, acted as gatekeeper for all tests and referrals. There were financial disincentives for the primary doctor to refer patients to subspecialists, order lab work, admit patients to the hospital, or prescribe non-approved brands of medication. The most positive spin on this system was that it discouraged doctors from careless utilization of resources, and in that respect kept the HMO's costs down. But the unavoidable negative side of this corporate style of practice was the glaring conflict of interest. At virtually every decision point in the doctor–patient relationship, deciding one way would have negative financial impact on the physician, and the other way would not, regardless of what was the right decision for the patient. It was a stunning departure from my navy experience.

Jessica was a one-year-old who was brought to the after-hours clinic by her worried mother because of fever. At this point in my career, I could tell a great deal just by how a child looked. I had been watching this child since I opened the door to the exam room—her flushed face pushed into her mother's chest, the droopy lids, the shallow panting of fever. When I approached her, she cared enough to grimace and whine and made a halfhearted gesture with her arm to push me away. But by the time I laid my stethoscope on her back, she seemed to decide she wasn't up for a fight. She chose instead to simply turn her head away. There were no abnormalities on the exam to explain the fever, which can be worrisome. It is tricky to blame a fever on a harmless virus when there are no viral symptoms to support that diagnosis.

There are plenty of definitive—and often controversial—guidelines as to when a pediatrician should run blood work or other labs on a febrile child; fever over 102.5 is an example. What about cases that don't fall within those guidelines? Jessica's temperature was only 101.8, but she was behaving in a worrisome way. She was too disinterested in me, too resigned.

Technically, I was not one of the doctors in the gray flannel lab coats. As a doc-in-the box, I was among the hourly help that allowed the regularly employed physicians to leave the office by 5 PM. So although the administrators could wave paper at me in an attempt to bring me in line, my paycheck was not at stake the way it was for regular employees. On clinical grounds, of course I ordered the lab work. I needed to see her blood count and her urine studies. If she didn't perk up after some acetaminophen and fluids, I would move on to additional, more expensive tests. But if this happened more than an allotted number of times, as recorded in my physician's "profile" for that month, the cost of the extra lab work would be removed from a pot of money that would have gone to all the regularly employed physicians in the group. The HMO was off the hook; no one was telling doctors they *couldn't* order tests on a sick child. But they reserved the right to declare in hindsight that the tests were unnecessary. The good news for Jessica was that she did have a self-limited viral syndrome after all. The bad news for the doctors at the HMO was that a slew of expensive tests were ordered to diagnose a harmless infection. Their pot of money got a little bit smaller.

To be fair, the HMO's practice guidelines did not come out of thin air, and in fact these organizations conducted some ground-breaking clinical studies that made us all take a second look at the cost-effectiveness of our various practice styles. If our nation is going to have a health care delivery system that is worthy of its medical science, then health professionals need to pay more attention to clinical cost-effectiveness and come up with strategies to translate these findings into everyday practice. At the same time, study results cannot simply be translated into a standardized cookbook for medical practice. Yet this is often the approach taken by health insurers. Clinical judgment is what separates the doctor from the health administrator, and practice guidelines are corrupted when they are determined by nonmedical managers. They are further corrupted when the threat of malpractice suits hangs over every patient encounter. This tangled web I found myself caught up in at the HMO foreshadowed the corporate intrusion I would wrestle with for the rest of my career in medicine.

If I had mixed feelings about the HMO setting clinical practice guidelines, I was equally ambivalent about acting as gatekeeper for subspecialty referrals. Doctors in these arrangements frequently found themselves between a rock and a hard place. Frequency of referral to specialists was monitored and penalized as much as lab utilization was, and the PCP was limited, except in extreme circumstances, to referring to specialists who were part of the HMO. Parents tended not to share such concerns. For many parents, getting a specialist's opinion, even when it is not medically necessary, is synonymous with getting the "best" care for their children.

Ramone was a rambunctious two-year-old brought to the clinic by his tanned, muscular dad. Father and son wore Washington Redskins T-shirts over sweatpants, and Ramone put his sneakers to good use, charging up and down the hall at breakneck speed while I talked with his dad. The problem was that Ramone's feet were turning in when he walked. The child was passing all his motor milestones with gusto and by his dad's description was no more klutzy than other children his age. But Ramone's dad worried this "in-toeing" would affect his son's agility, and he wanted it fixed. I sent Dad running after Ramone to snag him for an examination. Once I coaxed the squirming little boy up to the table, my exam revealed a very common condition called internal tibial torsion. The shin bones of his legs were turned inward, and this made the toes point in. His feet were fine. With Raymond wriggling on his tummy, I held up his legs bent at the knees, and showed his dad the reassuring anatomy.

"Look how flexible the feet are," I pointed out, smiling. I went into my well-practiced explanation of tibial torsion. "It's a common developmental condition," I explained, a model of pediatrician partnering with parent. "All those old cures—special shoes, braces, X-rays—they won't do a thing. And this will most likely improve on its own as Ramone gets older."

Dad watched me more than listened, and as I wrapped up my little lecture, he took a moment to gather his thoughts. "But he's pigeon-toed," he said finally. "I don't want him growing up pigeon-toed. I want him to see an orthopedic doctor."

"Yeah . . . ," I said, regrouping. I tried again, in a couple of different ways, but the expression on his face didn't change. Meanwhile, the fearless Ramone scrambled down the side of the table and stood, pigeon-toed, on a chair, clearly contemplating the pros and cons of a leap.

"Well, an orthopedist won't really have anything to offer," I resumed, but I already knew this was not going to go well. I prepared to fall on a sword. I just needed to decide whose sword it would be— the parent's or the HMO's.

HMO policy gave some muscle to the correct clinical decision, which was not to pursue this any further for the time being. Such policies meant, presumably, that fewer children were getting their feet X-rayed for harmless toeing in, or getting sent to ear, nose, and throat doctors for surgery just because they had a few ear infections, or getting an extensive bowel workup because they had a tummy-ache every morning just before it was time to go to school. Here was another example, in my mind, of "You go to a muffler shop, you get a muffler." Many specialty referrals automatically meant a routine battery of tests or procedures. So the HMO policy that discouraged referrals had all the hallmarks of a win–win situation: Fewer unnecessary tests and procedures had to be a good thing for kids, and there was less waste of expensive medical resources.

However, pediatricians, operating by insurer's rules or simply by the rules of good medical practice, usually end up referring to subspecialists for one of two reasons. The first, obvious reason for referral is that the doctor views it as clinically appropriate. The other, just as common, is that the pediatrician knows if she doesn't make the referral, the parent will either drive her crazy or shop around until a more accommodating doctor is found. With the right insurance policy, the parent may bypass the pediatrician altogether and go straight to the orthopedist for that funny gait. The navy's health care system had a flaw here, too. Since there were no immediate costs to anyone for a specialist evaluation, it was all the more tempting to choose the path of least resistance and hand disgruntled Dad a referral. On the other hand, in-toeing would have been deemed "low priority" over in the orthopedic clinic, and in the six months it took to get an appointment for such a diagnosis, the family would often have read up on the issue, talked about it with others, and maybe would even have observed the problem correcting itself. There was a good chance they would cancel the appointment themselves. Although many US patients base the quality of health care on, among other things, how quickly they can see a specialist, the fact of the matter is that for nonurgent issues, just the opposite is often true.

At the HMO in DC, my choice, which should have been a clear clinical one, instead came down to getting a parent very upset with me, or taking the hit and making an unnecessary referral that muddied my monthly profile some more. Again, the financial disincentive had little impact on an hourly employee such as myself. The squeeze that I was feeling was more on the shape of my future than it was on my pocketbook. When I read the complaint that Ramone's frustrated father wrote the next day about my refusal to refer him to an orthopedist, I was reading the writing on the wall. My patients' families would understand the need for cost containment—but wouldn't always be willing to have it applied to their own care.

More and more in the coming years, the decisions I made for my patients were going to be calculated to cause the least amount of repercussions—in patient dissatisfaction, or legal liability, or insurance hassles—often at the expense of charting the best clinical path. But back then, even with both feet back on US soil, I saw this breed of frustrated, demanding parent as a quirk of the HMO approach to health care, rather than seeing it as part of the sea change that it really was.

TWELVE

To Have and to Have Not

A year and a half after we returned from Japan, Randy found a private neurology practice in Newport, Rhode Island, that appealed to him. The location suited both of us, and I was confident that there would be plenty of pediatric opportunities as well. The Kozel family was again on the move, as were our careers.

A drenching, unrelenting rain welcomed us to Rhode Island. We arrived in Jamestown late at night, and drove up and down an unmarked road for half an hour trying to locate the vacant house we had purchased on a weekend visit. Finally, Randy decided to try his luck on a gravel indentation from the road, and as the car turned in, our future home appeared on the rise ahead of us, lit up in a spray of headlight. The next morning, our three-year-old, Caitlin, and our ten-year-old black Lab, Elwood, looked equally bewildered as they stood at the sliding glass doors in back of the house, taking in the expanse of wet greenery that glistened with sunlight before them. In Bethesda, with six lanes of Connecticut Avenue at our doorstep, neither of them had been allowed to venture outdoors without being attached to an adult. But within moments of being nudged out of our new home, girl and dog became animated with the delight of fresh freedom, with Molly watching wide-eyed through the window from her high chair.

I was anxious to find a private practice to join but realized I was going to have to establish myself in the medical community first. With this in mind, I spent my first year in Rhode Island working at Wood River Community Health Center. Community health centers are private, nonprofit organizations that meet specific criteria for federal support. For instance, they must operate in underserved areas, provide comprehensive primary care services, and see all patients regardless of ability to pay. All employees, including health care professionals, were salaried. In return for meeting federal requirements, the health centers received a higher rate of reimbursement from government programs such as Medicaid than private practitioners did.

Wood River Community Health Center was located about forty miles from our home and involved only clinic work, no hospital coverage. Here, in a small building at the edge of a small town, a collection of talented primary care physicians and very independent nurses delivered expert, state-of-the-art care. It was a medical Brigadoon rising from the surrounding woods and swamps. I shared the workload with an eccentric but dedicated pediatrician from Connecticut who divided his time between gentleman farming and a relentless fight against childhood lead poisoning.

Because the clinic accepted Medicaid and its fees were based on a sliding scale for the uninsured, we served a disproportionately large number of poor families. This was 1990, several years before the federal government began acknowledging how many low-income American children had inadequate health care because their families, the working poor, made too much money to qualify for Medicaid, yet not nearly enough to purchase private coverage. This situation would improve in 1997, when the Congress established SCHIP (State Children's Health Insurance Program), which granted matching federal funds to states that provided Medicaid-type health coverage to children in a broader income range than Medicaid alone covered. I watched SCHIP change the landscape of health care for poor children in Rhode Island almost overnight. Private practitioners could afford to see more poor children, which meant these children now had medical homes, instead of bouncing around hospital clinics and emergency rooms. They were more likely to be seen at the recommended times for well-child care, were more likely to be adequately immunized, had fewer emergency room visits, and were more likely to receive standard-of-care treatment for chronic conditions such as asthma. Lead poisoning was discovered sooner, iron deficiency prevented, developmental delays identified. Their parents in turn received much more safety and well-child-care education. But that was still a few years down the road.

In 1990, Medicaid not only left too many children in the dust, it also reimbursed physicians miserably, to the point that it sometimes *cost* a doctor in private practice to see a child with this coverage. Medicaid rates started at what private insurers would offer and then scaled down from that. To make matters worse, Medicaid took its cues from insurance models like Blue Cross Blue Shield. Not only did it pay less overall, but it used a counterproductive business model that paid considerably more for an ingrown toenail than a breast-feeding issue. Medicaid also denied claims for trivial reasons, meaning many visits went completely without reimbursement. In addition, handling the required paperwork meant the physician had to hire additional office staff, beyond what was needed for the private plans. But cost-effectiveness was not built into the Medicaid mind-set. As a result, many private pediatricians did not accept Medicaid.

Politicians shamelessly ignore these realities when they proudly introduce legislative bills to control health costs by reducing Medicare or Medicaid payments to doctors. The implication is that taxpayers will save money, patients will still get the same care, and those rich doctors won't even notice if a little more is shaved from their income. But none of those things is true, and politicians know it. Doctors cut back on the number of government-insured patients they can afford to see. With less access to doctors, these patients are more likely to defer their care until there is no choice but to go to an emergency room, and taxpayers end up paying the exorbitant cost of problems left untreated for too long.

Poor children on Medicaid have several strikes against them. Not only will they find fewer doctors to take them on, but they often are on Medicaid because they are special-needs patients, or in foster care because of abuse and neglect, or from impoverished circumstances that have put them at risk of malnourishment, or exposure to lead or smoke. These are the most labor-intensive patients in a pediatric practice. It is an unhappy fact that the vulnerable children who generate the least income for a doctor also generate the most work. How well they are cared for is the measure not only of a pediatrician, but also of a society.

One of my first patients at Wood River was three-month-old Jennie. By the foster mother's description, Jennie had had a generalized seizure—a convulsion—at home. She was in foster care because of her own mother's drug abuse problem, although we didn't have many details. Her physical exam was completely normal for her age. She smiled responsively for me, tracked my movements with her bright eyes, and wriggled with excellent body tone. I called the only pediatric neurologist in the state at that time, and faster than I could say "foster care" he understood the kind of reimbursement he could expect. He insisted he did not need to see the child or do any tests. I was shocked. No EEG? No imaging studies? No spinal tap? I had read consultation reports of his in other patients' charts. This was the same doctor who performed highly questionable but expensive EEGs on insured headache patients before he even evaluated them.

"What's the point?" he challenged impatiently. "The mother is a drug addict; you don't need to rule anything else out. This was probably a withdrawal seizure. Load her up on phenobarbital." Phenobarbital is a sedating drug that back then was commonly used to treat seizures in children, but we usually looked harder to find a cause for the seizure before we settled into therapy—especially with a young infant.

I was angry, and backed into a corner. Medicaid patients could not be referred out of state, and this baby needed to be evaluated by a pediatric neurologist. I told Dr. Do-Little that if he would not see her then I would refer her to the ER at the Rhode Island Hospital, and let them contact him. He was on the staff there and would have no choice but to respond. Do-Little begrudgingly relented but got his way in the end. He was rude to the foster mother and did only the most cursory exam on the child. He started medication without doing any tests.

I was thus forewarned when a few months later Kyle, a seven-month-old patient with Down syndrome, started having a particular kind of seizure known as infantile spasms. This type of seizure causes an infant to jerk suddenly into a flexed position. Its diagnosis and treatment are very different than for Jennie's type of seizure, but the pitiful insurance coverage was the same. I didn't waste time on the pediatric neurology specialist this time. Kyle needed a good evaluation quickly.

"He's how old?" asked Randy as I started to present Kyle's case over the phone; he usually did not see patients under twelve. But he didn't interrupt again through the rest of the story, and I knew he was hooked.

"Well, right off the bat, he needs an EEG. And if it shows hypsar-rhythmia [a very specific brain wave abnormality that is diagnostic for this type of seizure], we have to get him going on treatment right away."

Randy, who had privileges at nearby Westerly Hospital, arranged to have Kyle admitted to the pediatric service there, with him as consultant to the pediatrician. I helped him with the sedation doses for the studies Kyle needed. The CT scan and blood tests were normal, but the slow, intense waves that discharged across Kyle's EEG confirmed the diagnosis of infantile spasms. We slowly started him on medication. Sweet little Kyle not only stopped having those frightful jerks but over the next few months made amazing progress in his developmental milestones, like sitting up without support. His follow-up EEG was normal, and I had the pleasure of watching his continued development over the next decade.

If working in the HMO, fresh out of the navy, served as a wake-up call for me when it came to the business end of civilian health care, working at the health center was like a slap in the face. Randy and I had been trained to take our responsibilities as physicians seriously, and practicing in the navy had given us the tools to do that—and no excuses not to. Now, no matter how strongly I felt that my patient should receive a certain service, I might not be able to get it for him, because of his inability to pay. It was the first time in my medical career that I knew what a patient needed yet had to settle for something less.

It's not just about children, either. One of Randy's colleagues, a private neurologist, had what he dubbed "Medicaid clinic" every Wednesday afternoon. In the span of three allotted hours, he would see however many Medicaid patients had been referred to him that week. The more patients, the shorter the visits. It was a simple business model: He could still claim to accept Medicaid but limited the financial risk. Meanwhile adult, developmentally delayed patients from "group homes" were driven in from all over the state to see Randy for their seizures and headaches and dizziness, because he scheduled and treated them the same way he scheduled and treated all his other patients—making less money than his colleagues as a result.

Randy and I were facing, for the first time since medical school, the haves and have-nots of health care. The "haves" had good health insurance. The "have-nots" were marginalized, with government programs that allowed the rest of us to feel as if we could look away in good conscience, but with inadequate coverage to fully address their needs. And the doctors were caught in the middle, struggling to remain medically conscientious and morally responsible in a system that carried disincentives for both. For Randy's patients as for children in foster care, and many others, a large portion of our country's safety net would amount to relying on the kindness of strangers.

THIRTEEN

Brian and Billy

One of the first patients I met when I began working at Wood River Community Health Center was a six-year-old cyclone named Billy. As I pulled his chart off the wall rack outside the exam room, I heard a chair fall over on the other side of the closed door, followed by a swelling cacophony:

"Billy Robinson," shouted an adult female voice, "you stop that right now or we are not going to Burger King."

A squealy, laughing kind of sound was the first response, then a crash of some object against the wall, and the final percussive note—the dull *thud* of a bottom being whacked. Shrill strains of "That's it! No french fries for you!" and then a stomping and a low, slowly building wail, "Noooooo. I wanna go to berr-ga-king," in unison with an unexpected background trill—the unmistakable cry of a very young infant.

The pediatric nurse joined me in the hall, arms folded, smirking, her presence having no other apparent purpose than the entertainment my facial expressions were providing.

"Just how many kids are in there?" I mumbled out of the corner of my mouth. "In there" was an exam room the size of a walk-in closet.

"Oh, you'll get to know the Robinsons," she said, still smirking. "There are six of them."

"Six Robinsons?" I asked cautiously.

"No, six kids. They come from the housing project down in Branford. Dad's a big-time drinker. No job. Finally had his license taken away, thank God. Of course Mom can only get up here now when she can find a ride. Mom gets SSI [Supplemental Security Income] for some mental health disability, and the kids are all on Medicaid. She just had another baby, as a matter of fact."

"So I hear." The newborn's wails were all but drowned out now by the little boy's sobbed pleas.

"Pweeze Mom. I'll be good. I pwomiss!"

"No!" snapped the mom. "Now you've got your sister crying. Why do you always do this? Wait till I tell your daddy. You want a spanking when you get home?"

Billy began crying in earnest. "No! You won't tell Daddy!"

I took a deep breath; I needed to get in there. I had already kept them waiting too long. A quick glance at the chart revealed that nothing was filled in for weight or vital signs, just a notation in red ink: *Patient uncooperative.* There was similar brevity in the explanation for the visit: *hyperactive.* I flashed the nurse a thanks-loads smile and pushed into the room.

There were four children there. In the far corner, a quiet, watchful, stringy-haired girl of about eight was mothering her stringy-haired little sister by feeding her from a bag of candies. Mom sat on a chair with the baby flat on her lap, as if it had just dropped out of the sky and landed there. Billy sat on the other chair, whimpering, refusing to look at me.

Mrs. Robinson jumped up and flashed me a broad smile. She had no front teeth.

"Hello, Doctor," she gushed warmly, eagerly. This signaled she was poor more than her insurance information, or her disheveled children, or her gap-toothed smile. Though I had left her waiting in a tiny room for half an hour, with a very rambunctious child, she betrayed no signs of impatience, as if it was just so nice of me to show up at all.

I introduced myself, shaking her hand, and apologized for the long wait.

"So, this must be Billy." I smiled, crouching down in front of the whimpering child. He wouldn't meet my eye. His breaths were in heaves now. An orange stain that matched the spilled juice on the floor bled across the front of his Batman T-shirt.

"Billy, say hello to the doctor," prompted Mom, sounding worried that this might not go well.

"It's okay," I told Billy, instinctively wanting to let him off the hook. "Your mom and I can talk." The two little girls in the corner were silent and still, watching me like deer.

"Hi. What are your names?"

The older girl whispered, "Annie and Liz."

I crouched down to meet her face, really working the room. Their clothes smelled of mildew, and they were both covered in scratches and insect bites. Some of those bites looked infected. "Which one are you?" I asked, smiling, meeting the older girl's eyes.

"Liz," she said, so quietly she was practically just mouthing the words.

"Hi, Liz," I said to her. "Hi, Annie," I said to the little one who had been wordlessly following my every move. She used two fingers to slowly massage the goo from her nose. Annie looked to be about two years old.

"She doesn't talk," Liz offered cautiously.

"Never?" I asked, still careful to smile, trying not to frighten them.

"She's my quiet one," cackled Mrs. Robinson. "Doctor, it's actually Billy we're here about."

"How old are you, Billy?" I asked, turning back to him, my knees starting to ache. This had been one long crouch.

No answer from Billy. Just a pout.

"Tell the doctor how old you are," pleaded Mom, as if she feared I might end the appointment right then and there in the face of such stubbornness.

"Are you in college yet?" Tiny chuckle. "Married?" Giggle. I could see how decayed his front teeth were.

Billy then jumped up and proudly boomed, "I AM SIX YEARS OLD!" Had I unwittingly freed his inner Tasmanian devil? Still, we were making progress. In fact, everyone was smiling tentatively as I stood up and turned back toward Mom, preparing to get down to business. But there was so much need in that room, I hardly knew where to begin.

"He just can't sit still. He gets on everybody's nerves. He's not happy unless he's getting into trouble. He's driving us all crazy. And now with the new baby . . ."

I listened, mentally ticking off follow-up questions I needed to ask as soon as I could get a word in. And I watched Billy. There was a slight flicker of his eyes or flinch of his head as each complaint registered, even as he stomped around the room making grunting noises or turned the water faucets on and off. He was listening. He was probably hearing this litany for the hundredth time.

"Billy, will you *stop* that!" Mrs. Robinson snapped as he roughly pulled on the paper towel dispenser. "Do you see what I mean, Doctor? There is no controlling him," she whined. She was at the end of her frayed rope, looking to me for support, as in *Yes, you're right, I see what you mean. I don't know how you are coping.*

But I was playing for Billy's team, and I wanted to run interference for him. He reminded me of my brother, Brian, as a child.

My brother Brian was only eleven months old when I was born. Irish twins we were called, with a wink and a nod. We even looked like twins—the same facial features squeezed by our temperaments into different expressions. We were inseparable until Brian, a mere five years old, started first grade. Even then, reunited in the afternoon, we'd sit at the top of the stairs, out of harm's way, and Brian would use his schoolbooks to teach me to read.

Within a few years we began to part ways. By the time Brian started school, he had been assigned the role of Troublemaker in our family, while I was the Saving Grace. Our older siblings, Johnny and Helen Marie, had all but abandoned the sinking ship we called home by the time they reached high school, so Brian had to step up as the reason my parents drank and fought. Even the fact that nobody ever fixed the upstairs toilet or that the screen door had been off its hinges for years could be traced back, if need be, to how miserable Brian had made our lives.

"You're useless, just like everything else in this goddamn house!" our mother screamed at him if he dropped a bottle of milk or broke something he wasn't supposed to be playing with. She mocked him for being so puny, blamed him for ruining her life. "Why can't you be like Maggie?" she would demand. It would be my father's job to "do something about him!" when he got home. He spanked Brian with a bamboo cane that we had brought home as a souvenir from the World's Fair. I would run to my room to hide, sick to my stomach, afraid to stick up for him.

One stifling summer evening when I was six years old, our parents arranged a cookout. We packed a cooler with burgers and Cokes and Ballantine beer and headed to the town beach. The lusciously cool sand was no sooner pushing its way up between my grateful toes than my mother began shrieking that someone forgot to pack the mustard.

"Get the hell out of my way!" she shot at Brian as she reached into another bag. Brian and I snatched some rolls and ran down to the ocean to feed the hovering seagulls. This was my favorite time on the beach. The wind wildly bearing down on us, the waves pounding and pulling at our legs released us from the breathless space my family preferred us to live in.

Dusk was creeping in from the east by the time we gathered around the picnic table, and for a while we all behaved, focused as we were on keeping our paper plates and napkins from blowing away. Then Brian got the ball rolling. "So where's the mustard?" he tossed out, grinning as he chewed. Even the sullen teenagers snickered.

"Sure, go ahead and laugh, you little twerp," my mother snapped back. "Like you could ever do anything right."

"Oh, Mother," chimed in Helen Marie from stage left, "have another beer." Malice curled a corner of my mother's mouth. Brian and I took our cue, grabbing our cans of soda and running over to one of the scraggy pine trees that canopied the picnic area. Their lower branches were the perfect height for hoisting ourselves up, and soon we were lost in an airy game of hide-and-seek.

It was dark by the time my mother produced a bag of marshmallows for us to roast. Johnny had stomped off to town to be with his "no-good friends," and Helen Marie had withdrawn to a bench in the shadows, so it was a few minutes before our fractured group realized that Brian was not there.

"Where the hell is he?" demanded my mother.

"Oh for God's sake," whined Dad, and then they both looked at me. A feeling of dread congealed in my stomach.

"I don't know where he is," I said. "I haven't seen him in a while." Just saying this terrified me.

We fanned out, yelling "Briiii-an! Briiiii-an!" But there was no answer, just the empty space that followed our calls. Even my parents began to look worried.

"Oh my God," cried Mom, suddenly horrified, "He wouldn't have gone in the water!" We hurried down to the ocean's foamy edge, screaming his name into the wind. Nothing. Back at the picnic site, the neglected fire cast menacing shadows across the sand. My mother was hysterical.

"Where could he be?" she cried, clutching her head with her hands.

We resumed our aimless circling in the darkness, frantically calling for him, as if hoping he just hadn't heard our desperate cries the first time.

"John, get the police," my mother wailed. My stomach jolted, and I tried to concentrate on breathing through my mouth so I wouldn't throw up. My father started to walk toward the car.

"Hey, I'm up here!" shouted Brian from the heavens. Everyone stopped, stunned and confused, looking up to the night sky. His voice had shot down from one of the dark pines. There was a rustling and a shaking, and we saw the silhouette of his little monkey frame drop down to the sand from a low-hanging branch. Then it was chaos. My parents began shouting and didn't stop.

"What the hell did you think you were doing?"

"You had to ruin everything, didn't you?"

I hung back, already too worried about the unfolding battle to allow myself a moment of relief—and angry with Brian for setting another rampage in motion. Brian insisted that he had fallen asleep up there in the twisted, knobby arms of the pine tree. But I knew that wasn't true. I understood exactly why he had crouched silently in that miserable tree, peering through pine needles at the drama below. He had been listening carefully as the night wind moved in to winnow our frantic calls, bringing him only our love and grief, and carrying the rest away.

Seven-year-old Brian, like Billy Robinson, could have been Dennis the Menace in a cartoonishly healthy family, an adorable imp who stood wide-eyed in front of a broken window, the incriminating slingshot still in hand, while his mom and dad decided if he should be made to go sit in the corner. Nobody called Dennis "hyperactive," like it was a disease. But neither Billy nor Brian had the good sense to be born to Mr. and Mrs. Mitchell. They were born into broken, overwhelmed, addicted families that didn't know what to do with them, that only knew how to behave badly in response. So I had a soft spot in my heart for Billy, even as he drenched the floor with water and emptied the paper towel holder into the sink.

I couldn't say if there was anything "wrong" with this little plumber. I knew that I didn't want him to spend his childhood listening to such litanies. And I knew that children's behavior is usually just a mirror held up to their families—their genetics, their attitudes, their emotional health. This was too much to try to sort out in a twenty-minute appointment. But I learned long before, from Dr. Cahill, that the only way to deal with pain is to look at it square in the eye and, if nothing else, at least name it for what it is.

"So, how long have you been concerned about Billy's behavior?"

My question to Mrs. Robinson sounded so casual and bland. But I knew I was inviting a dam to break open.

"From the day he was born," she said, waving him away. Impatience slipped through her voice. Any fool could plainly see the problem. "You gotta do somethin', Doc. He's like this all day at home. He's just wild, I guess you'd say. And we can't take it no more."

Pediatric residency seemed so theoretical and far away now. We learned about ADHD—attention deficit hyperactivity disorder—in lumbering lunchtime lectures, watching videos of kids bouncing off the walls, followed by discussions of precise diagnostic methods and the multidisciplinary approach to treatment. This involved coordinating the efforts of the pediatrician, the neurologist, and the school, and of course it included family therapy—regular sessions over an eight- to twelve-week period to teach parents behavioral and environmental strategies for coping with the disorder.

This was ivory tower medicine at its most disconnected. There was nothing precise about the diagnosis of ADHD, there was no magical network over which care could be coordinated, and there was precious little money for anything that smacked of "mental health" service. Military medicine was the closest I would ever come to having the scheduling flexibility and outside resources that this approach required. At Wood River, I was a long way from military medicine.

Attentional problems and hyperactivity were among the most common concerns that brought parents into my office in my years as a pediatrician. ADHD is the most commonly diagnosed chronic disease of children, and various studies estimate the prevalence among children in the United States to be anywhere from 4 to 12 percent.[8] The statistics for the percent of patients seen in a pediatrician's office for this diagnosis are similar—about 3 to 11 percent. The causes are as individual and as complicated as the child. The current approach to evaluation and treatment requires a great deal of time, batteries of imprecise tests, and, if we are honest, guesswork that then drives trial-and-error management. The fact that ADHD is real, and serious, does not mean that we are good at identifying or managing it. The fact that it is increasingly diagnosed and managed by primary care physicians does not mean that this is the most effective approach.

Imagine that doctors were called upon to diagnose pneumonia without being able to examine the patient for physical findings or do any laboratory tests such as blood counts or X-rays to look for infection. The only data they could collect would be in the form of questionnaires handed out to family members and nonmedical professionals, asking a lot of subjective questions such as "Does he seem more run-down to you?" Then imagine that all the parties have secondary agendas of their own. Parents know that they will be able to sleep better at night, and teachers know there will be less coughing to disrupt the class if the little darling gets some of that codeine-containing cough medicine. And just to make it all interesting, lots of people, it turns out, not just children with pneumonia, would like to get their hands on that cough prescription. They might enjoy it themselves or sell it to friends. Meanwhile, pharmaceutical companies are making a bundle of money on an ever-expanding variety of drugs to treat the cough, so marketing cough syrup for the questionable pneumonia has become a full-court press. Even the parenting magazines in the waiting room carry full-page glossies. Interestingly, as pharmaceutical production increases, so does the diagnosis. Free-market health care.

The doctors, of course, might well be wrong as frequently as they might be right in their diagnosis and treatment of pneumonia under these circumstances. Just as significantly, they would be overlooking and undertreating other causes of cough, such as allergies or sinusitis or foreign bodies in the airway.

Pediatricians work very hard at diagnosing ADHD, but the objective data that we try to tell ourselves we have is not very objective. It's often not even data.

Many children react to emotional overload with impulsive, excessive activity. That means that children who are depressed, unlike their adult counterparts, are often bouncing off the walls. So are children who are anxious, a net that gathers children of alcoholics, children of angry or abusive parents, children who are neglected, and children browbeaten by overly controlling parents. And children in all these circumstances can also have ADHD. This is the puzzle I am supposed to get to the bottom of.

And so I continued with Billy, drawing little on my formal pediatric training. I plodded through the developmental history, opening with an easy one.

"How old was Billy when he first walked?"

Mrs. Robinson's momentary look of confusion suggested she was sure I missed the point of the visit, but she was willing to indulge me, kind of. "Oh I ain't worried about him in that way. He can climb like a monkey. Now, this one," she added, pulling Annie front and center, "she's the one who wouldn't walk. And she still don't wanna talk neither."

Oh boy. Mental note to get an appointment for Annie, for a visit unlikely to be reimbursed. Meanwhile, I was burning through our allotted twenty minutes before I'd even established Billy's eating habits. As for the behavioral disorders? Family dysfunction? The learning issues? I couldn't imagine how we were ever going to get through this. The standard approach in outpatient clinic during my residency was: If you didn't have enough time to cover a complicated problem, then you just explained to your patient that you had to reschedule a follow-up visit. Parents apparently would be more than willing to follow this reasonable plan.

Hah to that. There was no way Mrs. Robinson was going to be able and willing to repeat today's monumental effort in the interest of academic purity. And Medicaid—or any other insurance—wouldn't pay for a to-be-continued second visit anyway. So I soldiered on, working my way through the family social history as delicately as possible. I couldn't draw her out about Dad's drinking, only that Billy seemed to be at the root of Dad's bad humor. Mrs. Robinson shyly admitted that she was being treated for depression but said little more about it, brushing it off even as her face slackened and she seemed to forget that she had a baby in her arms. Another note to self.

Discipline in the Robinson household seemed to mostly involve the parental version of banging one's head against the wall—lots of yelling and spanking and frustration, with little result. Billy's nutrition made me wince, although it wasn't that much worse than that of a lot of kids I would see from wealthier backgrounds, where juice boxes are considered to be a reasonable substitute for fresh fruits and vegetables. When she thinks of it, Billy's mom takes the vitamins that she gets for the younger children on the WIC program (a nutrition subsidy program for poor women, infants, and young children), and gives him some.

"How is he doing at school?"

"Oh, his teacher says he has that ADD thing."

Great. He's just starting kindergarten and already needs fixing.

I proceeded with the physical exam, methodically, urging myself to be conscientious even as the clock ticked away. When all was said and done, I found nothing that was medically definitive. I ordered some lab tests to rule out conditions like iron deficiency and lead poisoning. I gave Mrs. Robinson referrals for social agencies with long waiting lists and limited resources, and pamphlets about nutrition and discipline, but I wasn't even sure she could read. I offered her the name of the only dentist in southern Rhode Island who accepted Medicaid. And I handed her what was the cornerstone of ADHD diagnosis: questionnaires for her and for Billy's teachers about his behavior.

"Isn't there something you can give him, Doc? My husband's ready to kill him."

"My concern here is Billy, Mrs. Robinson. Are you worried for Billy's safety?" I went too far. A shadow came over her face.

"No, nothing like that," she said quickly. "He's just driving us all crazy. There must be some medicine you can give him." She was pleading.

I offered more advice, more strategies, more encouragement, temporizing while we waited for lab results. And as I watched them all trudge out the door, seemingly dazed by the lack of a fix to this godawful mess, my heart sank. I knew better than Mrs. Robinson how little this visit had accomplished, how little difference any of this was likely to make in Billy's life. He would probably end up, at least for a while, on a trial of one of the stimulant medications, like Ritalin, that are used to help ADHD patients focus. The medication might help some of his behaviors, or not. It certainly wouldn't help all of them. It wouldn't change his natural temperament or his environment. He would almost certainly continue to be a scapegoat. His parents would engage minimally, if at all, with social services and would not find parenting classes practical, affordable, or appealing. Billy was unlikely to be evaluated in any meaningful way for depression or anxiety.

I heaved a deep sigh after they all cleared out. There were a number of children I saw that year at Wood River whom I felt I had been able to truly help. I could not kid myself that Billy was one of them. A pediatrician was only one small piece of what Billy needed. But it's the only piece that gets paid for, and I was beginning to see that health funding is what drives our health practice. If the problem didn't come under the traditional "health" umbrella, our only choice was to make it fit, just like Mr. Williams's invisible string back in med school. We used questionnaires and practice guidelines endorsed by our professional organizations to convince our patients and ourselves that we were practicing good medicine. The approach made sense if we closed one eye and squinted, imbuing an anemic strategy with color.

There was very little in that room overflowing with Robinsons that I was trained to treat. In four years of medical school, and another four years of internship and pediatric residency, I barely brushed the surface of topics like nutrition, emotional trauma, behavioral disorders, or learning differences. The greatest risk to pediatric health, poverty, isn't even a medical school topic. Poor children in our society are the ones most likely to be malnourished, be exposed to environmental toxins and violence, be under-immunized, and have inconsistent access to medical and dental care. To view childhood poverty as a separate issue from children's health is like turning our backs on contaminated water supplies during an outbreak of dysentery, waiting instead to treat patients as they become ill.

I was well trained, to be sure. If one of the kids in that room happened to be wheezing, or have a genetic syndrome, or needed me to explain what his bone marrow biopsy revealed about his leukemia, then I had a wealth of experience and scientific thought to draw upon. If one of them was lying ill in a hospital bed, getting her nutrition through an IV, then I just needed to write some orders in the chart to come to the rescue. But back there in that crowded little exam room at the health center, five years after completing my specialty training, I had barely begun to acknowledge an important reality: The doctor I had trained to be—scientific, conscientious, and skilled in diagnosing and treating specific kinds of pediatric illness—was not what many—perhaps the majority—of my patients were going to need. I, Brian's sister, knew better than most what Billy needed. But now in civilian practice, with its narrow, physician-based definition of health care, I was no longer positioned to reach out of the exam room for help.

FOURTEEN

Family Ties

O ne morning at the health center, I was seeing a four-week-old with an incessant cough. She was breathing rapidly but otherwise looked well. The crackling sound of fluid in her lungs suggested that, despite her happy demeanor, she had pneumonia. I ordered an X-ray and stepped back out into the hall where the nurse was waiting for me, looking tense and anxious. "Your aunt Dorothy is on the phone" was all she said.

Dread started filling my chest and closing my throat before I even knew whom I would be grieving for. By the time I reached the phone, Father Gallagher, the parish priest, had been handed the phone on the other end; he had come to sit with Aunt Dorothy as soon as he'd heard. "Maggie, I'm so sorry to have to tell you, but your father has passed on, God rest his soul." Dad had just been up to visit us the previous week, constantly short of breath, hardly able to read a bedtime story to the girls, his heart and kidneys debilitated by a lifetime's assault on his arteries. Seventy-five years old, he had seemed dismayed at the way his body was betraying him, but I hadn't expected him to die so soon.

I quietly cried through the details. He had been brought to the hospital in congestive heart failure and had passed away while the nurse stepped out to arrange TV service—he had insisted on watching the Giants game. I asked Father Gallagher to put Aunt Dorothy on the phone so I could sniffle a few reassuring words to her before I hung up. Although Dad rarely had a kind word for his younger sister, I knew his death would hit her hard.

By the time I went back out in the hall, I was red-eyed and puffy from crying, in no shape to reassure a worried mother but weirdly able to slip into a detached state where I could explain to my internist colleagues how to take care of the infant. The X-ray, which looked much worse than the child, showed fluffy infiltrates across both lung fields. It was a classic case of chlamydia pneumonia, which a baby can contract from an infected mother during childbirth. It was usually a self-limited illness, but infants recovered more quickly with treatment. "She just needs a prescription for erythromycin," I explained to my colleagues, writing out the dose, stopping to blow my nose. "Have her come back tomorrow for follow-up. Teach the mom how to count the baby's respirations. She needs to go to the ER if her respiratory rate goes up, or she stops feeding, or looks sicker in any way. Okay?" As I talked, I was aware of feeling like I was just going through the motions, an actor playing a doctor on TV. The two internists, wide-eyed with uncertainty, turned together to the exam room where the baby and her mom were waiting, finding strength in numbers. I went back to the office and called Randy. We headed to Point Lookout that night—but not before I made one more phone call.

I had sniffled on the phone a few weeks earlier for a different reason. My brother Brian, whom I hadn't seen in years, had called from St. Louis to tell me that his marines reserve unit was being sent to Kuwait, for what we would later refer to as the "first" Gulf War. He also told me that he had gotten married to a woman named Marian, a woman I had never met. I told him to be careful, and he teased me when my voice cracked.

As Brian and I had grown away from our childhoods, an awkward strangeness had settled between us. The bonds that had held us close in childhood had been stretched so thin, I almost forgot they were there at all. When I made my escape to college and then to med school, Brian hung back in our hometown, working on a clam boat by day, finding dinner and companionship in the bars along Point Lookout's boulevard by night.

By the time I graduated from medical school, in May 1980, my parents were the only family members for whom I needed tickets; my siblings had flung themselves as far from Mom and Dad as they could get. Helen Marie had all but disappeared into Miami, preferring rooming houses and even homelessness to life in Point Lookout.

Johnny wished me well from afar; I understood by then that our relationship could only exist out of firing range from Mom and Dad. I lost touch with Brian when he had enlisted in the marines and was sent to Okinawa.

As I hovered on the stage steps at the Kennedy Center on graduation day, waiting for my name to be called, I waved at classmates and sent a thumbs-up to Randy. The cycle of applause revved up and died down as I stepped toward the podium. Then, in the brief quiet between clapping and diploma, there came booming down from the balcony, across an ocean of graduates and their families, "Way to go, Maggieeeeeee!" The audience tittered as I stopped mid-stage, stunned, and looked up to find Brian, tall and broad in his crisp marine khakis. He had bargained for some last-minute leave, took an endless series of military hops, and somehow charmed his way into the hall in the nick of time. My commemorative photo of the moment shows the dean of the medical school shaking my hand, smiling at me. My face, however, is looking away from him, away from the camera, upward, smiling at Brian in his perch.

Now, ten years later, I was calling the Red Cross to have Brian sent back from Kuwait. He arrived in Point Lookout less than forty-eight hours later, still in his desert camouflage, and his new bride flew in from St. Louis. Johnny came right away, too. Helen Marie by this time was already in Point Lookout; she had recently moved back from Miami to live with my father, claiming the tiniest room upstairs as her own and sleeping on a mattress on the floor.

It was the first time the four of us had been together in twenty years. We didn't congregate in the sad, squalid little house we had grown up in. Instead we crowded into Aunt Dorothy's cozy rooms, let her fuss over us, ate her roasts with gravy and canned vegetables, drank screw-capped wine out of her tiny crystal glasses, and laughed at crazy memories until Aunt Dorothy hushed us, "out of respect for the dead."

We trekked up to the nursing home in Long Beach to tell our mother that Dad had died. Shrunken and yellow-haired, strapped to an oversized high chair, she hissed at us, not knowing who we were. After the funeral, the four of us hugged one another, glad to have been together, not sure if it would become anything more. Johnny and I talked practicalities about the house. Brian headed back to a faraway desert, and Marian returned to St. Louis. Aunt Dorothy and Helen promised to drive up to Rhode Island soon for a visit. We would spend the next few decades slowly, cautiously, weaving our lives back together, with cousins getting to know cousins, and birthday cards arriving from aunts and uncles who previously had been just names occasionally mentioned. We created a family where there had been none.

FIFTEEN

Mae

I had been at Wood River for almost a year when a private pediatric practice closer to home contacted me. Narragansett Bay Pediatrics had one of the best reputations in the state, and it was losing a pediatrician. A young doctor who had worked there only a few years had decided, as do many who start out in general pediatrics, that primary care was not for him. He was headed for a fellowship in allergy/immunology. The two remaining doctors, Celeste Corcoran and Bob Maltz, asked if I was interested in joining them.

Working at Wood River Community Health Center had given me a wonderful opportunity to provide health care both to children who otherwise had trouble gaining access to it and to well-insured children who happened to live nearby and chose the center for convenience. But there were two drawbacks: The job paid very little, and I had no hospital affiliation. When a child needed admission, I had to call one of the private medical doctors in the area and beg him or her to admit the child to Westerly Hospital. The usual resistance to this was understandable. These pediatricians had more than enough work of their own, and the low Medicaid reimbursement for the poorer children was insulting. I hated making the calls; the private docs hated getting them. Working for Narragansett Bay Pediatrics, I would not only work much closer to home, but would also have privileges at nearby South County Hospital, share night and weekend call, cover the newborn nursery and ER—for all pediatric patients, not just our own—and make considerably more money (about as much as a Rhode Island public school teacher at the highest pay grade, but without retirement benefits).

I sat down with Bob and Celeste in their cramped storefront office. They had sent out for pizza in my honor, and we chatted in a rambling way, slowly uncovering what we needed to know about one another.

"I have several complicated patients I'm following now," I told them cautiously. "Most are foster children on Medicaid."

"They're welcome here," said Celeste, without missing a beat. Petite and business-like, she filled me in on their call schedule and patient load. "We don't make a lot of money, but the practice is growing. We take Medicaid, unlike some of the other practices around here," she added with some annoyance, "and if the family is uninsured we set them up with a payment schedule."

"What kinds of problems have you been seeing out at Wood River?" asked Bob, much more intrigued by the clinical stories than the insurance details. He looked totally relaxed sitting there in his jeans and sneakers, absentmindedly fingering his Mickey Mouse tie. Smiling, self-effacing, he was a young Woody Allen version of a doctor. "Don't worry about getting in here from Jamestown," he told me with a wave. "If you think you can't get here fast enough for an emergency, call me. I'm close." I pictured that was the way he talked to patients. *It's no big deal. You can handle it.*

I liked both of them. A lot. And when I made my move over to Narragansett Bay Pediatrics, Kyle, Jennie, and a multitude of other insurance-challenged children came with me.

My maiden voyage into the land of private pediatric practice began on a Fourth of July weekend in 1991. My new partners had been overworked since the departure of their former colleague, and both were looking forward to holiday getaways. Celeste was going sailing; Bob was heading to New York to visit family. So after a day or two of orientation, I was handed a beeper and a list of emergency phone numbers. I was on my own and scheduled to start hospital coverage at eight o'clock Saturday morning.

I was awakened, however, by an ER call around 4 AM. A four-year-old girl from a nearby health center had presented with high fever and an alarming petechial rash—a rash that looks like countless tiny broken blood vessels all over the body. The pediatric consultant on call had been brought in; he apparently was distinctly unalarmed and dismissed a lab test showing a very low platelet count in her blood. He had advised the ER staff to "have her follow-up with Narragansett Bay"—code for "not my practice"—in the morning. It's impossible to know what was going through that doctor's head, but what is clear is that if this very symptomatic child turned out to have a harmless viral illness, the pediatrician would get a tiny amount of reimbursement for diagnosing that in the middle of the night, regardless of how much work it took to rule out more dangerous things. And very significant to the management of acute illness in pediatrics, insurance companies would not pay for any follow-up visits that occurred in the first twenty-four hours after the initial assessment. As I was quickly learning, insurance providers, whether government-funded or private, set up all kinds of disincentives to providing good care, with punitive policies for ruling out serious conditions in a child who will turn out to have a benign illness, just as occurred in the HMO, and refusing to pay for visits to reassess a sick child at frequent intervals. To make matters worse, malpractice lawyers make it risky for a doctor to willingly take on dangerous illness—especially in unknown patients. Many physicians legitimately view that scenario as a lawsuit waiting to happen. Any doctor who ignores these disincentives in the interest of good, equitable medical care deserves respect. Fortunately, the (salaried) ER doctor who saw Mae that night felt uncomfortable sending her home and decided to get a second opinion from the new doctor at Narragansett Bay Pediatrics, a few hours ahead of schedule.

I was excited to be summoned in the predawn. As I backed my Ford Escort out into the dark, the crunch of gravel breaking the silence of the sleeping street, I was eagerly scanning my brain for all the possible explanations for fever and petechiae. I met the headlights of the newspaper deliveryman for the first of what would turn out to be hundreds of times. Twenty minutes later, I found my way to the hospital's emergency room. It was the first time I had seen it at night, and nobody there knew me. The nurse at the front desk directed me to a darkened cubicle. When I drew the curtain aside, I saw the still figure of a small, sick child wrapped in sheets on the bed.

Pediatricians have their own definition of sick. It is not fever or vomiting. It is a dullness, a disinterest. A screaming child with a temperature of 104 who has to be held down by three adults in order to be examined is probably not a sick child. Not scary sick. But this little girl, hot and dry, watched me sadly, whimpered at my approach, looked to her parents helplessly; she had my attention. Her skin was dotted with the tiny spidery lesions of petechiae. I had to cross the first hopeful possibility off my diagnostic list: The rash had not been misdiagnosed. I wondered why the pediatrician who had seen her earlier was so dismissive. Was this how things were done in private practice?

A young Korean couple stood next to the gurney, poised with worry. "Thank you. Thank you, Doctor, for coming to see Mae. She is so sick. We are very worried." The father's desperation was thicker than his accent.

"How long has she had the fever?" I began.

An urgent flurry of Korean questions and answers passed between the parents before the father translated. I learned that Mae felt slightly ill with low-grade fever for a day or so before she suddenly took a turn for the worse. They normally brought her to the local community health center, but of course it was closed for the holiday weekend.

"Is anyone else at home feeling ill? Has she had her vaccinations? Has she taken any medicine?"

"No, Doctor." Exchange of Korean. "Yes, Doctor." More worried Korean from the mother. "No, Doctor. We are sorry we are not more helpful."

I reviewed the lab work, and it refused to be anything other than what it was. The red and white blood cell counts were slightly depressed; the platelet count—the component that affects blood clotting—was dangerously low. The results of her blood cultures, which would tell us about infection, were hours, perhaps days, away. I suspected a platelet disorder, but I could not rule out a dangerous bacterial infection, or even leukemia. It was too risky to do a spinal tap given her blood's poor ability to clot, but meningitis was a real concern. I had to blindly start treating her for the most dangerous possibilities first while I waited for the test results that would help me sort it all out.

I started IV antibiotics and then paused to orient myself. This child was going to need a pediatric intensive care unit, and I sure didn't remember coming across one on my hospital tour the previous day. She was also going to need a pediatric hematologist and a bone marrow biopsy—interesting challenges since I didn't yet know where to find a cup of coffee in this place, or even a restroom. I found my way back to the front desk and was directed to a phone; I called the number Bob Maltz had given me for his family home in New York. He was handed the phone by a sleepy-voiced woman and laughed into the receiver before I could say a word.

"What happened?"

By the time I had finished telling him why I was calling before I was officially on duty, about a complicated patient who did not belong to our practice and who had already been seen once by the pediatrician actually on call, we were both laughing. "So, this is what it is going to be like, working with you," he teased, but within minutes I had all the names and even the phone numbers of the people I needed to contact. Bob was funny and pragmatic, and, I couldn't help but note, too gracious to bad-mouth the pediatrician who had deposited all this in our laps. My faith in private docs was being restored. By the time I had found my first cup of coffee, a beautiful summer morning had dawned, countless sails were unfurling over Narragansett Bay, and Mae was safely tucked inside an ambulance that was screaming its way up I-95 to Rhode Island Hospital in Providence, where the chief of pediatric hematology was awaiting her.

Mae, it turned out, had a very common viral infection that in her case took an uncommon turn, temporarily wiping out her platelets. The same virus that produced the usually harmless fifth disease in children had not-so-harmlessly attacked her bone marrow. She eventually made a full recovery, and I had the pleasure of watching her grow into a lovely healthy teenager who worried her parents endlessly about her eating habits but had them beaming with pride over her schoolwork. When her younger brother was born, it was to the now eight-year-old Mae that I directed my questions.

"Does he cry too much? Does he wake you up at night?"

Such a soft voice and sweet smile. "Not too much."

"Does he poop a lot?"

Giggles. Even her parents giggled.

Four years earlier, a smart pediatrician had unfairly diagnosed Mae in the middle of the night as an income liability, and she had been passed off to me. Fortunately, I had been trained better than that to begin with, and my years in the navy meant that the economics of the encounter weren't really on my radar screen anyway. I needed to summon a great deal of my particular skills and experience that night; in return, caring for Mae had been thrilling and rewarding. Dr. Duval-Arnold's favorite saying had stayed with me since my residency days at Bethesda: If you're not conscientious, smart is no good at all.

SIXTEEN

Nuts and Bolts

Private practice is by necessity a firsthand lesson in medical economics. What quickly becomes apparent is that the shorter the visits are, the more money you make. Monetary rewards go to visits with reimbursable diagnoses that can be evaluated quickly, and are lost to any complicated issue that runs over the allotted time or pulls you out of the office. Also, procedures pay much more than talk and, in a pediatrician's office, tend to take less time; think wart removal as opposed to breast-feeding advice. Most insidious of all, the fastest way to burn through your schedule is not to get caught up in lengthy discussions that try to talk parents *out* of intervention, such as antibiotics for a cold, or unnecessary X-rays for feet that turn in.

I was ten years out of medical school by the time I joined Narragansett Bay Pediatrics in 1991, and I was earning a salary of forty-eight thousand dollars a year for my "part-time" position. I worked in the office twenty-four hours per week and covered nights and weekends, which would add on average another hundred hours a month to my schedule. The hours on call were long and exhausting but generated very little income for the practice. A pediatrician could stay up all night answering phone calls and not earn a dime. Or she could trek into the ER at 2 AM to see a worrisome child who turned out only to have a cold and have the reimbursement denied because of the final diagnosis; colds shouldn't be seen in the ER. Even if she does get paid, the radiologist who comes in the next morning to officially read the X-ray that was ordered (and read by the pediatrician) on that child will earn more for that reading than the pediatrician will earn for the hours she spent with the patient providing diagnosis and treatment. Or that pediatrician, the Rodney Dangerfield of medicine, could spend half an hour doing a spinal tap on a sick infant (a moving target, by the way) in the middle of the night and get paid $40 for it, while her husband, a neurologist, could do a scheduled spinal tap on a cooperative adult in his office and receive $120, because his patient was an adult. Throughout the spectrum of office visits as well, from physical exams to treatment of illness, little patients drew less reimbursement than adults did, for no other reason than because insurance companies said so.

I was not yet a partner in the practice, and I understood that the more money the practice earned through me, the more my salary would increase. The key was in finding ways to be more efficient without compromising patient care. How much emphasis a doctor puts on either side of this seesaw shapes her practice as much as her expertise will.

At Narragansett Bay Pediatrics we took all patients, regardless of insurance, and we tried very hard to balance the need for efficiency with a determination to do the job right. We each had spouses who worked in the health profession, and with that, we all earned enough money to lead comfortable, middle-class lives. But the choices we made meant that we didn't earn nearly as much as comparable pediatric group practices in the area.

Shortly after I joined the practice I met a new patient, the young infant of a drug-addicted mother. Josh's foster mother brought him in, along with a roomful of her own children. I was confused when I looked for the names of the siblings in the chart. None were listed.

"Oh, that's because they aren't seen here." Mom started her explanation matter-of-factly but grew more uncertain as she went on, as if the callousness of the situation hadn't occurred to her until she described it out loud. "They see Dr. _____, in East Greenwich, but, well, he doesn't take Medicaid, so I have to bring Josh here." Perhaps the stunned look on my face helped move her thought processes along. In any event, the entire family of children eventually transferred over to our practice.

Of course Dr. _____ didn't take Medicaid. Medicaid paid only about two-thirds of what private insurers like Blue Cross Blue Shield of Rhode Island did, and in order to get paid even that, you had to run a gauntlet of paperwork designed to avoid payment. A large number of claims were denied by inexpert people for trivial reasons and would need to be submitted and resubmitted. If the question wasn't resolved within ninety days, the claim was closed, as if this were a game show and the buzzer went off because you ran out of time.

Insurance source isn't the only consideration; volume is just as important in generating income. In general, if you are going to see a lot of patients, you have to see them quickly. Unfortunately, the easiest way to do that is to give the parents a quick fix—antibiotics, for example—in a way that will generate little discussion or challenge. That means writing the prescription for the overpriced broad-spectrum antibiotic—

"This is really powerful."

—before Mom has even settled into her chair, congratulating her for bringing her child in so soon.

"That eardrum looked like it was about to burst!" Doctor to the rescue.

It means treating any unexplained ache or fatigue as the demon du jour, Lyme disease.

"Fortunately, we caught it so early."

"Oh, thank you, Doctor," gushes Mom as she is ushered out of the room six minutes after the doctor swooped in, relieved at the decisive action. A deeper conversation to tease out the vague symptoms and a recommendation for watchful waiting would have taken much longer, and in all likelihood, a much less satisfied mom would be making her way to the checkout window.

Quick patient turnover means telling stressed-out nursing moms to just switch to formula.

"You've done everything you could. Some women just can't breastfeed. Let's get you a free sample case of formula."

What else is good for rapid patient turnover? Vitamins as the quick solution for a picky eater, cough syrup with codeine for colds, and knee-jerk Ritalin for "out-of-control" kids. The child's condition will follow its natural course mostly unaffected by the intervention, while eroding reimbursement rates will be more than offset by the healthy volume of well-insured patients. On top of the financial disincentives to doing the job right, no one should underestimate the pressure pediatricians feel not to disappoint parents, or how seductive it is for a pediatrician to have herself seen as coming to the rescue.

Being conscientious has its price.

"This is a viral infection. You need to understand why antibiotics won't help, and may actually cause resistance . . ." Or:

"We have a lot of experience with Lyme disease here, and I don't think this is it. Why don't we follow this closely over the next few days. Call me if . . ." Or:

"Why don't you go ahead and breast-feed your baby now, so I can get a firsthand look at how he's nursing . . ."

Insurance companies don't pay for ". . . ," and parents may leave the office annoyed because they feel they have wasted their time and money. Practicing good pediatrics is a moment-by-moment struggle to stick to the truth, compassionately. Most of the heroics in modern pediatrics are found not in the delivery room or the ER but go unnoticed, and unrewarded, in the little decisions of every-day care.

SEVENTEEN

Between the Lines

My patients' charts chronicled the day-to-day events of my professional life. Like a series of snapshots, they were accurate in only a two-dimensional way—the reasons children came into the office, the data we gathered, my physical findings, and so forth—nothing that went too much below the surface. The nurses could add some texture to the story—that I was usually in good humor, for example, and that the parents generally liked me. But a knowing eye, flipping through the charts, could piece together much of the real stories, like a detective poring through someone's credit card bills. One of the first things the detective would surmise about my workday was its rather mundane character, how ordinary many of the worries were, how rote the responses. Over and over again he would have read about developmental milestones, and when to introduce solid foods, and bicycle helmets, and when to use Tylenol for fever. This was not the stuff of a TV drama. By the end of the day, this detective would almost be ready to start seeing patients himself if nothing out of the ordinary came up.

The chart was always there waiting for me as I approached an exam room, a peripheral brain in a Plexiglas holder. On the inside cover I found the child's name, the names and occupations of his parents, and a list of the names and ages of his siblings. This was followed by pages of entries summarizing visits or phone calls. The thirty seconds or so that I spent stooped over the folder outside the exam room allowed me to smoothly step into the parent's universe when I opened the door. Much of the really useful information was between the lines.

A little guy named Matthew was my first patient one typical morning. His chart indicated that he had been a healthy eight-pounder when he was born two months previously. The simple data began to conjure up an image for me before I even stepped into the room. He was delivered here at the local hospital, rather than traveling "up the road" to Women & Infants in Providence.

—suggests a certain relaxed attitude on the part of the parents.

Delivery was attended by one of the obstetricians, not a midwife.

—relaxed, but not New Age.

His newborn exam was unremarkable—and he was circumcised.

—Dad's American.

This two-month well-baby visit was scheduled exactly two months to the day after his birth.

—Mom's organized and attentive.

Mom is a teacher,

—of course she's organized; also well educated and well insured, with good maternity leave. Good odds that she's breast-feeding.

and dad owns a landscaping business.

—two incomes, financially stable.

That's just the inside cover.

There had been three calls, all handled by nurses, about mild fussiness, and one about a "possible" diaper rash.

—these new parents have joined the ranks of "the worried well."

But they never felt the need to bring him in.

—worried, but not excessively anxious.

There was one nighttime call to me, which I didn't recollect, about the baby not sleeping. The note I filed the following morning indicated that the baby seemed very healthy by the parents' description, and that I "offered reassurance."

—great doctor!

Weights and measures recorded by the nurse that morning indicated that the infant was acquiring the shape of the Michelin man. Before I even turned the knob on the exam room door, I would have put money on the likelihood that the baby arrived in a brand-new car seat, and that there would be more than one doting adult and at least three changes of baby clothes in the room. Matthew would probably not end up with lead poisoning, would get all his vaccinations on schedule, and would be well prepared to enter school in a few years. Society likes to chalk these accomplishments up to parental virtue, but my patients' charts suggested it was more socio-economic. My patients from poorer circumstances, and with inadequate insurance, were simply less likely to be healthy in all the ways that Matthew was. Race and ethnicity seemed less significant than economic variables. Virtue was barely in the equation.

"Good morning! I'm Dr. Kozel," I began as I walked in the room, shaking hands with the parents. "Hey there, Matthew!" I scanned him as he lay undressed on the table. Someone had placed a small blue blanket over him. I started to touch him gently, stroking his cheek, working my way into his good graces even as my eyes turned back to the eager parents. "I know we've talked on the phone. It's nice to meet you all in person." Then, to the smiling gray-haired woman standing in the corner holding everybody's jackets: "You must be Grandma. Congratulations!" And back to the parents, "So how's Matthew been sleeping since that night we talked?"

This could sound disingenuous, but I was attempting to establish an important relationship within the impossible confines of a twenty-minute office visit. The family needed to know that I recalled who they were and what events had transpired between them and the health care system—even if it was the chart that had to do the "remembering" for me. They saw that I cared enough to get the details straight before I walked in the room, and I hoped they felt my genuine warmth and interest in our interaction.

Sometimes I got nailed, usually by a six-year-old.

"Hello, Ashley! Boy, are you getting big! Are you in first grade yet?"

"How do you know my name?"

Oops. We didn't really know each other; she usually saw Dr. Bob. I was busted.

"Well, Ashley, you've been coming here a long time—since you were a baby."

"But I don't remember you."

"Wellll," I stalled, quickly thumbing back through the chart, "it looks like I saw you the summer before last when you had a cough." Ashley stared at me, unconvinced. I was embarrassing myself.

I rarely lie to children. I am among a lonely minority of Christians who think Santa Claus is one of the weirdest things we do to our children. Lying is almost never to their advantage. So I 'fessed up to Ashley. "Actually, your name is written right here on this chart. That's how I knew. This chart tells me all kinds of things about how healthy you are."

"Let me see."

So I showed Ashley the chart; all was forgiven, and we moved on to discuss the wart on her foot.

There is potential risk in placing the patient into some workable context before entering the room; it could bog the doctor down with false assumptions. Patients and their families are not, after all, statistics. There are plenty of poorly educated women who decide to breast-feed their babies, just as affluent, well-educated ones may opt for formula. Poor, unemployed women bring their husbands/partners to well-child checks. A mother in the most ideal of economic situations can be abused or suffer postpartum depression. But experience and statistics do have something to teach us. Babies of educated, financially secure parents have less of an uphill road. It's the way life—and our wealthy but unequal society in particular—has laid out the odds. Doctors can't pretend to practice medicine in a vacuum. The more we recognize the external forces that shape a child's health and well-being, the more effective we can be.

When I saw from the chart that a new mom was seventeen years old, I went into the room already expecting to devote a good part of the visit to the benefits of breast-feeding. She was likely to need education and support. If the information sheet indicated that Mom was a thirty-year-old lawyer—

—*reflex paranoid shiver.*

—breast-feeding probably was not going to be the focal point of the visit. I certainly asked her how feedings were going, and if she had any concerns; but when she'd indicate that no, the four books she'd read on the subject covered it quite nicely, and that she had already calculated how many ounces of formula she could supplement without suppressing her breast milk production, we moved on. Hallway impressions couldn't write the script for the visit, but they suggested focus, prepared for parental expectations. To go in without these was to go in as unfocused as a medical student reading from a script: *Does his hair ever seem unusually brittle to you?*

Our pediatric office was a busy place, vibrating with the sounds and movements of patients, siblings, parents, doctors, and nurses. Lab results were constantly being called or faxed in, parents were phoning in for prescriptions. Vaccinations were drawn up and dispensed in dizzying numbers. In every room weights, measures, temperatures, and blood pressures were recorded. The patient's chart was the key to imposing order on all this commotion. It was the thread that connected visit to visit, doctor to doctor. This was important, because sometimes doctors had to be the detectives themselves, looking for clues between the lines. There are a million families out there who need help, and they don't come with signs on their forehead. Careful, complete, reliable records can be lifesaving.

I had a lovely little girl in my practice who had been born very prematurely and had suffered some developmental delays. This is a huge stress on any family. Annie's young father always brought her in for her appointments. In the fifteen months I took care of her, I never set eyes on her mother, even though she was the primary caregiver. This was unusual, but Dad always appeared polite and concerned, even solicitous, and in the burgeoning age of involved dads I thought this was sort of sweet. When I would inquire about Annie's mom, he always had a reassuring response at the ready.

"I thought I'd give her the afternoon to relax."

At about a year of age, Annie started falling off her growth curve— she was growing at a slower rate than she had been previously. Her expected developmental milestones, like walking and talking, began to lag, and her parents started to miss her appointments.

If my nurse had told me that one of our healthy fifteen-month-olds with a beautifully dull history and appropriately thin chart had missed his appointment, I might have recommended simply noting that he would have to catch up on his immunizations at the next visit. But Annie's chart came with its own alarm system. Premature. Delayed. Mother notably absent. The missed appointments now took on an ominous significance.

For the next few weeks our office kept calling Annie's home, and the parents kept rescheduling visits that they didn't keep. We decided to get visiting nurses involved, but before that could happen, Annie returned. A woman from the family's church had been watching Annie grow more and more sickly over the weeks and couldn't overlook the increasing number of bruises and burns over her body. Annie's mother confessed that she had indeed been abusing Annie, and the friend brought them in.

Annie was starving, her body shape defined by the bones that protruded at every angle from her sad little body. She had cigarette burns over her face and chest, bruises on her back; her expression was vacant. When the nurse picked her up to weigh her, a wordless Annie wrapped her stick-arms around the nurse and wouldn't let go. I pored over her chart, again and again, re-reading the histories I recorded at each visit.

Dad brings Annie in. Mom not feeling well.

Dad loving, very involved, following physical therapy plan. Parents do not see need for visiting nurses at this time.

Annie looks thin, but Dad describes adequate intake.

Should I have seen this coming?

There was no question that the child had to be admitted to the hospital under protective custody. Dad descended on me with a fury, outraged that we accused his wife of abuse, insistent that he was perfectly capable of protecting his own daughter. Intimidating. Bullying. Angry. His menacing eyes bored a hole through me.

How did I not see through his act?

Annie flourished in the hospital. She gained weight so fast, we had to slow down her feedings. She took her first steps and even began to talk that week. A plastic surgeon advised us on burn care to minimize scarring. She still clung to any set of outstretched arms that appeared.

Then one morning I received word from the nurses that DCYF had approved her release. The Department of Children, Youth and Families. They never spoke to us directly; apparently they didn't feel they had to. Dad was "such a nice young man" and so concerned, and besides, the parents "didn't fit the profile of abusers," explained the twenty-something-year-old caseworker when I got her on the phone.

"What profile is that?" I asked, wondering what criteria could trump cigarette burns to the face.

"It's a written test that we give the parents. It's very accurate. And I saw the pictures of her taken in the hospital," she continued. "We feel the sores on her face are more likely impetigo, which confirms what the parents told us."

"I'm telling you that both her pediatrician and the plastic surgeon who examined her feel these are cigarette burns. This looks nothing like impetigo."

"I'm sorry, I disagree."

I had to hand it to this young caseworker: What she lacked in expertise, she more than made up for in overconfidence. I refused to discharge Annie.

We were never advised of her hearing, although we heard later that the family's pastor showed up to vouch for the couple. The judge compromised and released Annie to the friend from church. These disturbed parents soon regained custody and immediately moved out of state, out of DCYF's jurisdiction. We never heard from them again. Annie's chart was filed away under "inactive" in our storeroom, the string of clues and warnings, like their author, left dangling, rendered useless.

Pediatricians and parents are usually partners, even when they don't agree. The whole relationship is based on trust. When a parent throws up smokescreens, the system breaks down. It would be great if troubled parents were annoying and healthy ones were nice, but I never found any such associations. I noted all the red flags in Annie's story, but at the end of the day, I was fooled; throughout Annie's first year of life, I was pretty comfortable that her parents and I were on the same side. It wasn't until Dad's smokescreen faltered, and he stopped bringing her in, that I started to see the truth that was waiting for me between the lines in her chart.

This is why my charts, like most pediatricians', were peppered with subjective comments that might offend a parent: *Dad's angry at being kept waiting. Child has missed three well-baby visits. Mom not holding baby.* These observations make their way into the chart not because we want to show our disapproval or annoyance—as tempting as that may be at times. They are only appropriate when we are concerned they have a larger significance for the child. These comments were the markers I left along the way, in case later someone had to find their way to the truth through smoke.

Medical science, and the health care delivery system that has grown up around it, is becoming increasingly complex. We not only have more kinds of therapies to offer, but we are able to individualize those therapies to a greater extent than ever before. The key to utilizing these resources and tracking their outcomes lies in continuity of care, and this in turn requires two things. First, all children need a medical home. This means that pediatric patients are receiving their care not only in a consistent physical setting, be it office or clinic, but that they are also being consistently seen by the same group of health professionals with whom they have an ongoing relationship. Secondly, effective health care delivery requires a system of record keeping that allows the various branches of health care to communicate with one another. The navy, with its single-payer system, had this system down, even back in the day when everything was handwritten. Complete medical records that included doctor encounters, consultations, test results, and hospital summaries accompanied personnel everywhere they went. Unfortunately, civilian records are much more fragmented, resulting in wasteful duplication of effort, poor communication, and, too often, critical information falling between the cracks.

Fortunately for Annie, she had a medical home, at least for a while. Unlike many disadvantaged children, she had not been bounced around from clinic to ER to clinic again. Until her parents moved away with her, she had one primary physician, one who was part of a practice that would continue to follow her no matter her financial status and that, just as important, put a high premium on record keeping. That meant there were also the five other pediatricians in the practice, a dozen nurses, and an office full of staff who had complete and reliable records to work from, and who considered it their job to watch out for Annie, even if I wasn't around. If those records could have followed her to the next place Annie's family sought care, they could have continued to protect her there, too, but Annie's parents were unlikely to make that happen.

Unfortunately, our civilian system of transferring records is inconsistent and often unreliable. Getting records transferred from one practice to another often takes a monumental effort by motivated parents. So many children have their care interrupted or, just as bad, duplicated because of lack of communication between their doctors. We need a national, electronic system in place, the kind that would have allowed Annie's doctors access to her records from birth no matter where she resurfaced for treatment. Every child in this nation needs a medical home, where professionals know the child and the child's history, and every child deserves medical record keeping worthy of our capabilities and our responsibilities.

EIGHTEEN

The Best Defense

The medical chart was my servant and my master. After I finished up with my last appointment of the day, I would head into the small office I shared with Bob and slump into my swivel chair. Off to the side of my desk would be a high, neatly piled stack of charts, left there by nurses and office staff, a phone message or lab report paper clipped to the cover of each one. My office hours were over, but I had forty or fifty stories on that desk that would require a note, a phone call, or some sort of analysis.

Most of my desk, however, was covered with charts I had been strewing haphazardly across my desk all day. During a patient visit, I barely had time to jot down a few key words in the progress note—just enough to stimulate recall at the end of the day when I completed my notes:

A: URI [assessment: upper respiratory infection or "cold"]
P: sx tx [plan: symptomatic treatment]; discussed expected course

I would also carefully note any medication I recommended, or any lab tests ordered. I would fill in the details later.

Bob stood out as the only one among us who got most of his charting done while the patient was still in the office. He didn't rely on handwriting so much as a series of hills and valleys stretched across the page that, if surveyed long enough, would somehow divulge useful patient information. His signature, two hilltops followed by a gently sloping plain, was instantly recognizable, if illegible. My handwriting, which had deteriorated sharply over the previous two decades, was only slightly better.

It wasn't penmanship that slowed me down compared with Bob as much as it was an inclination toward prose. Bob, the Hemingway of medicine, hammered out his notes; I composed mine. They weren't long. They just weren't fast. So an hour and a half after "finishing for the day," I would still be hunched over my desk, chewing on my pen, finessing an encounter between me and little Davey's runny nose, or capturing the essence of a phone conversation with Stephanie's snippy mother about toilet training. Bob, having added his last little squiggle to an entry, was long gone.

If I was late to pick up the girls after school, or exhausted from being on call the night before, I would scoop up the load of folders and wobble out the back door to my car, dropping them unceremoniously in the backseat. Until I finished with them, they went where I went. (This predated HIPAA prohibitions on road trips for medical records.)

My family knew that when I walked in the door with an armload of charts, I was home only in the technical sense. I was there to relieve Christine, our babysitter, put something in the oven, and try to compress a day's worth of affection and interest into a half hour reunion.

"Show me the headdress you made in school today, Caitlin!"

"Mom, Mrs. Murphy told us that a lot of Native Americans died of measles when the Europeans came." Caitlin's forehead creased with concern. She was a happy child but always seemed to understand that the word was a serious place. She looked to us for rational explanations like other children look for cookies.

"Well, that's true, honey. Lots of people, especially children, died of those kinds of things before we had vaccines."

"You mean shots?" she asked, even more serious. Caitlin always requested to get her shots at the start of a doctor's visit, so she wouldn't have to think about them during the checkup.

"Yep. You never have to worry about getting measles, 'cause you got your shots."

"I hate shots!" chimed in Molly, who then started laughing at her own exuberance.

"You do, huh?" I responded, tackling and tickling her, inviting Caitlin to join us on the floor, soaking in bits and pieces of their childhood like it was the first sunlight I had felt on my face in months. After a while, I helped them on with their jackets and boots and sent them out to the yard with Elwood. Then I grabbed the charts that required phone calls and headed into the home office. I could put off writing notes and reviewing lab reports until the kids went to bed; the lab results were mostly routine screens that just needed my initials. On the nights I returned home late, I often wouldn't finish the charts. The accusing stack would be waiting for me on the sticky, cluttered kitchen counter when I stumbled downstairs the next morning.

My relationship with my charts mirrored my relationship with the patients and families whose stories were detailed in them. First and foremost, the purpose of my notes was to document and communicate. But just as important was the reality that charts are legal documents. Lurking in the background of every patient encounter, even the most genial one, is the threat of a lawsuit. The chart, which we craft with such care for our patients, is also a tool that can and sometimes will be used against us. In every note we write, we are on the defensive. We make sure to write that the child was "alert." We document that the parents were advised to return the next day if their child wasn't improving. We make clear what we didn't see—the neck was not rigid, the rash was not petechial, the optic nerve was not swollen. Even with all this protective language, there is not a chart entry in the world that a reasonably intelligent lawyer could not find a hole in.

"You say you didn't see a petechial rash, Doctor, but nowhere did you state that you specifically looked on the abdomen for the rash. Can you say with 100 percent certainty that you looked on the abdomen of this patient [that you examined three years ago]?"

"I always undress the patient and inspect the whole body."

"But do you specifically remember examining the abdomen of this patient at that particular visit?"

Malpractice law is not about poor care. If I prescribe antibiotics for a child with a viral infection, that's poor care, but no one's going to sue me. Malpractice is about poor outcome, devastated families, and lawyers making lots of money. Sometimes that poor outcome is due to a doctor's negligence or incompetence. Often it is not. If a child dies of meningitis, and a pediatrician saw him earlier that day for a school physical, she better contact her lawyer. The fact that the child appeared perfectly well in the office and that the doctor did nothing wrong will be irrelevant.

"But, Doctor, you yourself admit you never checked him for neck stiffness."

She will get dragged into a legal battle, the family's grieving process will be poisoned by the conviction that somebody is to blame, and the insurance company will settle out of court—it's almost always cheaper that way. The doctor is left feeling angry, helpless, and crushed. If we sued lawyers every time they lost a case, regardless of how professionally they conducted themselves, the playing field would be a little more level.

We all make mistakes. To err is human—unless you are a doctor. This is a lesson that began in med school. If something went wrong, someone else was to blame. Attending physicians blamed the residents, who blamed the interns, who blamed whomever else was within range—med student, nurse, patient. We gave lip service to learning from our mistakes, but in morning report or on rounds, those left standing were the ones who most effectively pointed the finger at someone else. There is no greater pain a doctor can experience than that which comes from making a mistake that causes harm, so we try anything to convince ourselves we did nothing wrong, to protect our sanity. Once we are out in practice, this unhealthy denial goes beyond the personal. The threat of a malpractice suit means we must never, ever acknowledge our fallibility. The wolves are at the door.

I made a terrible mistake when I was an intern in internal medicine at Bethesda Naval Hospital. I was on call in the coronary care unit—the CCU—supervised by two residents. B. C. was the junior resident, two years out of medical school. The senior resident, Roy, was responsible for B. C. Roy reported to the chief resident, who took call from home. Roy and B. C. must have been very busy that night with other patients in other parts of the hospital, as I was left alone with the CCU nurses minding a very busy store.

There were six patients in the unit, each of them lying almost motionless on a mechanized bed behind glass walls. A web of lines connected their arteries and veins and chest walls to banks of screens and monitors that flashed around their rooms and across the nurses' desk in a constant illuminated display. Large flow sheets the size of opened newspapers sat at the foot of each bed, documenting pulse and oxygen levels, IV fluid rates, and medication orders. The constant electronic beeping was reduced to a background noise in my brain. The scene took on a certain eeriness at night, with overhead lights dimmed to help the patients rest, and the staff talking in hushed voices. The beeps and monitor lights rose to fill the void in an uneasy standoff between vigilance and catastrophe.

I moved quietly from patient to patient that night, watching the watchers—the blood pressure monitors, the EKG tracings. I scanned the elaborate flow sheets to assess vital signs and urine output. Looking at the patient was almost superfluous.

One of the patients, Mr. P, began showing signs of decreased cardiac output a little after midnight. He had been admitted earlier that day after suffering a heart attack. Now the catheters that threaded far into his arteries and veins were transmitting signals that his heart was not pumping blood as effectively as it had been. I paged B. C., but he must have been tied up because he didn't answer right away. So with Mr. P's nurse hovering anxiously over my shoulder, I called Roy. We agreed on a medication, Nipride, that would help Mr. P's heart pump better. I calculated the dose by hand and wrote the order. His nurse efficiently sent the order down to the pharmacy "stat," meaning we needed it urgently, and in a short while a small plastic bag containing the Nipride arrived in the unit and was connected up to Mr. P's IV. In all those transactions, no one noticed that I had written for ten times the recommended dose.

I watched that patient closely for the next several hours. Mr. P showed signs of improvement, and I let Roy know that when he called to check in. By 3 AM, all the beeping and buzzing and tracings had settled into a constant reassuring rhythm, and I crawled into an empty bed so I could catch a nap. I dozed uneasily over the next two hours, so when the nurse jostled me awake just before dawn, I wasn't sure if I was dreaming. She looked worried and told me the chief resident wanted to talk to me; there was a problem with Mr. P.

I hopped off the bed and into defensive mode. The chief resident, Carl, was a brilliant superhuman who rolled his filing cabinet around the hospital with him so that he would have instant access to all his cutting-edge journal articles in this pre-cyber world. I imagined that with black-rimmed glasses he would even look like Clark Kent. He didn't usually waste a lot of effort on facial expressions, but as I hurried toward him across the CCU I could read fury and contempt in his face.

"Nice dose of cyanide you gave Mr. P," he said as soon as I was within civilized earshot.

I was still trying to shake the half sleep from my brain; I couldn't make sense out of what he was saying. One of the dangers of using Nipride is that it is metabolized to cyanide in the body. Even appropriate doses of Nipride need to be monitored with blood testing for cyanide. An overdose could be lethal.

"You wrote for ten times the correct dose."

"No way," I protested as my shaking finger ran down the order sheet. I blinked at my handwriting—the neat feminine cursive so appreciated by the nursing staff—and began to recalculate the dose, but Carl had already done that and shoved his scratch sheet in front of my face. My stomach contracted, and my own pulse roared through my head as I took in the enormity of my mistake. I stood defenseless as he drove his message home:

"You could have killed him, you know. Didn't you wonder why his oxygen requirements were increasing?"

"I didn't know he was having a problem," I answered weakly. I glanced over at the nurse—I would have expected her to let me know if the patient's oxygen levels were dropping—but she just stood there, tense. There would be no help from her corner.

B. C., my phantom resident, had been hovering off to the side with the medical students but now chimed in. "Why didn't you notice? What were you doing?" Of course, he knew perfectly well what I had been doing, so this was a safe avenue to chase me down.

"I was asleep," I mumbled, as if I was admitting to getting high off the anesthesia machine while my patients screamed for help. "No one notified me . . ." I trailed off. The nurse waited silently at the bedside now, watching closely to see which way this ill wind would blow.

"But you're the doctor," B. C. hammered at me. I wanted to smack him.

"You know, we generally don't try to kill our patients here," added Carl in disgust.

I was utterly defeated, just a white coat and scrubs draped over the shell of a lousy doctor. "I'll change the order right away." My voice sounded as if it were coming from far away.

"Never mind," spat Carl. "I thought I'd stop the drip myself before he started turning blue."

I turned without another word and walked into the break room, shutting the door behind me, and began to sob as quietly as I could. I had the sudden feeling that over the past four months I had been fooling everyone into thinking I was a good doctor. In fact, I had even fooled Georgetown into thinking I should have been admitted to medical school. What would that admission committee think now if they could see what a danger they had unleashed upon the world?

A few minutes passed, and then B. C. walked in, closing the door behind him and settling into the opposite chair. "Shouldn't you get out there and see to your patient?" he asked gravely, a caricature of a wise old TV doctor—though only a year older than me.

Screw you! I thought. I was in no mood for melodrama.

"You know," he restarted, "I almost wrote a wrong antibiotic order once." There was a hesitation as he chose his words. "But then I caught it before I sent it off. But still, it could have been serious, I suppose."

My breath caught, and I stopped crying. A slow burn worked its way up my chest and into my face. "Are you consoling me by telling me that once you almost made a minor mistake, but then you were smart enough to catch yourself?"

"Well . . . yeah." He shrugged. I could tell he had no idea how furious I was—or that I had just found him out. B. C. had made a mistake last night, too—maybe even bigger than mine, because he should have known better. He should never have left an inexperienced intern in charge of six critically ill patients. He should have been checking on us all night or called for help if he was too busy. It turned out he had been too involved in an "interesting case" from the ER; he would make a big splash at morning report.

"Leave me alone, B. C." My voice had gone flat and cold. "Mr. P is fine now. Carl took care of him. I'll be out in a minute." He tried to offer another pearl of wisdom, but I cut him off. He had already helped me more than he realized.

What an asshole! I thought as I washed my face and blew my nose. These guys weren't any smarter than I was (except maybe for Carl), but now I suspected that B. C. had made plenty of mistakes, and I was pretty sure that everyone else had, too. But nobody was talking. Blame was deflected, rationalized, minimized, swept under the rug—anything to avoid the horrible epiphany I had just endured: We were all capable of royally screwing up, and that was as good as we were ever going to get.

Mr. P did miraculously well—so well, in fact, that he was transferred out of the unit to a "step-down" bed the following afternoon. His cyanide levels had risen briefly but then cleared. My troubles lingered. On attending rounds later that day, shaken and exhausted, I had to relive the experience with the cardiology attending. Later that evening, I asked the senior resident if the cardiologist had said anything to him about me. Roy was a kind soul and took no pleasure in squashing an errant intern. He hesitated but then opted for the truth. "He said, 'If I ever collapse from a heart attack, don't bring me here.'" I swallowed hard, and moved on to finish my tasks so I could go home. It had been a long thirty-six hours.

I trudged home alone that night, slowly making my way across the large expanse of lawn that rimmed the navy base as the sun set behind the high-rise buildings across the way. I was parched, and my head throbbed as I walked in slow motion toward the traffic lights of Wisconsin Avenue. I kept playing the course of events over in my mind, trying to find a way to let myself off the hook. The residents had left me alone with desperately ill patients. Why hadn't one of them stopped by the unit to check my orders, see for themselves how this critical patient was doing? And that nurse must have transcribed hundreds of orders for Nipride in her career. Did she think we were treating a gorilla this time? What about the pharmacy? If they didn't know drug dosages, who the hell did? This reasoning might have held up in a court of law, but none of it relieved the sickness in my stomach, the ache in my chest.

Blame was a tricky thing. It didn't get rid of guilt. It just wrapped it up in a package, stored it safe from the light. There was so much I had to learn; finger pointing and making excuses wasted precious time. As much as I hated to admit it, B. C. had been right about one thing. I was the doctor now. The fear of making a mistake would follow me the rest of my career. It would be the caution that made me double-check orders, the defensiveness I would have to keep under control when patients questioned me, the meticulous documentation that would follow every clinical encounter. I had discovered the greatest and loneliest burden a doctor carries.

Fortunately, in all my years as a pediatrician, I was never sued. Pediatricians have some of the lowest rates of malpractice suits in the profession and therefore pay the lowest premiums. By the time I left practice, I was paying about $13,000 a year for malpractice insurance—a drop in the bucket for obstetricians or neurosurgeons, who pay that much in a month. There are a number of theories for why pediatricians are the specialists least likely to be sued. One is that we are more likely to have connected with the family on a personal level. But meticulous charting helps, too, even before an issue has the chance to land on a lawyer's lap.

"Dr. Kozel," accused Mrs. C in an imperious voice through the phone line, "we told you months ago that Jamie was having headaches, and you told us it was nothing. Now the neurologist is sending us for a CT scan. Why didn't you do something back then?" I could tell over the phone that this mother was loaded for bear.

"How did she end up seeing a neurologist?" I asked.

"Well, I had to do something. The poor child was suffering."

"Mrs. C," I began, already fighting the anxious defensiveness that flared up reflexively, "I am looking at her chart right now. Jamie had a very normal neurological exam at that visit. If you remember, I went over her from head to toe. You have a family history of migraines. We talked about that and the likelihood of this being childhood migraine, especially since they seemed to be triggered by sleepovers. I asked you to have her avoid sleepovers, use ibuprofen as needed, and call me in two weeks if things were not improving. It doesn't look like you called back. But I agree with the neurologist. If she's continuing to have problems, she should have an imaging study."

Mrs. C mumbled her way out of the conversation, my record keeping having removed most of the wind from her sails. Even if the CT scan, God forbid, showed an abnormality, my records would support my stepwise evaluation—although I would still almost certainly get sued. But I hardly felt vindicated for doing a good job, just adequately armored. I sat staring into space for several minutes, feeling defeated by something unseen, knowing I had to switch gears, see the next patient, try to connect. Two weeks later, I got a letter from the neurologist stating that the CT scan was normal and he had diagnosed childhood migraine. Brilliant. Mrs. C started taking her daughter to another doctor in the practice.

For surgeons and obstetricians, lawsuits are a way of life, like broken noses to boxers. But all kinds of doctors can get sued, and when they do, it can suck the lifeblood out of them. One highly regarded colleague, a close friend of mine, was asked to consult on a patient of his who had been hospitalized with an infectious disease. The consult was for a minor intestinal problem the patient had had for years, unrelated to the mysterious fever for which she was admitted. Her current doctors were checking to make sure they didn't need to address that intestinal condition while she was being treated for this infection. The family later sued about some controversy around the diagnosis of her infection; the gastroenterology consultant was named in the suit. He was sure there was some mistake. When he asked his lawyer why he was included, the answer was quite simple: "Because your name was on the chart." It cost that doctor over a thousand dollars in legal fees to get his name dropped from the suit. The greater, hidden cost was the bitterness and frustration that settled into his gut. "I gotta get out of this goddamn business," he said.

So when I sat down at the end of the day to fill out my charts, it was with more than healing in mind. I had come a long way from my teenage image of a doctor, from that naive image of a gifted healer, reaping the gratitude of patients. Much of what I put down on paper was written because I might need protection from the very patients I was trying to treat.

The relationship between healer and patient, which relies so heavily on trust, has become too often, in a very fundamental way, adversarial. The cloud of mistrust is such a constant in daily practice that its wisps and curls go almost unnoticed in the day-to-day business of treating patients and documenting events. The defensiveness I felt as I constructed my chart entries—and for that matter in all my professional encounters—was not enough to suck the lifeblood out of me. It was more like a slow, barely noticeable trickle.

We have to deal with the reality of medical malpractice, but the process needs to focus on caring for the injured party and improving quality of health care. The current process is driven by how much the malpractice lawyer stands to gain (on average, over half the award), with secondary emphasis on the patient's well-being and none on improving medical care. Cases should be arbitrated by an independent panel of health experts, lawyers, and patient advocates who can assess the circumstances in the context of acceptable standards of practice. Disciplinary or remedial action should be directed toward doctors who have practiced negligently, and victims should receive capped compensation from a general fund that doctors pay into. Medical schools could teach, right from the beginning, constructive ways to critique ourselves and our colleagues; once we are no longer target practice for lawyers, trends in poor outcomes could be made transparent, and they could be studied so that we could find more effective ways to deliver care.

It is a sad paradox that the politicians who are most willing to tackle health care reform also tend to be the least likely to take on medical malpractice. They will say it is because malpractice suits do not have a significant impact on health expenditures, but such arguments are just grasping at statistical straws. Doctors spend billions in tests every year for no other purpose than to protect themselves from lawyers. It is why so many of us still order MRIs for uncomplicated back pain. It is why the C-section rate in this country has been on a steady rise. A recent study in the *Archives of Internal Medicine* reported that 91 percent of physicians admit to ordering more tests and specialist referrals than they think are necessary because they are practicing defensively.[9] A 2008 Pricewaterhouse report estimated the cost of such defensive medicine to be $210 billion annually.[10]

Politicians are, for the most part, lawyers, and they rely on the support of their fellow lawyers. By their very nature, most cannot imagine a bad situation that would not improve with a lawsuit. Tort reform gives them acid indigestion. I say to these political leaders, grab yourself some of those expensive reflux medications that your excellent insurance plan pays for, roll up your sleeves, and do the tough work that needs to be done. Provide this country with a rational, responsible approach to medical malpractice—one that will protect the health of both patients and medical practice.

NINETEEN

Leaning into Pain

Professional charts chronicle only one side of the patient–doctor encounter: the patient's story. But as everyone knows, there are always two sides to an encounter, and a story. The doctor's story—her personal reactions, judgments, feelings—has no place in the medical chart. Elaine, on the popular sitcom *Seinfeld,* was sure her doctors were commenting in her chart on what a "difficult patient" she was, but in reality doctors are smart enough to leave out extraneous information. For one thing, it's unprofessional to comment on, say, how annoyed a parent makes you. For another, it's malpractice suicide to put in writing anything that indicates you may not have been 100 percent on the patient's side. So you try to distinguish between your emotional reactions—like anger or frustration with a rude parent—and stick to observable facts and medical reasoning, including subjective comments only if you are concerned that it is relevant to the well-being of the child—like if Mom's detachment raises concerns about depression. The ability to draw a distinction between how we feel about a parent or patient and what we need to communicate in the chart for the child's benefit, is a measure of our professionalism, and so most doctors work very hard at getting it right. But every patient, every illness is seen through a lens that is unique for every doctor, crafted by her own temperament and personal experience. On a bad day, this lens could blind us to a truth we do not want to face—like a problem with our own child or an anxiety we don't want to admit, so we might sound dismissive or uncaring in the face of a legitimate concern. When we are at our best, however, our personal lens can focus beneath the layers of an encounter, allowing us to see a hidden wound that needs healing.

No one reading my charts would have any idea that Mrs. G lambasted me in front of an entire waiting room one Saturday morning for hustling her out of the room when she had more questions. As she made clear to her audience, she didn't care if I was busy. The way she saw it, that's what I was being paid for. Didn't I know she paid my salary? I obviously didn't care about Amanda. The only thing I was concerned about was finishing up so I could go home.

It wasn't the first time I had been subjected to such accusations, but it certainly was the most public.

"Mrs. G," I said, half pleading, my face turning bright red, "like I told you, we only do urgent visits on Saturday mornings. We treated Amanda's asthma. If you want to talk about how she's doing in school, you have to set up a regular appointment during the week."

"Well, excuuuse me if your time is so important. Isn't my time important? Why should I have to come back just to ask you questions? I have to work, too, you know. And I suppose I would have to pay another co-pay, wouldn't I?"

There was a deadly silence in the waiting room. Even the kids were quiet. The only sound was the soft *suck-click* of a small patient breathing from an oxygen tank. Poor Amanda was squirming with discomfort. I guessed this was not the first time her mother had behaved this way. I also knew from experience that if there is one thing worse than watching your own mother make a total fool of herself in public, it is hearing her do it ostensibly on your behalf. Been there. Amanda seemed to grow smaller and smaller as the spectacle dragged out. She looked like she was about to cry.

If there had been a nurse around, she would have escorted Mommy Dearest to a private place to play out her temper tantrum. But I was flying solo, and for me to stop and do that now would have meant doing exactly what I was trying to avoid—prolonging her visit at the expense of children with more immediate needs. And I was getting mad—mad that she was treating me this way, and mad that she so easily ignored the pained, embarrassed look on Amanda's face.

"I have to go now," I said. I briefly caught Amanda's eye and smiled at her and then walked out of the waiting room, struggling with a volatile mixture of rage, confusion, embarrassment, and sadness. Over the remaining two hours of patient visits, Mrs. G left two phone messages. I didn't answer them. I knew Amanda wasn't in medical trouble, and Mrs. G would have taken her to the ER if she had been.

When I wrote up Amanda's chart several hours later, I described her symptoms and findings, and then added a final sentence: *Amanda's mom quite upset that we couldn't talk about school issues; advised to make appt. during regular hours.*

This was for the benefit of whoever had to deal with her next, to give them some context. It was a tone that served the professional purpose of the record. But as was often the case, the doctor's story parted from the patient's here. The anger, the indignity, the sense of defeat that lingered within me the rest of that day and into the next was left unnoted, irrelevant to the narrative. The chart was for Amanda's story, not mine, and not her mother's.

My heart ached for Amanda. Just as patients like Billy Robinson reminded me of my brother Brian, bullying parents reminded me of what it felt like to be in Amanda's shoes when I was young. I knew firsthand the pain and public humiliation that a mother's out-of-control anger could cause. The best I could offer Amanda during that spectacle was to look her in the eye, give her a reassuring smile, and let her know that I knew this wasn't about her.

Meanwhile, my own mother's story was about to fade to black. If a doctor carries her personal baggage into the exam room, she also carries her medical bag back into her personal life. I was sitting in the office I shared with Bob Maltz a few days after my encounter with Mrs. G, catching up with evening phone calls, when Barbara, the nurse working with me, hurried in. "Dr. Shapiro, from a hospital in New York, on line one," she said. My dad had been dead two years. My sister, my aunt, and my mother were the only family left down in Point Lookout. *Who is it this time?* I wondered with dread.

"Hello, Dr. Kozel. This is Dr. Shapiro calling from the ICU. Your mother was just transported here from the nursing home with what looks like an intestinal obstruction. She's pretty sick, Dr. Kozel. Her blood pressure is extremely low. She's probably in shock. Now, we know she has severe Alzheimer's. We need to know how you want us to proceed." He was asking me if they should do exploratory surgery, to try to see what was going on, or just let her go.

"Does she seem to be in any pain?" One advantage to medical training at a moment like this is that it gets you right to the heart of the matter. Loving family members might be tempted to first ask about what was causing the problem, or what were the chances for survival. But doctors and nurses know what *really* matters to patients: Stop the pain and suffering. This was not the moment to lock horns in some ideological battle with Mother Nature. My mother had been suffering the misery of relentless agitation and confusion for years. I couldn't bear the thought that she was in physical pain, too.

"She seems comfortable," answered Dr. Shapiro. "If she does seem to be having pain, we can always treat that with morphine."

"I have to call you back," I told him shakily. He didn't like that answer—another busy doctor trying to deal with what was in front of him without delving into all that human emotional mess.

"Well, how long do you think that will be?"

I bristled at the hint of impatience in his voice. "I need to think," I snapped. "I'll call you back in a little while."

What I couldn't explain to the ICU doctor was that I might not be the person he should be asking. I wasn't so sure I was playing for my mother's team.

For years I had felt that it was absurd, even inhumane, to keep my mother alive in the nursing home, meticulously monitoring her blood sugars and adjusting her insulin doses. Perfect diabetic control allowed her to continue to sit there, day after day, babbling, diapered, tied into her "Gerry" chair.

My aunt Dorothy and I went to visit my mother in the nursing home one evening after my father's death. My brother John had been to Point Lookout the previous week, sorting through the disarray of our parents' home, tossing decades' worth of broken, soiled furniture into a Dumpster. I had spent this day cleaning the emptied house so we could sell it, scraping out dried cat shit from the closets, scouring years of human residue from the bathrooms. With the sour taste of the afternoon still in my mouth, I sat quietly next to my mother in the hallway of the nursing home, watching her rock in her chair and babble, "Oh Lord, Oh Lord, Oh Lord." I thought, *Hello, Lord. That's you she's calling. What are we waiting for here?* Ever faithful, ever sarcastic.

Every once in a while, as if finding a brief window of lucidity, my mother turned to me and her face would darken with malice.

"What the hell are you looking at?" she snarled, startling me, still able to hurt me.

"She doesn't know what she's saying, Maggie," Aunt Dorothy quickly interjected, pained to see me wounded.

"I'm not entirely sure about that" was all I could say.

On the ride down in the elevator I started to cry. Aunt Dorothy stood by looking sad and helpless. "I don't know why they have to keep her diabetes in such perfect control," I said. "High blood sugar isn't a bad way to go."

"Maggie!" gasped Aunt Dorothy. I was instantly sorry that I had said that aloud. Aunt Dorothy, loyal and infinitely forgiving, was the last person I wanted to cause distress. But I knew in my heart that my mother would never have agreed to the prolongation of her life in this way. The visit must have affected Aunt Dorothy as well. To my surprise, she asked for and signed some advanced directives for end-of-life care at her next doctor's appointment, and asked me to accept medical power of attorney for her. "If it's your time to go," she asked, "why suffer?"

Pediatricians know about a special kind of death—the death of a child. In the course of my career, I have presided over a failed attempt to resuscitate a nine-year-old-boy who the day before was perfectly well. I have sat at a baby's bedside with parents, stroking the child's hand, subtly watching the EKG tracing on the silent monitor, whispering, finally, "He's passed on." I've been to funerals for my friends' children. Any of us who have witnessed such loss—doctors and everyone else—surely cannot help but feel frustration that exhausted lives like my mother's grind on while children slip from our fingers. But no matter how untimely a death seems to us, doctors and nurses understand the sacred experience of a passing life. We want to save lives, but not at the expense of desecrating death. Patients, together with their doctors, are in the best position to know just where in life's course they are and to understand when enough will be enough. And those conversations need to happen, in an atmosphere of trust and respect, while a patient still has a voice.

My parents, unfortunately, had never discussed end-of-life issues with their doctor. So Dr. Shapiro, a stranger, had to sort things out and called me for help. Well, I didn't want her to suffer; that was absolutely true. But the sooner my mother departed from this planet, the better for everyone, I felt. I wasn't sure that qualified me as her strongest advocate.

I called Randy.

"C'mon, Mags. You know this is the right thing—no matter what your feelings are toward your mother. It would be crazy to operate on her at this point. Why make her suffer more? And you know she probably wouldn't survive the surgery anyway. This is her time, Maggie. Let her go."

Let her go.

Bob, having overheard all this, rolled his chair next to mine as I called back Dr. Shapiro; and Bob, one of the gentlest, kindest doctors I knew, reassured me I was doing the right thing. The other doctors and nurses hovered outside the office door, offering support and sympathy. There was no room in this circle for detached ideologies, or absurd legalistic debates about feeding tubes or IVs. There were just decent, honest people who knew the truth, firsthand, about life and death. I called the ICU and told them to keep my mother as comfortable as possible, and I made plans to leave for New York early in the morning to bid her farewell.

I didn't get there in time and shed some unexpected tears at the news of her death. I wasn't crying because I would miss my mother; I grieved for the enormous waste that was her life, and for all the pain she inflicted, and because I finally had to accept that the story of this doctor and her mother was never going to have a different ending.

TWENTY

Follow the Money

How much *should* a doctor earn? It's hard to discuss health care costs without having that question pop up in one form or another. A 2009 study by the Kaiser Family Foundation estimated that 21 percent of health care expenditures goes to "physicians and other clinical services."[11] Physician income is a relatively small piece of the health industry pie, but for many people it is the easiest to pinpoint, and it often gets discussed in very simplistic terms. What—and how—we pay doctors is incredibly important in terms of physician workforce, but not necessarily as important in terms of overall cost containment. For example, the 21 percent cut in Medicare payments to neurologists (the similarities in the two percentages cited are coincidental) that Congress temporarily allowed to pass into law in 2010 would have devastated neurology practices across the country, would have decreased access of Medicare (think "elderly") patients to this critical specialty, and would have given doctors-in-training one more reason to fight over those prized dermatology residencies that lead to very lucrative and less harried careers. But the cutback would not have made a dent in the trillions of health care dollars we are now spending annually and was rescinded a month later when lawmakers stopped to consider the ramifications.

There is little rational basis for the way we pay doctors. It is not based on the number of years of training required, the typical workload that a specialty carries, or, significantly, the overall impact that specialty has on our health. For reasons that seem not to be based on either free-market forces or medical necessity, radiologists earn three times as much as pediatricians, doctors in Nevada earn much more than doctors in Rhode Island, and Medicaid reimburses a fraction of what private insurers do. Supply-and-demand theories fall apart: primary care doctors, of which there are critical shortages, and who arguably have the greatest impact on our nation's health, are paid the least. Meanwhile, surgical procedures, even when they are of unproven value, make doctors rich.

Business models are also distorted: Medical professionals have to provide a service first and then go begging to be paid, at whatever rate they can manage to get. If we were to look at end results, and use a pay scale that reflected our health care goals, hours worked, and skills required, physician income comparisons would look very different than they do now. But physician income levels and workloads, like our health care policy in general, have often been allowed to drift far from a rational set of goals and priorities. We can't have an intelligent conversation about health care reform unless we understand who is making money doing what. Randy's experience as a neurologist gives some perspective on one aspect of the scramble among hospitals and doctors for health care dollars.

With both our practices well established, Randy and I built a house at the edge of a pond in Jamestown. We bought the land with my share of the money from the sale of my parents' house in Point Lookout. Our new house was no bigger than the one we first bought in Jamestown, but it had a stone fireplace and a screen porch and a home office. We loved it. Randy staked out a vegetable garden and surrounded it with a stone wall. We set up a swing set in a grove of trees for Caitlin and Molly, now ten and eight years old. Seven years into our life in Rhode Island, we were comfortable.

We loved our newly adopted state, too, but not because of its high reimbursements for doctors. In fact, Rhode Island has some of the lowest levels of physician income in the country, relative to cost of living. But by 1997, sitting in our custom-built house on our Crate and Barrel furniture, this two-doctor family was solidly at the upper economic end of the middle class. In our garage were a late-model Ford Taurus and, my personal indulgence, a leased Mustang convertible. The Mustang didn't last long. Our two girls were long, tall drinks of water, and by the time they got into middle school, their kneecaps were hammering their chins when they rode in the backseat. We replaced the convertible with a Subaru wagon.

There were annual ski weekends in New Hampshire and two trips to Disney World. We traveled to St. John after collecting enough travel miles on our credit card, and we used the last bit of my father's estate to take Aunt Dorothy and my mother's cousin Irene to Ireland; it was the first time the eighty-year-old Dorothy had ever been on a plane.

And we took advantage of professional trips whenever we could, Randy and I tagging along to each other's medical conferences with the children, the four of us cramming into paid-for hotel rooms in Washington, DC; Boston; and New York. A necessary mixing of work and pleasure, these getaways provided welcome relief from our everyday worries.

One of my everyday worries was Randy; he was burning out. He was employed by Newport Hospital then, and hospitals by that time had taken on the mantle of big business. The bottom line reigned supreme.

Randy, in a departure from other neurologists in the state who were in private practice, opted for a fixed salary as an employee of the hospital, similar to his work setting in the navy. It limited his income on the one hand but spared him the uncertainties of private practice. He didn't have to arrange for office space or pay a receptionist or pay his own malpractice premiums. He didn't have to submit and resubmit and resubmit again claims for payment that were being routinely denied by insurance company employees with no medical training. They were still denied, but now that was the hospital billing department's problem.

Randy paid a price for his unconventional practice setting—one that went far beyond the lower pay. In a way that was very different from his military experience, Newport Hospital needed to make money off Randy. Medicare and private insurance companies put the squeeze on hospital payments in the late 1990s and into the 2000s, making it a challenge for hospitals everywhere to stay afloat.

As the staff neurologist, Randy was responsible for seeing as many outpatients as he could in the office and then doing whatever neurology consults were requested on hospitalized patients. As time passed, he experienced growing pressure from the hospital administration to see more and more patients.

At the same time, there was a national movement among internists and hospitals to utilize a growing genre of specialists called hospitalists. These doctors, made up largely of young physicians recently out of training, took over the care of internal medicine patients once they were admitted to a hospital. The patients' personal physicians let go of their care until they were discharged again. This was logical in a lot of ways. The care of hospitalized patients has grown increasingly complex over the last decade, and it makes little sense for a doctor with a busy outpatient practice to be managing these hospitalized patients over the phone from his office. Also, just as in pediatrics, insurance companies reimburse for hospital care at a much lower rate than for office visits, so primary care doctors earn more if they focus all their energies on outpatient medicine. Last but not least, complicated inpatients require a lot of a doctor's time, so letting go of this responsibility significantly improves internists' quality of life.

Hospitals also benefit from their growing relationship with hospitalists. One of the most important features of cost management for hospitals is the ability to discharge patients as quickly as possible. With hospitalists on site to coordinate tests and consultations, and to discharge patients at the earliest possible moment, rather than waiting for the community physician to stop by after finishing at the office, hospitals save money. In a symbiotic relationship, hospitals supplement the low insurance reimbursement that hospitalists receive by also giving them a salary, making their overall earnings more attractive.

Use of hospitalists has brought unintended consequences as well. These doctors have no outpatient relationship with their patients, and therefore little sense of the continuity of their patients' care, so many of them tend to order specialist consults early and frequently. If a patient came in with a urinary tract infection but had seen Randy two years previously for migraines, that generated a neurology consult. If a patient with well-controlled seizures came in with chest pain, the instructions were sure to include, "Have Dr. Kozel see this patient." It was the quickest, easiest way for the hospitalist to deal with that history, and it cost the hospitalist nothing. It got to the point where Randy was consulting on seven or eight inpatients every evening, and most of these were medically unnecessary.

Being as meticulous as he is, it was hard for Randy to complete any of these—necessary or not—in less than an hour. In an opposite trend from that of his internist colleagues who had removed themselves from inpatient work, Randy now had to work longer and harder, and do more of the lower-paying inpatient work, than was the case before hospitalists came on the scene. He began ending his outpatient schedule at three thirty, so he could finish the hospital work by eight or nine at night. Fewer outpatients meant less money for his employer, the hospital. Unnecessary inpatient consults also meant less money for the hospital because the insurance companies refused to pay for them. Randy was working harder than he had as an intern, he was getting only a 3 percent cost of living raise each year, and he was being hassled to increase the number of reimbursable office visits he scheduled. It was a catch-22.

Night after night, Randy trudged in the door well after the girls had gone to sleep, looking tired and defeated. His briefcase dropped like a bowling bag to the floor of the front hall. As he emptied out his lunch bag and made a cursory glance at the mail, he'd bitch about his day. He found little joy in patient care these days. His successes were reduced to how much the patient encounter grossed for the hospital—the ultimate perversion of what was important to him. As he hurried from patient to patient, he hardly had time to hear their expressions of appreciation. They followed him, unheard, in his wake, making their way back to him only through the grapevine. "Mrs. H's family said they really liked you, Dr. Kozel."

Dr. Kozel learned to live with a baseline level of anger and resentment. When he told the hospital administrators that he needed help with weekend and night coverage, they told him the money they spent on that would be money they couldn't pay him. Randy was surprised that they were being so unreasonable. I wasn't. They were getting everything they needed: He was doing the work of two or three excellent neurologists for the price of one modestly paid one. It was good business.

Many of his colleagues found ways to do a good business, too, promoting niche clinics for diagnoses such as headaches or ADHD that relied heavily on encounters with nonmedical professionals as well as a wide range of testing procedures, and that offered services not covered by insurance (translation: lucrative). These neurologists were doing nothing that was unethical. They designed their practices in response to the rules that someone else was making up. And they were rewarded accordingly.

A few short years later, Randy would leave the hospital and open up his own private practice. Neither of us was foolish enough to believe that this would be the answer to all his woes. He would continue to fight the good fight against health insurers, writing stern letters and making phone calls he didn't have time for, on behalf of his patients who had been denied coverage for visits or referrals or prescriptions. He would continue to see the Medicaid patients whom so many other physicians ignored. He would listen calmly to the halting narratives of octogenarians, wait patiently, smiling, as frail, bent figures made their way slowly down his hallway. His net income stayed about the same as it had at the hospital, but he was able to make his own choices about whom to see and how to schedule their visits, and when Randy left the employ of Newport Hospital, our lives got better overnight.

Overall, Randy and I felt privileged and blessed. I don't think we questioned ourselves too much about whether we were happy. We were doctors, after all, so we assumed that exhaustion, aggravation, and miserable schedules went with the job. And for the sake of our sanity, we tried not to think about who was getting rich in health care, and for doing what.

How much *should* a doctor earn, and for what kind of workload? The complexity of the question mirrors the complexity of our cumbersome, often misdirected health care system. We won't be able to address one without taking a bold look at the other.

TWENTY-ONE

Tilting at Obesity

The most pervasive health problems that American children face today are also the ones that pediatricians are the least effective in dealing with. This is not just because we have relatively little training in these areas—which is true. It is also because by their very natures, the solutions to these problems ultimately cannot be found in a doctor's exam room. Nevertheless, we are the professionals who get paid for dealing with them. So we do the best we can.

At the top of this list are "lifestyle illnesses," those illnesses that are acquired because of the way we live. Diseases caused by smoking and substance abuse are examples. Obesity is the most glaring of such illnesses, with the rate of obesity in children increasing five-fold over the last several decades. Studies suggest that more than 30 percent of US children are currently overweight,[12] placing them, and the affordability of our health care system, in peril. Widespread obesity can be expected to produce an epidemic of secondary illnesses such as diabetes and premature heart disease in the near future.

Pediatricians have been ineffective in stemming this tide, even though, as the problem has grown, so have the time and energies that we have allotted to it in billable office visits. The sad result, for pediatricians and their patients, is that our mission and our livelihood center more and more on a condition over which we have little influence.

Our approach to treating obesity in children is like Mr. Williams's approach to the invisible string. There is a devastating health problem out there and no easy solution for it because its causes are rooted in the very fabric of our society. As a society, we are not really set up to deal with health issues outside the paradigm of the traditional doctor–patient relationship. What we know how best to deal with—and by that I mean what we know how to pay for—are disease states that are treated in the doctor's office. So we look for an answer that fits the way we typically address and pay for health problems, and thus weight concerns will be one more topic to squeeze into the twenty-minute office visit with a physician.

The American Academy of Pediatrics, the professional organization for pediatricians that has long been dedicated to the well-being of children, has dutifully responded to the challenge, publishing treatment guidelines and urging pediatricians on as the "best advocates for your patients." Experience, though, has told us loud and clear that relying primarily on doctors' intervention is not effective. The societal forces that influence a child's eating habits and activities far outweigh a pediatrician's influence, regardless of how caring the doctor is, or how loving the parent. Pediatricians didn't install seat belts in cars or remove lead from paint. The medical community appropriately called attention to these issues, and we decided as a society to take steps to address them—steps that cost money. Pediatricians were then able to reinforce these measures in their clinical practice. Likewise, pediatricians are not going to change the way Americans eat or how much TV they watch. The statistics are clear on that. History teaches us that no progress will be made until we address these complex issues as a society.

As an analogy, imagine that pediatricians were tasked with tackling childhood poverty, because of the very real and terrible impact poverty has on children's health and well-being.

The American Academy of Pediatrics could publish guidelines on just what the criteria are for diagnosing childhood poverty.

Okay, this sounds like a scientific approach to the problem.

This would be followed by suggestions for diagnostic tools, like a screening questionnaire for household income and a scale on which to rate the quality of health insurance.

Yes, objective data. I feel good about that.

Then there would be the standard recommendation to take a complete history and do a physical exam, to rule out any co-morbidities.

I knew we would find a way to tie in medical school.

And then the official AAP recommendations: Educate parents on the danger of poverty. Suggest ways they could increase their income. And finally, advocate for your patients in the community, pushing for economic development, living wages, and more research on the root causes of poverty.

Huh? But wait, how exactly do I do that? Tell them to get a job? Or find one that pays more? Do I sit down and go through want ads with them? Where do I find the time to be a community activist? How do I go about it, and who will pay for it? What does any of this have to do with my training or my skills?

And the most uncomfortable question of all—

Have I actually helped my patient, or am I just going through the motions?

Doctors are a pretty adaptable, quick-learning bunch. As the nature of health threats changed in our society, from illnesses that a vaccine will prevent or a pill will treat, to challenges like preventable accidents and lifestyle-related illnesses, our society, including the medical profession, presumed that doctors would be well positioned to take on the new challenges. But the history of modern medicine is full of examples, such as seat belt use and lead eradication, where the solutions to serious health threats were found in muscular public health policy, not the individual doctor's office.

Not too long after I started private practice, little Robby came in for his five-year-old check. It was pretty clear he was gaining weight at too fast a rate. His height had been progressing steadily along the 50th percentile for his age since he was two years old, but his weight had been climbing and now was close to the 90th percentile, meaning he weighed more than 90 percent of his peers did who were at the same age and height. A grandmother would call him pudgy, but the clinical term was *overweight*. Despite this, one of his mother's chief concerns for that visit was that she "could not get him to eat." This is the double-edged sword that cuts into our attempts to deal with overweight children: Just as many Americans have lost their ability to determine appropriate portion size, they have by and large forgotten what the normal body shape for a child is. Robby's mom was confused and insulted that I thought her child was overweight.

Feeding their children appropriately is one of the most primal drives that parents have. To suggest that they are not doing it well presses buttons—a big one being the denial button. During my years in private practice, I had many of my own patients switch out of my care because I had brought up the subject and just as many transfer into my care because another doctor with two horns and a tail had done the same. It was a giant revolving door of avoidance. And the more revolutions a family made around that door, seeking a doctor who would forgo all that nonsense about excess weight, the fatter the child tended to grow.

So I knew from the start that I would have to approach Robby's weight gain with delicacy. To me it was a quantifiable health problem; to Mrs. T, it was about what kind of mother she was, and how adorable Robby was. I began on fairly safe ground, asking how much TV Robby watched.

His mom looked at me skeptically. We were supposed to be talking about how Robby "won't eat."

"He doesn't watch that much TV," she said, not sure what I was getting at. "An hour or two in the morning, another hour or so when he gets home from kindergarten. But I don't let him watch TV in the evening, Doctor. If he wants to watch something while I'm making dinner, he has to watch a video"—a distinction without a difference that I have always found interesting.

"Any time in front of the computer?"

"Oh, yes, Doctor," she said proudly. "He's a whiz at the computer. We got him one for his room and sometimes he spends hours on it. I have to make him turn it off so he'll go to bed!"

I then took a nutritional history, and it followed the same script as that of most of the children in my practice who "won't eat." Lots of sugar, in everything from flavored milk to breakfast foods to the desserts that are used to bribe the kids to eat what is good for them. Lots of soda and juice. Very few grains, fruits, or vegetables. America, land of plenty.

Next I had to convince Mrs. T somehow that Robby was overweight and that this was a condition that got harder to reverse the longer it went on.

"But, Doctor, look at him. He's not fat."

Robby stopped walking his action figure up the wall and turned to look at us.

"Robby's great," I said to him, flashing a big smile in his direction, and then I turned back to Mom, showing her the growth curve, trying to talk in percentiles, and growth trends, using words that will cause Robby to lose interest. I could see that Mom was overweight, which added to the challenge. Weight issues are often a family condition, and if just the child in the family is singled out, the problem is likely to worsen, not improve. I found out that Dad was overweight, too, and that while the parents worked, Robby was looked after by a grandmother who "spoiled" him.

"She fixes him snacks all day long, just trying to get him to eat. And she probably lets him watch a little bit more TV than I would. It's hard. She's getting older. She doesn't want to chase around after a five-year-old, and I can't blame her."

Neither can I.

Other than his worrisome body mass index, Robby had a normal physical exam.

We moved on to recommendations, though Mrs. T was still skeptical. We talked about how lifestyle affects many aspects of a child's health, and about how time spent staring at an electronic screen—whether it is TV, videos, or a computer—is directly related to being overweight (not to mention poorer school performance). I recommended that Robby not spend more than an hour a day in front of a video screen.

"But what will he do? He'll be climbing the walls."

"He'll get used to it, Mrs. T. And he'll play. He'll get more physical activity, which he badly needs."

"What about educational shows?"

"It's the inactivity that is unhealthy, Mrs. T. It doesn't matter what the show is. Robby shouldn't be spending that much of his day being mentally and physically passive."

Then came the most-asked question I got at this point in a visit: "Do you have kids, Doctor?" Mrs. T. had decided I was clueless.

I rarely brought my own kids into exam room discussions. For one thing, we are all entitled to our privacy, and I'm as entitled as the next tired/indulgent/neurotic parent to have my flaws. For another thing, there is always the danger of sounding smug.

My daughters aren't overweight, because I . . .

This is the last thing parents need to hear. But TV viewing is one of the rare topics for which I will recruit my family. I suppose it is because the issue is so pervasive, and the solutions, unlike for many aspects of child rearing, are fairly cut and dried. Any of us, regardless of our parenting styles or temperaments, can follow them.

"Yes, I do, Mrs. T. Two girls—one in second grade, one in fourth. We have one TV in the house, and they don't watch it at all on school nights. When they can watch TV, they are each allowed to pick one show. And we watch it with them."

Mrs. T looked at me like I'd recommended breast-feeding Robby through adolescence. And we hadn't yet come to how the whole family had to work toward a healthier nutrition.

"He'll drive his grandmother crazy."

"She doesn't have to entertain him. Boredom can be a good thing for kids, Mrs. T. It fires up the imagination. When my kids complain about being bored, I offer to let them do chores. Boy, does that bring whining to a halt. Next thing I know, they've figured out 320 uses for an empty cardboard box." I was going for lighthearted, trying not to sound preachy.

We covered a lot of ground, but there was a good chance little of it would take. In eight years of medical training, the amount of time I spent considering TV viewing habits, or the quality of day care activities, or even the recommended nutrition for the school-aged child, could be measured in minutes. But obesity is the health crisis of the day, and doctors are expected to deal with it. We still get paid the same flat rate for a well-child visit, but we now have to focus more and more of those precious minutes on body weight, and all the lifestyle issues that go into it, talking as fast as an auctioneer to fit it in.

Why did I doubt I had any impact? The causes of obesity in our nation, with rare exception, are social and economic, political and psychological, and the solutions for them are not found in medi-

cal school. We are a society that has confused prosperity with glut-
tony. Our economy relies heavily on selling us things that are bad
for us, and our advertising industry supports that by marketing
those things directly and indirectly to children. We the people, ever
distrustful of regulation, stand by like cows in a field watching a
runaway train speed by.

Pediatricians are painfully aware of the scourge of obesity on our
patients and their families; roughly one-fifth of our patients are
overweight. We can see the horrible consequences awaiting many
of our obese patients down the tracks—cardiovascular disease,
diabetes, social rejection, to name a few. We can also see the crushing financial burden this will place on all of us in the future. The
CDC, Centers for Disease Control and Prevention, estimated in a
2009 report that over ninety-two billion health care dollars were
spent in one year on obesity-related illness, and more than half of
these dollars came through Medicaid and Medicare.[13] And we can
do what medical professionals have been doing for the last several
decades—stand on the platform waving our hands, shouting "Get
out of the way!" But we know, *we know,* that most of the time the
patient can't hear us over the roar of the engine. If societal trends
tell us anything, it is that the social forces that promote obesity—
sedentary lifestyles, excessive TV watching, unrelenting food marketing, and constant access to cheap, processed food of low nutritional
value—are accelerating, that the solutions are complex, and that to
effect them will require large-scale changes. As individuals, doctors
will have little impact on slowing that train down. This is why I was
not optimistic about Robby.

For primary care doctors like me, who are the steadfast foot
soldiers in this tragedy, spending enormous amounts of their time
attempting to do what they are ill equipped to do, against all logic
and to little avail, the effort can become soul crushing. I did not
expect to be constantly engaged in medical drama, like that night
in the ER with Mae, but I expected to be doing more than going
through the motions for my patients.

As for Robby, that visit went about twenty minutes overtime, and
Mrs. T, to her credit, seemed to be really trying to give me some

benefit of the doubt. I asked her to bring Robby back in six months for a follow-up. If the family bought into my advice, they would show up for that visit. If they maintained the status quo, which was more likely, then they would cancel that follow-up appointment and schedule his six-year-old visit with some other doctor in the practice. This is in fact what happened.

Later, as I wrote up Robby's chart over lunch—a blueberry muffin the size of a softball washed down with an extra-large iced coffee—I was, the good doctor, able to correlate my intervention closely with the official AAP recommendations:

I identified the excessive change in Robby's weight. Objective data. *Check.*

I encouraged healthy eating patterns for the child and the family as a whole. *Check.*

I promoted physical activity and limits on video time. *Check.*

I made plans to track Robby's progress. *Check.*

Advocating in the schools and community blah, blah, blah: *Maybe someday . . .*

TWENTY-TWO

Uncommon Sense

As far back as 1959, Dr. Julius Richmond published an article in *Pediatrics* warning that traditional pediatric training programs, which focused on the evaluation and care of sick children, were not necessarily the most appropriate training for pediatricians headed out to office practice.[14] He talked about the "new pediatrics," which emphasized children's growth and development, as well as the treatment of transient or minor illness. Dr. Richmond cautioned that residency programs needed to address this shift in focus, perhaps by shortening a general pediatrician's training, while doctors interested in a more "scientific" and specialized path could pursue specialty fellowships. By this time, Dr. Spock's revolutionary book *The Common Sense Book of Baby and Child Care* had become wildly popular with parents, as hungry as they were for an expert's advice on routine child-rearing issues, packaged in a gentle, nonjudgmental way. Both men's works were prophetic in their own ways. General office pediatrics in the latter half of the twentieth century gradually took on a new direction, one that emphasized prevention, education, and management of routine complaints. And parents, especially well-insured ones, began to expect a less clinical or authoritarian attitude from their pediatricians; child-rearing issues and pediatric medicine started to blur into each other. We didn't change the way we trained professionals to deliver this new care, however. Pediatric training programs focused on ever-more-complex illness and sophisticated treatments, widening the gap between training and practice even farther than in Dr. Richmond's day. Meanwhile, the burgeoning appearance of third-party payers discouraged the use of other highly qualified and less expensive professionals, such as nurses, to do the "new" work of pediatrics.

I wonder what Dr. Malinski, the doctor of my childhood back in the 1960s, would think if he observed the way I spent my day in a pediatric practice at the start of the twenty-first century. He would certainly be impressed by the growing complexity of medicine, as evidenced in my charts—an ever-expanding range of diagnoses, a dizzying array of therapies, a new emphasis on prevention.

Granted, he was a general practitioner, not a pediatrician, but I picture him scratching his head as he read my chart entries about obesity, and juice intake, and sleeping through the night, and what age to start kindergarten. Had there been a sudden glut of cheap physician laborers whom we needed to find work for? Had grand-mothers gone on strike? Or when he read between the lines, would he picture an entire generation of primary care doctors wanting to bang their heads against the wall? Wait till he read the staggering number of entries about constipation.

If obesity is the lifestyle illness that parents most frequently avoid dealing with, constipation must be the one that they obsess on the most. Constipation, that battleground where peristalsis meets pancakes, is front and center on parents' minds. As obesity presses the denial button, a sluggish bowel pattern presses the panic button.

Constipation, the passage of hard, dry, often painful stools, is a lifestyle illness because it mostly results from poor dietary habits and a sedentary life. Treating adult constipation is a booming over-the-counter business in America, but pediatricians try to avoid medi-cines to treat lifestyle illness in children. Instead we get into long (greater than five minutes) and questionably effective conversa-tions with parents about healthier living: avoiding a lot of processed flour and sugar, excessive cheese, chocolate. We encourage whole grains and dietary fiber, fresh fruits and vegetables, plenty of water, and exercise. The reason I say "questionably effective" is not that parents don't listen. They do listen, and nod in agreement, their brows furrowed in guilt. Unless they have been living in a cave, they know all this already and know that they—most of us, in fact—are falling short.

"You're right, Doctor. We are really going to try and do better. [Pause.] But what about the constipation?"

Constipation makes parents anxious, and they want it to go away.

A plan to serve more brown rice and enroll the child in karate just doesn't relieve that anxiety. Surely there must be a concoction of some kind that will send Betty Poop skipping off happily to the bathroom every morning.

There is a relationship between constipation and toilet training. Normal child development suggests that most children are physiologically ready to control their bowels at about three years of age. Grandmothers' anecdotes and experts' best-selling books will provide many variations on this theme, but what is striking is that, no matter when it is attempted, toilet training in our uptight society goes so badly so much of the time. Partly this is for the same reason that we have trouble "getting" our kids to choose healthy foods. We often send the message to our young children that this whole business of where and when one poops matters way more to us, the parents, than it does to them. It's in the tension in our voice and our posture. It is in the way we talk about it ad nauseam to the child and to any other adults who will listen. It is in the way we would schedule our own open-heart surgery around the time of day little Betty usually gets the urge, if we had to. Oh, it matters to us all right. So Betty, who wants nothing more at this age than to feel some power and control, refuses to poop. What should be a milestone of self-mastery becomes a power struggle in which the parent, by definition, will lose, and Betty, by definition, becomes constipated. Her parents become crazy in the process. And drive her pediatrician crazy.

Aside from diet, exercise, and a little cultural neurosis, another constipating influence in our society is our national tendency to rush around on a tight schedule. We are a people in a hurry.

"Does Betty sit on the toilet for a while after meals?"

Mom is taken aback by this, like I must have been born and raised on a different planet.

"Well, she usually eats breakfast in the car on the way to day care."

"What does she eat?"

"I'll give her some dry cereal and a sippy cup full of milk."

"And then will they sit her on the potty when she gets to day care?"

"Well, they'll ask her if she needs to go. We're really trying to encourage it because to be in this day care after you turn three, you have to be potty-trained. That's why this is such an issue."

You got that right. But that's smug me thinking in italics, as the clock on the wall ticks away. Deep down, I can sympathize with this woman. She's working full-time, running a household, feeding her family in the dysfunctional way that our culture has normalized, and rushing her youngest off to day care first thing in the morning. I'd be surprised if Mom has enough time or intestinal roughage to poop. And now day care is adding to the pressure to get Betty's bowels in line.

If things have gotten really bad—and they can get really bad, with chronic abdominal pain, urinary tract infections, and even soiling of clothes from leakage of liquid stool—then we have to treat the child with stool softeners and laxatives, retraining the bowel to work properly. But the only thing that will help in the long run is to improve the child's lifestyle. Offering that to parents as the solution is about as well received as recommending that obese patients and their families eat less and exercise more.

The task here is explaining to Betty's parents, in a convincing way, that the constipation culprit is the American diet, combined with watching *The Lion King* video three times a day in its entirety, and not allowing enough relaxed time to actually sit on a toilet. Because of the narrow way our health care is conceived and paid for, this task falls on a person with board certification in a medical subspecialty, who may be able to allot all of three minutes to this in the course of the well-child visit. The pediatrician's involvement, in itself, raises the stakes further. If discussing Betty's stooling pattern is a fitting topic to dominate a high-priced physician visit, then it must be a serious medical concern. The Circle of Life.

From the vantage point of five decades later, I would respectfully disagree with Dr. Richmond that the solution to meeting the demands of the (no longer so new) "new pediatrics" is to scale back physician training. Rather, I am convinced that the solution is to train other, less expensive and better-suited professionals to provide that kind of care. Dr. Spock's (and later Dr. Brazelton's) work addressed what had been an unmet need in pediatrics; namely, providing reliable commonsense advice to parents, backed up by clinical evidence. But that does not mean that a pediatrician is necessarily the most effective professional to meet that need in the office.

Delivery of modern pediatric care that is both clinically and economically effective requires a team approach. The problem is that if our insurance system is not aligned with this approach, it cannot happen. As a pediatric resident-in-training, I studied constipation with the understanding that it could be a sign of more serious conditions, such as Hirschsprung's disease, where the large bowel has abnormal nerve supply. Someone on the team caring for a child needs to have that information. And the rest of the team needs to know when to refer children to that person. In the downsized reality of my everyday practice, however, my primary role was no longer to distinguish serious pathology from the routine travails of childhood. Reality required me to be a high-priced, fast-talking lifestyle coach, passing out rote advice that people didn't want to hear or could do little about. Not very effective. Not very efficient. Not very satisfying.

Bowel habits. *Check.*

TWENTY-THREE

Fast Talk

My day, like the days of most office pediatricians, was filled with routine questions of when to start rice cereal or how to treat a bug bite. Most of our savvy nurses would have handled these issues with at least as much skill as I did, but they didn't, because they couldn't bill for it, and it made no financial sense for us to pay nurses to do that out of our own pockets when insurance companies would pay doctors much more for providing the same service. The physicians in our group, at least during my tenure, earned less than the national average for pediatricians, which was about $132,000. None of us were looking at ways to whittle our income down a little further by paying nonphysicians ourselves. As was true everywhere else in health care, our practice methods were determined by whom insurers would pay, and for what.

In the midst of all the routine work, I tried not to take my accomplishments for granted. It is a strong testament to the beauty of modern medicine that we have grown so complacent about treating some common illnesses. I made a habit of reminding myself, as I casually wrote out an amoxicillin prescription for what was probably a bacterial pneumonia, that I might very well have just saved a life. It might have been a commonplace, "no-brainer" patient encounter, but a few decades earlier that child may have died. Often, on my drive home in the evening, I would go back over the day and try to find the genuine, important differences I made. I would think of the child with congenital hypothyroidism who, if it weren't for timely treatment with thyroid medicine shortly after birth, would have had a life of mental retardation ahead of him. I would remind myself of the toddler whose respiratory efforts were deteriorating in the subtlest of ways, and who might have landed in real trouble but for my timely intervention and close follow-up. This wasn't particularly

fodder for my ego; for the modern pediatrician, the
are indeed no-brainers. But if I paid attention to tl
they helped to give some purpose to my day, like
It's a Wonderful Life taking stock of what could have in ,
had not been around to prevent it.

Much of modern pediatric medicine is, appropriately, prevention and education. Back at Yokosuka, when a military family
came in for a well-baby check, they would spend much more time
with the nursing team than with me, learning about nutrition,
child development, and safety and immunizations—part of Dr.
Richmond's "new pediatrics," or "anticipatory guidance," as it is
now known in the profession. The pediatrician's job was to oversee
the whole program, choose resources, keep the team current on
practice standards, monitor quality, and of course provide specialized services. It all seemed so sane and rational. And effective. But
now I was expected to accomplish the work of that entire team,
speed talking like those disclaimers at the end of erectile dysfunction commercials. Anticipatory guidance had become the verbal
"fine print" of the pediatric visit. A 2006 study pointed out that
there were by that point 142 AAP policy statements—on everything from tobacco use to poison prevention—that each carried a
recommendation to bring up the issue at routine well-child visits.[15]
There is no way that this can be realistically accomplished by a
single provider in the confines of doctor visits, and yet we continue
to go through the motions, always falling short, working within the
system we know.

Appropriate car seat use was one of those things on my expanding laundry list of topics to cover during well-child visits. Parents
need to understand how important car seats are for their children.
Under our health care system, doctors who have spent eight or so
years of their lives learning how to treat disease are the people who
can most easily get paid for teaching parents about car seats; so
it becomes, by default, our job. If we chose to pay nurses to do it,
that would come out of our own pockets. The doctors are certainly
not going to get paid more for adding it to their other tasks during
a well-child visit, so we have to squeeze in the extra information

during the allotted block of time, relying on printed brochures and hastily answering questions. On every patient's record we have placed a small box labeled "car safety" as a reminder.

Check.

In this process of trying to fit a square peg into a round hole, we as a nation approach car seat safety—a hugely important public health issue—in the most expensive and minimally effective way we can. I could so easily imagine a national health care system in which well-paid nurses went into the home to discuss safety issues with parents, pointing out the potential toxins, warning how a toddler might drown, demonstrating—yes, hands on—how to restrain their child properly in a car seat. Imagine the effectiveness that would result, the money that would be saved by not insisting that only a person with a medical degree can deliver the information. Pediatricians would have a more appropriate role. When it came time for the doctor's visit, we could lend gravitas to the process, voicing our strong support for what happens on those home visits. And we could use more of our time doing what we are good at.

The misdirected economics of our health care system is not the only obstacle to finding a more rational approach to prevention. There is a prevailing sense of entitlement that has grown up in our society. Our health care is often a "benefit" of employment, and many of us want to make sure we are getting our money's worth, trying to overfill our plates at an all-you-can-eat buffet. We expect a pediatrician to advise us on everything from developmental toys to diaper choice. Nothing but the "best" (most expensive) advice will do. A visiting nurse may not sound special enough to some people—especially if it is government-funded. That this type of care has worked well in European societies may not be a welcome example to the more conservative-minded among us. A shift to a more rational approach to pediatric care may require a wider cultural shift, with a clearer realization that the *last* thing our US health care system is giving us right now is our money's worth.

It is ironic that the safety nets the government provides to poor children are called "entitlements." This is the least entitled segment of our society. Uninsured or underinsured children, or ones on Medicaid, may have trouble finding a practice to accept them. They are more likely to use public clinics and never be seen by the same practitioner twice. Their parents are more likely to hold off bringing them to care until it is absolutely necessary. They are more likely to wait for hours in a crowded ER for a common ailment, because they have nowhere else to go.

Entitlement, from my perspective, means demanding that your doctor do an ear check at ten o'clock at night because your otherwise well three-year-old seems fussy. Entitlement is expecting that your doctor will see your child at 5 AM to diagnose a rash, so you will know if the child can go to day care or not. Entitlement is insisting on going over, one more time, the pros and cons of keeping a cat when you know your child has cat allergies, as the ticking of the clock competes with the sound of all those kids hacking and coughing out there in the waiting room.

"Well, no, we'd rather not keep his door closed at night, Doctor. And I hate having him on all this wheezing medicine. Is there some kind of vitamin he could be missing that makes him allergic?"

I get so good at suppressing screams I hardly even know I am doing it.

"You need to get rid of the cat, Mrs. K. Really."

"But how do we know that will even take care of the problem . . ." Mrs. K has all the time in the world, and can't imagine a better use of her doctor's time than to come up with a solution that will fit comfortably in her life.

Connecting the word *entitlement* to poor kids is a contradiction in terms. There are plenty of entitled people in our society. But they drive Volvos and send their kids to Montessori schools and fret inconsolably when one of their children bomps another child over the head at playgroup.

"Could it be because there was too much sugar in that oatmeal cookie he ate at playgroup?"

The poor kids are likely to be the ones sitting patiently out in the waiting room. Their mothers have learned that they will have to wait for their "entitlement."

Get a life, for God's sake. That's cranky me in italics, nerves wound tightly after a long night on call. My cranky thoughts were seldom directed at the "welfare mom" in the waiting room. She had her own story. They were directed at the Mrs. Ks of the world, whose obsessive parenting wore down my patience. As time went on, I grew worried that my italics were not staying in my head anymore but written plainly on my face.

I felt my well of compassion was beginning to run dry, and it both saddened and frightened me.

TWENTY-FOUR

Johnny, James, and John

One of the most common issues a pediatrician faces every day is discipline. Nowhere else does a pediatrician's own temperament, style, and experience filter through the advice we give so freely. Discipline is part lifestyle issue, part counseling and should be added to the growing list of things pediatricians advise about with little formal training. It makes some sense to talk to us about discipline; we are smart, and generally kind, and have broad experience in what is considered normal behavior for children. But mostly what we are offering is common sense and perspective; as is true with other common topics like nutrition and education, our credentials don't take us much farther than that.

Practically speaking, there is a strong "preaching to the choir" factor in discipline discussions. Parents with pretty healthy child-rearing skills will be receptive to our advice. The parents who are in the most trouble will be looking for ways to change their children, not their behaviors, and will hardly hear a word we say. If parental substance abuse is fueling the problem, they are unlikely to even ask for advice. Like so many other important issues of childhood, serious discipline issues are not effectively dealt with in the doctor's exam room. Yet as with obesity, and poor nutrition, and learning issues, physicians are usually the only ones whom insurance will pay to treat the child. We can make referrals for counseling, but more often than not what will be available will be too little, too late and not covered by the patient's insurance plan.

Rare indeed would be the pediatrician whose own childhood does not resurface somehow in conversations about behavior and discipline. I for one have an honorary degree in child rearing from the University of Crazy Parents. My childhood experience, with two angry, alcoholic parents, provided more of a cautionary tale than a how-to manual. Fortunately for me, there were a number of others in my life who helped me survive. One of them was my aunt Dorothy. Another was my brother Johnny.

Johnny had always been the mysterious older man to me. When I first stepped on a school bus at five years of age, Johnny was the eighth-grade bus monitor. He was a grown man as far as I could tell, and he hung out with other fourteen-year-old men. They sweated and cursed when they played basketball and had no use for little girls. Even when he was home he wasn't really there. If he had been, he would have had to listen to the litany of his failures. Yet as detached as he was, he had a way of slipping tenderness into the lives of his younger brother and sister—a hidden dollar bill on our birthdays, a missing stuffed animal found and gently pressed next to me as I slept.

Johnny was brilliant in many ways, not the least of which was his way with the piano. As a young kid, he could look at a single line of notes on a page and instantly turn it into a two-handed orchestration. My parents hated that he "never did anything with all that talent." They hated his rowdy friends even more, and when Johnny's grades started to slip in school, my father said he would have to hang his head in shame when he walked around town. When Dad enrolled his oldest son in a military high school in New York City, Johnny seemed to just give up on us.

When I was in grade school, I went to bed every night in fear. I was afraid the devil would come and take me, because that's what Sister Adele Marie said would happen to "the likes of you, Miss Keavey." What other conclusion could she come to given that I found it hard to sit still or stop chatting in her class? I was also afraid I would unwittingly step into quicksand, like those poor people in *King Solomon's Mines.* Sometimes what frightened me was so vast I couldn't even name it. Lying alone in my disheveled bed, I had to cross a horrifying chasm to get from wakefulness to sleep.

Then Johnny would sit down at the dusty upright piano outside my bedroom door. "Play 'Sentimental Journey,'" I'd call to him, "and 'Blue Moon.'" These were not his favorites by a long shot, but he never hesitated. The familiar strains would flow into my room, gentle oscillations like arms wrapping around me, soothing me, bringing me peace. The teenage Johnny moved like a phantom in our house, but night after night he would play those tunes for me, rescuing his baby sister one night at a time.

Johnny had to get out of Dodge, and he didn't come back. By the time he got his driver's license, the piano sat untouched, collecting layers of dust and clutter, its strings falling as far out of tune as the rest of the noise in our house. He moved to Buffalo to go to college when I was ten years old. I saw him occasionally over the next few years, but by the time I finished high school we were completely out of touch.

Then one Sunday afternoon in my first year of med school, I was sitting around my DC apartment doing nothing in particular when Johnny called. Caught completely off guard, I was instantly six years old again, flattered and grateful for my big brother's attention. He was calling out of the blue to see how I was. He was calling to invite me up to Buffalo, to be with his wife and three children for Christmas.

I had a moment of guilt at the thought of not going back to Point Lookout for the holiday. If I didn't go back, there would be no tree, no lights, no presents; I had been the only one to go to all that trouble for years, never giving up hope for a happy Christmas even as my mother cursed the presents I bought her, and my father pouted over his drink.

"Yes," I finally said. "I'd love to come."

John, as I tried to remember to call him—nobody up in Buffalo called him Johnny—made chocolate mousse for me my first night there. We sat at the small Formica kitchen table with my nephews and niece, decorating Christmas cookies and catching up. Johnny still seemed ticked off at the world; I still felt like I personally had to make everything okay. I wasn't sure he would recognize—or care about—the young woman I had become. I was so different from the little girl he had left behind in Point Lookout a decade earlier. Yet privately I was still battling the anxiety that had taken hold of me in childhood. But he did still know me. And as I relaxed, it felt good to be in the same room with him, sharing the same space, the same memories, crossing a chasm that I had thought was too wide to cross.

Shortly after that visit to Buffalo, a psychiatry professor of mine, Dr. Grande, tossed me another lifeline, just as Johnny had with his music when I was a little girl. I sat in Dr. Grande's office, sweating and shaking, unraveling the story of my childhood. In a few short weeks of visits with him, I learned a magical truth that I was able to share with hundreds of patients in my future: Take that anxiety out of your head, give it the light of day, and just name it. It melts, like the Wicked Witch of the West. I may be doomed, by nature and/or nurture, to be a lifelong worrier, but I have never had another anxiety attack. As the demons of my childhood were sent scurrying to their corners, my heart opened—to family, to patients, to Randy.

I see a few silver linings in the story of my childhood, which was much more horrific for my older brothers and sister than it was for me, the "baby." My Quixote-esque attempts to make my family happy probably shaped me as a high achiever, paving my way toward med school. My experience also led me to develop some pretty clear views on what children need from their parents, a clarity that served me well as a pediatrician.

In my daily practice, it was quite common for frustrated, guilt-ridden parents to bring their kids to see me because they felt the children were spoiled or defiant or out of control, because they were fighting with other kids or getting into trouble at school. Effective discipline comes naturally to some parents. For many others it requires education, and that education should start early—not force-fed in the short span of a well-baby visit but provided by trained nurses or other professionals on a regular basis, right from birth. Those professionals can provide good guidance in a context condu-cive to learning and could identify families that need extra help. It is the only way to break the cycles that keep regenerating between angry, abusive, substance-abusing, or mentally ill parents and their children, and it is the only way to support parents, especially young ones, who want to be good parents but don't really understand child development and what that means for discipline. This would require a small investment by our society for big gains. Putting into practice a rational model of child-rearing support for parents, however, like so many other worthwhile health interventions, requires that we take a fresh look at what it means for a family to be healthy, and what professionals we will pay to foster that health.

Over the course of twenty years of pediatrics, I watched some children blossom and others lose themselves. I was impressed that children's success in life seemed to have little to do with whether their parents were strict or indulgent, authoritative or permissive, or even whether or not they used "measured" physical discipline (which I, as well as the American Academy of Pediatrics, oppose). It didn't seem to matter necessarily if there were tons of rules in the house or just the basic safety precautions and nutritional goals. I have seen overbearing parents cause as much damage as inattentive ones and rules be used more for control than for teaching. My patients taught me that it's not the recipe that matters so much. It's the ingredients.

Authoritarian child-rearing experts, like John Rosemond and James Dobson, have all the answers, and being "faith-based" they claim a moral high ground that appeals to a wide readership. By combining a little finger wagging at "*today's* parents," some spanking to teach your child how to use reason instead of acting out, and some snide potshots at those newfangled notions of self-esteem, the books of James and John suggest that if you are not raising a perfectly behaved child, in an emotionally healthy and financially secure two-parent family, well then, you're just being irresponsible. Perhaps even un-Christian.

I never was man enough for their schools of thought.

Having been invited into the private lives of thousands of children and their families, there are only a few things about raising children that are absolute to me. Obviously, if children are being abused, we need to rescue them immediately. Beyond that, I know that alcoholism produces damaged children, and yet parents live in a constant state of denial about this. I know that ugly divorces that don't put the child's need first are poisonous. I know that chronic anger, one of the most insidious of parental flaws, is toxic to anything that grows in its midst. On a larger scale, I know that poverty is a huge, messy, complicated handicap that begins at birth. When I look at my own children, before I can take any credit for their emotional health and successes, I have to factor in all these broader circumstances that they have been spared.

There may be as many right ways as wrong ways to raise a child. In the end, regardless of other circumstances, the best predictor of outcome seems to be how much respect and kindness a child witnesses and receives. If I were to write a book on child rearing, this would be my bottom line, not a specific behavioral outcome. And I would dedicate the book to Johnny, Brian, and Helen, and maybe even to myself. And to that little Tasmanian devil, Billy Robinson.

TWENTY-FIVE

Codes to Live By

Narragansett Bay Pediatrics grew by leaps and bounds in the 1990s. We moved from our small storefront, to a larger space in a shopping plaza, to a suite in the hospital's new medical office building, all in the span of ten years. We gradually expanded to a staff of six doctors, seven or eight nurses at any given time, and—to meet the needs of an insurance industry that was expanding faster than we were—a large clerical/receptionist staff. Our administrative costs continued to rise as reimbursements remained flat. We even opened a satellite office, and five years after I joined the practice, I became a partner. The doctors were all working hard, and making decent money, but certainly not getting rich. We each were typically on call six nights or weekend days or holidays a month. We could have each made more money with fewer doctors, but we were all raising young families. The more doctors in our practice, the more nights and weekends we could spend at home.

Medical practices are businesses; rent was due every month, employees expected paychecks, and malpractice premiums increased each year. For a typical primary care doctor in private practice, 50 to 60 percent of her gross income goes to administrative costs. As my idealism moved over to make room for the nuts and bolts of earning a living, I became less apologetic about trying to make money. But keeping that goal in line with my practice ethics was a constant challenge, as it is for every other primary care doctor in the United States.

Primary care doctors refer frequently to the ten-minute visit or the twenty-minute visit. In reality, insurance companies pay by diagnosis, not time. The term *twenty-minute visit* really refers to the fact that if you are only going to get paid so much per visit, you need to consider what you think you have to earn in a day, then fit that many visits into the day. For a pediatrician it was typical that well-child appointments would be allotted twenty minutes, "sick visits" fifteen, simple follow-ups, like for ear infections, ten minutes, and adolescent physicals anywhere from thirty to forty-five minutes. The number of longer visits you schedule has to be balanced by quick visits. At current reimbursement rates in general pediatrics, an average of 25 twenty-minute visits will usually come close to providing typical earnings.

Diagnoses are evaluated according to codes, not time required to treat. Anything that happens in a doctor's office is translated into an ICD (International Classification of Diseases) code, which is then linked to a payment scale. A simple cold will be coded one way. A cold in a child who is wheezing may earn a "higher" code and slightly more reimbursement, if the visit included a breathing treatment. A simple cold in a patient whose mother has three pages of questions and occupies your time for thirty minutes still gets reimbursed as a simple cold. The code system, as it is applied to physician reimbursements, is designed so that even someone with an MBA from Harvard would have difficulty understanding it. This is intentional: Miscoding almost always works in the insurance company's favor, since it likely results in denial of the claim.

To have a financially healthy practice in this health care system, a pediatrician needs to see a large volume of patients with good insurance and needs to see patients in the office, where the chance for insurance reimbursement is strongest. For many pediatricians that means, "Don't get involved in complicated cases that take you out of the office, even if the family has good insurance, but especially if they don't." Spending the day in the hospital next to a very ill young Medicaid patient on a ventilator was my job, but it sure didn't pay the bills.

Children with special needs do not fit neatly into our health care system. They will take a long time to get to know and will require weekly prescription renewals, scores of consults, and, quite often, hospital admissions for the common illnesses that their bodies just can't handle. In the late 1990s, Rhode Island, backed by new federal funds as a result of the enactment of the State Children's

Health Insurance Program, developed a state health insurance
coverage called Rite Care. It paid doctors more than Medicaid had
and covered a broader range of children. More and more poor
and special-needs children found a medical home, as pediatricians
across the state became willing to accept the improved reimbursement. But even Rite Care paid considerably less than commercial
carriers did. A few of our colleagues in other practices who began
to see more poor children under Rite Care would still say to parents
of a special-needs child, "She is much too complicated for this practice. You'd better have her followed at the outpatient clinic up at
Children's." At the children's hospital in Providence there were
clinics staffed by dedicated doctors and doctors-in-training where
any child could be seen—eventually. So instead of having a medical home, this second-class citizen and her family would have to
commute to the city, sit for hours in an overcrowded waiting room,
and more than likely see a different doctor at each visit. The private
practitioners who avoided these patients had good financial reasons.
Special-needs children take up roughly twice as much time to care
for as a child without special needs, and most of this time, which
involves paperwork, coordination of specialists, and a greater need
for prescription medications and treatments, is not reimbursable.

The irony of this is that primary care, even for special-needs children, and even at the rate at which commercial insurers would pay, is
relatively cheap. It costs so much less than controversial back surgery
or treating everyone who has acid reflux with the most expensive
drug on the market. Yet this is where the people who hold the purse
strings in health care choose to save money—where our moral obligation is clear, and where the cost–benefit ratio is lowest. These are
patients who are disproportionately poor, and whose families may
not be skilled in advocacy, leaving them without much of a voice. In
addition, their care will never make a lot of money for doctors or
hospitals, the way back surgery or imaging studies will, and marketing to this small demographic will never reap rewards for pharmaceutical companies the way medicines for erectile dysfunction will.

Narragansett Bay Pediatrics cared for many special-needs children, even before SCHIP. I followed one girl with severe brain

damage due to encephalitis she acquired as an infant. Sabrina, a foster child, related a little to the rest of us with her facial expressions, but she was developmentally delayed and had a seizure disorder. Her limbs were contracted into tight, spastic angles, and her bones were mottled by rickets—a softening of the bones—from disuse. She had a list of specialists a mile long, and her foster mother kept meticulous records of her doctors and medications. My job was mostly to follow her weights and measures, monitor her nutrition, refill the prescriptions, arrange subspecialty consults, check on her if she appeared ill, and draw blood from her when the specialists ordered tests.

When Sabrina was sick, she could come right in, bypass the waiting room, and get wheeled straight back to an exam room, the beeping of her heart monitor announcing her arrival. Sometimes, if all she needed was blood work, I would go to her house to draw it, to save her and her foster mom the complicated transport to the office. Most of the time, caring for Sabrina was work of the heart rather than of the brain. The reimbursement was insulting—perhaps a forty-dollar payment, low even for the standard twenty-minute visit, but totally inadequate to the hour or so of my time it would take to treat her properly. The occasional house calls I made to give her a quick look or draw blood were usually denied any reimbursement at all. But enabling a vulnerable child to be treated with the same dignity and respect as everyone else was the reason we were all there; the rent would have to come from somewhere else. I was fortunate in being part of a practice that adhered to this ethos, but when America's national strategy for caring for disabled patients relies so heavily on highly skilled professionals doing something for almost nothing, the result is a two-tiered delivery system. Our special-needs children should be able to rely on more than goodwill for their care.

Likewise, the rent will not come from a sick child who appears in the local emergency room in the middle of a busy day. Whoever runs over to see him will either leave a pile of patients fussing in the waiting room, and get backed up with appointments through dinner, or cancel scheduled patients.

One morning, a deathly ill newborn baby, who had not yet established care with a pediatrician in our area, appeared in the emergency room. The staff there determined that the baby's potassium level was dangerously high, and his EKG revealed a life-threatening rhythm. The physician on call for pediatrics was passing through the ER as the staff was accumulating this information. Janet Markham was a busy young woman; she had patients waiting for her in the office—where the money was. So she told the ER staff to call over to "Narragansett Bay." I got the stat page from the ER just as I arrived in the office that morning. I was confused, since our practice wasn't supposed to be on call for the ER that day, but crises are not the time to debate ER coverage. So I ran, leaving my scheduled, paying patients in the dust.

The newborn looked like he was in shock. I began life-support measures, giving him oxygen and fluids and warming him up. His serum level of sodium was dangerously low, and his potassium level was still frighteningly high. The baby had congenital adrenal insufficiency. His adrenal glands weren't working, and the electrolyte disturbance that this produced gave him a classic abnormal heart rhythm, the usual rounded hills of an EKG tracing appearing instead as sharp peaks.

I got the children's hospital in Providence on the phone. We discussed the infusion of glucose and insulin that would help lower the baby's potassium level and correct the heart rhythm, and they put their neonatal transport team on the road to come get him. By the time they arrived, a scary forty-five minutes later, the tiny patient's rhythm had stabilized and his skin was warm and pink with capillary perfusion. He was safely whisked away to the big city. I never saw the infant again, but we heard later through the ER staff that he did very well. By the time I got back to the office that day, several of my patients had been rescheduled, and several more were still waiting, with varying degrees of patience. I did not help pay the rent that morning. The other pediatrician, Dr. Markham, who had walked past that baby a few hours earlier, had probably billed for several hundred dollars' worth of office visits already that day—visits with satisfied customers who had not been kept waiting.

Perhaps more important, she hadn't risked her livelihood by taking on a malpractice suit waiting to happen. Getting involved with complicated patients carries more than financial consequences. It's ripe with opportunity for something to go wrong—for a malpractice lawyer to get that vacation home he's been drooling over. Thank God that baby came into the ER in time and did well. If he had not, then not only would an infant's life have been tragically lost, but the hospital, and I, would have been sued for millions. Guaranteed. It's not about the care. It's about the outcome.

Even with the good outcome, I wasn't completely off the hook. By the time I saw that sick baby in the ER, we had two more additions to our growing practice, Meg and Joy. Both were superb pediatricians who had recently come out of excellent training programs. The doctors in the group typically discussed our most challenging patients with one another, and Meg and I had an honest disagreement about my management of the newborn's arrhythmia. She felt strongly that I should have defibrillated the baby (used paddles to shock him) to get immediate results rather than taking the slower route of correcting the potassium level. My argument was that with the underlying electrolyte disturbance, defibrillation would have been useless. Meg arranged to have a neonatologist come to the next meeting of our hospital's Pediatric Department, which all the area pediatricians and family practitioners attended, to discuss the treatment of neonatal arrhythmias. Our guest's conclusion mirrored our own ambivalence: It wouldn't have been wrong to try defibrillation on that sick baby in the ER, but it probably wouldn't have worked, either.

Ah, if that were only the end of the story. But no. The drive-by pediatrician, Janet Markham, who had first been consulted about the baby, was now holding court over this departmental meeting, and I grew furious as I watched her second-guessing my actions and expressing her gratitude to the speaker for helping out the "old-school" pediatricians in the group.

Possessing neither the unwavering rationality of Celeste, nor the calmness of Bob, my two "old-school colleagues" in the practice, I let loose.

"Do you know why I am sitting here on the hot seat tonight? Because I showed up when they called. Not like you. You saw what was going on and you just kept walking."

This little outburst took place in front of most of the hospital's pediatric staff and our guest. It was foolish and accomplished nothing other than to make an enemy of Janet. If the ER had a beef with Dr. Markham, it was their job to pursue it. I did my job. The ethical challenges that arose for each of us, in a health care system loaded with ethical disincentives, as well as malpractice threats, meant that I had my hands full with my own clinical decision making, and my own code of ethics. I didn't need to go worrying about Janet Markham.

Every clinical decision that a doctor makes, especially a primary care doctor, is made in the context that spending more than twenty minutes with an ill patient, whether in or out of the office, is likely to cost rather than earn the doctor money. And as the risk of a malpractice suit goes up, the doctor's reluctance to take the case on will grow. We all need to be aware of these disincentives operating in our health care system; only then can we develop an effective system that minimizes them.

TWENTY-SIX

Fracture

Through these busy years, my bike was one of my favorite companions. There is a twenty-two-mile perimeter of roads around the island of Jamestown, and I knew every pothole, bump, tree stump, and stone wall on the route. I wore a ski mask in January and carried water in a sack in August. I grew accustomed to the different ways light glanced off Narragansett Bay in each season and knew to time my passing in front of Beavertail lighthouse so as not to get blown off my seat by the foghorn's periodic bellow. I rode in the predawn before work and entered road races without having slept the call night before. Even burdened with bags of groceries or racing to get to the bank before it closed, riding my bike made me feel like I was ten years old. I felt free and untouchable. Concerned parents found me in church, at the market, on the soccer field. They called me at home and distracted me at my children's school plays. But on my bike, no one could reach me. No one could stop me. No one could interrupt my rambling thoughts or the music in my head.

In July 2000, I was speeding down a hill near my home, with the glowing remnants of a perfect sunset lighting my way. Randy had joined me for the ride, a kickoff to our upcoming week's vacation. I hit the brakes as I rounded the last corner, noticing the long oil slick a moment too late. My bike and I went flying, one foot still trapped in its toe clip, and when I landed, my knee hit the ground first, cracking the top of my shinbone like a split log.

The medical term was a tibial plateau fracture, and the only alternative to surgery was to bear no weight at all on the leg for twelve weeks. I could hardly get out of a chair the first week; the slightest movement brought throbs of agony. My knee, filled with blood, was swollen to the size of a cantaloupe, and the strange foot that stuck out from the bottom of the brace was a sickly reddish purple.

I couldn't bathe or even use the toilet without some very intimate assistance. And I watched the clock in agony, waiting for the moment when it would be safe to take pain medication again. Overwhelmed with pain and helplessness, surveying my broken limb, it was hard to believe it would ever function normally again, but I badly needed to get back to work.

In an untimely coincidence of fortune that summer, two of our pediatricians were out on maternity leave. The rest of us had each staked out a week's vacation, stretching us as thin as we ever got. Sympathy for my mishap was thin, too—somebody had to see all the patients. Pain, immobility, and impaired hygiene couldn't lessen my feeling of responsibility. I told my partners I would start taking nighttime phone coverage as soon as I could get off the pain meds, and I would get back to the office in two weeks.

The challenge of not bearing weight on one leg is that you need two hands for crutches, making even the simplest task almost impossible if you are standing. So I rented a wheelchair, and we hired Jenny, the teenage daughter of our nurse manager, Maryellen, to shadow me from exam room to exam room, handing me otoscopes and tongue blades or picking up charts when they slipped off my lap.

Pediatrics is a seasonal business, and the business of summer is mostly school physicals and viral infections, with a bit of Lyme disease thrown in. I was dragging myself into the office every day not because of medical crises, but because kids can't go to school or camp or play sports without getting forms signed. Health maintenance visits are important, but their timing is mostly driven by paperwork. I was also dragging myself in because fevers of 103, as harmless as they may be, scare parents as much in the summer as they do in the winter. Still, the incredible effort that it took to go to the office that July brought into focus a much larger picture—the contrast between the level of medical necessity of an encounter and the personal cost for me to be there.

I hadn't previously realized how much I relied on body language to wrap up a visit: close a chart, pat an arm, move toward the door even as I offered my parting words. If there was a question tagged on—"Oh by the way, Doctor, his little brother, J. C., seems to be stuttering. Should I be worried?"—I would already be turning the knob as I answered.

"Well, when is J. C. coming in for his well-child check? See if you can schedule one in the next week or so instead of waiting till October."

By the time I finished a sentence suggesting an appointment for J. C. the following week, I was halfway out the door. Such exits frequently made parents unhappy, but it was the only way to stay on schedule; there was never enough time to give everybody as much conversation as they would like. I experienced the same thing when I went to my own doctor.

"Well, Maggie, everything looks good. I should see you again in a year." Dr. Schwartz, my gynecologist, pushed his stool back against the wall, closing my chart, grinning in summation. But he hadn't mentioned my thyroid function.

"Ummm—how about my thyroid tests? It's been a year now since I had them done."

Dr. Schwartz was visibly *not* reaching for the door handle, if such a thing was possible. I was, after all, a colleague.

"Doesn't Russ [my internist] follow you for that?" he asked, quickly thumbing back through my chart without landing on anything. His I-have-all-the-time-in-the-world-for-you tone turned to insanely distracted in a matter of seconds.

"I'll order them myself and have the results sent to you," I offered. I knew if I had questions, I could bring them up with Russ at the *start* of my next visit with him.

"Great." Dr. Schwartz smiled, relieved, closing the chart again and finally able to reach for the knob. "Say hi to Randy for me."

I was not offended in the least; I got it, even as I recognized I was being shortchanged a bit. He was probably an hour behind already, and his day was only going to get worse.

Sitting in my wheelchair during an office visit, trying not to fall hopelessly behind, body language failed me. I needed the families to clear out, or at least make way for me so I could exit. It was not my choreography anymore. I sat there helplessly listening to added stories, and new questions, tensely eyeing the hands of the clock, falling farther and farther behind schedule with each appointment.

During one of these standoffs, a friend from Jamestown, Lynn, checked in for her son's physical twenty minutes late. Lynn was always late for appointments; she saw it as the privilege of friendship. We had a policy in the office that if you were more than fifteen minutes late, you had to reschedule. This wasn't for the doctors' benefit: Rescheduled appointments are money down the drain for a doctor. If we didn't hold to such a policy, all the people who showed up on time for the rest of the day would be kept waiting that much longer. It wasn't fair to them.

So Lynn was told she would have to reschedule.

"Tell Dr. Kozel it's me. I know she'll see me."

The receptionist knew better and explained why the lateness policy was necessary now more than ever. She knew that I was lumbering around in the back, with my sorry leg sticking straight out like a lightning rod for every rambunctious kid in my path.

"I know all about that. But she's a personal friend. She'll see us." The receptionist called on my nurse, Barbara, to explain my difficulties again. But the more Barbara tried, the more annoyed Lynn became, and she refused to leave until she spoke with me directly.

"She's mad," Barbara said, looking uncharacteristically mad herself as she stuck her head in the room. I was in the middle of checking a very unhappy patient for an ear infection. Jenny had pinned the wriggling mass of child down for me; a line of sweat had broken out above my lip. "She won't leave until you talk to her."

I leaned back in the chair and looked at Barbara but pictured my "friend," Lynn. I was usually a wimp in such matters, tending to avoid confrontations in the office, but the kernel of me that typically tried so hard to keep people happy had cracked.

"Tell her to go home," I said.

By the time my office manager dropped me back home at the end of the day, my knee was pulsing with pain and I was dizzy and fatigued. Once I hobbled through my front door those first few weeks, I made a beeline for the couch, swallowed a couple of pain pills, gulped water to quench the thirst I hadn't been able to satisfy all day, and slept deeply for hours until Randy came through the door with take-out food. I must have seemed like a phantom to the girls, and as the weeks went on they made more and more arrangements to be at friends' homes.

Time truly did heal my wounds, with the help of some great doctors and physical therapists. By Labor Day I was flying around on my crutches like I was born with them and rarely needed even a Tylenol for pain. In just a few weeks more I was slowly putting weight on the ball of my foot, driving a car, and even hobbling daintily from bed to toilet without my crutches. As my good humor returned, so did my family's, and our house regained its former energy.

Those long months taught me a lot about strength and weakness, about being broken and being healed. They also taught me a lot about paying attention. Spending hours on the porch with my swollen limb propped up on a chair, I came to believe that being able to distinguish the different shades of green on the leaves of my backyard trees was as important an accomplishment for me as catching up on my professional journals. I was ready for truths beyond what could be measured in lab reports or documented in charts, for more meaning than could be heard in the clatter of a busy day.

TWENTY-SEVEN

Nothing Personal

One of the advantages to private community practice is that you can get to know your patients and their families; there is a chance to form a relationship with them. For many doctors, including myself, it is that relationship that allows us to keep going in the face of all the other obstacles we encounter in current medical practice. Over the years I enjoyed wonderful relationships with families, like with Mae and her parents. I received beautiful handwritten notes on a regular basis from a young single mother whose son had asthma, keeping me informed of his progress and thanking me for my help. I was kept well supplied with wasabi paste by a Japanese mother of a child I had treated for whooping cough. I had walls of crayoned art and was flooded with baked goods and greeting cards at the holidays. There were endearing smiles of recognition from small children as they passed me on the street, and kind words from parents on line at the grocery store about how helpful I had been. These were the things that sustained me. But doctor–patient relationships seem to have grown increasingly strained over the years. The economics of health care has had a depersonalizing effect on the doctor–patient encounter, and the crazy-paced lives of the families in my practice put a growing premium on convenience and quick fixes rather than on process and relationship.

I have no idea what percentage of my encounters with parents was overtly negative. It had to have been small—surely less than 10 percent. What is frustrating about such experiences is that they loom disproportionately large on a psychological level. In a relationship where trust and respect are indispensable, one or two angry encounters a day can be hard to shake off and can poison the day with a lingering sense of defeat and resentment.

I had been following Megan Smith in my practice since she and her siblings were babies, and I knew her mother well—she was intelligent, articulate, and reliable. Mrs. Smith brought ten-year-old Megan in one mid-July with fever and a stiff neck. That combination always gets a pediatrician's attention, since it can signify meningitis. Sure enough, I found a flushed, unhappy-looking Megan sitting on a chair in the exam room, her neck held slightly askew. Mrs. Smith explained that Megan's fever had been up and down for two or three days, and she had headaches only when the fever spiked. She vomited several times and complained of muscle aches.

Megan was alert, if miserable, and moved slowly onto the exam table for me. I checked her over carefully, noting that there were no signs of increased pressure in her brain, no rash, no lumps in her neck to cause discomfort. I was almost certain she had acute Lyme disease, and not meningitis.

If there was one thing we did exceptionally well at Narragansett Bay Pediatrics, it was diagnosing and treating Lyme disease. Southern Rhode Island is a hotbed for it, and July was when we saw the highest incidence of infection. Megan just "looked" like she had Lyme. Mom was very surprised at my impression but relieved that the physical exam suggested this was probably not meningitis. Still, Megan had to come in to the hospital while we sorted out what was going on. An hour later, I had performed the spinal tap, drawn her blood, started an IV, and ordered antibiotics that would cover Lyme bacteria as well as the common causes of meningitis, in case the spinal tap proved me wrong. Her preliminary lab work, however, supported my diagnosis. I drove home that afternoon with that gratified, energized feeling I always got when I felt I was actually being the doctor I had been trained to be. The next morning, I found Megan sitting up in bed playing video games and asking when she could go home. The parents were relieved and eternally grateful—well, perhaps not eternally. I recounted the story back at the office, and my partners shared in the satisfaction of medicine practiced well.

A week later, Megan was recuperating beautifully at home. She came in to see me, was switched over to oral antibiotics, and sent merrily on her way with a continued plan for close follow-up. A few days later, however, our office manager, Denise, came in to tell me that Megan's family was transferring out of the practice. She placed the medical records release form on my desk.

"What?" I almost shouted.

"Apparently she had a conversation with Donna at the front desk when she was here the other day, and it upset her, and she wants to transfer," Denise then elaborated.

"When she was checking out, Donna mentioned that she had a past balance due, and I don't know whether other people heard it or not, but Mrs. Smith got really mad and left. I asked Donna about it, and she said she was being polite. Mrs. Smith kept questioning it, and Donna kept trying to explain, but Mrs. Smith just kept getting madder and madder. Donna really feels bad."

None of this made sense. Donna was one of the most poised and mature people we had working on our staff. And I was smoothly seeing Megan through a serious ordeal. What the hell could have happened?

I called Mrs. Smith.

"I'm sorry, Dr. Kozel," she explained very matter-of-factly, "but I felt that it was very unprofessional to bring up our account at a time like that, with other people standing around."

"I'm sorry if we caused you any embarrassment, Mrs. Smith, but checkout time is when we bring those things up, and Donna is usually so careful in the way she conducts herself."

"I'm sure you're very fond of your receptionist, but I will not go to a practice where I am treated like that."

I felt stunned—and betrayed.

"Okay, Mrs. Smith, let's say for argument's sake that Donna was a complete jerk. I am trying to imagine what a receptionist would have to say to me to make me leave the practice of a doctor who had been taking very good care of my children. Maybe that he belonged to the Ku Klux Klan? It's hard to come up with something, Mrs. Smith. If I got really mad, I'd say something to the doctor, not transfer out of the practice."

"Well, we'll just have to disagree on that, Dr. Kozel. We appreciate everything you did for Megan, but as long as you employ people like that, I will not be bringing my children there." From my perspective, Mrs. Smith had chosen to react to the situation like a health care "consumer" and was dismissing me like I was the manager of an appliance store. There was no relationship between us that she saw any value in. She saw our interaction in terms of purchasing power, and let's face it, one appliance store is generally as good as the next.

What I was failing to acknowledge in the heat of the moment was that Mrs. Smith was caught up in the same health care dance I was. One could argue that her daughter's beautiful recovery had been sidelined by us, of all people, and had been reduced, in one insensitive moment, to the issue of when she was going to get around to paying for the service. Mrs. Smith and I had both been cast into roles here, pushed into a business relationship that neither of us had chosen.

Not able to see the other side of the story at that moment, I hung up the phone, stared at the records release form in frustration, and then signed it in my most careless chicken scrawl. This health care provider had to move on. More and more, it seemed to me, insults and feelings of betrayal had to be ignored for me to make it through a day.

TWENTY-EIGHT

The Worried Well

I graduated from medical school a doctor, but somewhere along the way I morphed into a health care provider. Shakespeare might have thought there wasn't much in a name, but he didn't have to search out his "preferred provider" when his humours got all out of whack.

Patients and their families, by necessity, have had to become health care consumers. Insurance premiums, co-pays, deductibles, out-of-pocket expenses, and just trying to keep track of who is in or out of network all mean that once you need a doctor, the next thought often is, "Who's going to pay what?" or, more to the point, "How do I arrange this so that it will cost me the least amount of money?" These are quickly followed by the thoughts that are likely to put the patient at cross-purposes with the "provider": "Did I get my money's worth?" and, sometimes, "Did you accommodate me enough?"

I was on call one September weekend when a massive nor'easter blasted through southern New England. Roads flooded and power lines went down; the governor asked that all non-essential person-nel stay home. Randy drove me to my office in his Jeep Scrambler, plowing through the waters that covered Route 1 like one of those amphibious duck boats that dip you in and out of the Charles River in Boston. I had canceled appointments that Sunday morning but needed to get to the office where I would have access to the hospi-tal's phone lines and be close by for emergencies.

By eleven o'clock that morning, I had fielded twenty or so calls from parents. No one was having an emergency; I was able to tempo-rize and reassure. Then Mrs. B called about her sixteen-year-old daughter, Kate. They lived up in North Kingstown, near our satellite office in Wickford. Kate had been having a sore throat for three or four days. It wasn't bad enough to keep her home from school, but it was dragging on and Mom felt it was time to get it cultured.

"Has she had any fever?"

"No, not that I can tell."

"Is it keeping her from eating?"

"No, her appetite seems fine, but it hurts her sometimes to swallow."

"Any cold symptoms?"

"I'm not sure." She was getting an edge to her voice. Mrs. B. was calling up for takeout and I was questioning her menu choice. "I just want her to get tested for strep."

"Well, that's not a bad idea. You could bring her to the Wickford office first thing tomorrow morning, and the nurse will swab her throat."

"But you're in the office now, and I don't want her to miss school tomorrow."

"Mrs. B, look out the window. I'm not seeing office patients today. I'm just here for emergencies."

"Well, I pay a fortune in health insurance every month, and I say this is an emergency. I want her to be seen today."

I tried to squash the first flames of anger that licked at my throat.

Taking a deep breath, I explained to her why this was not an emergency. Antibiotics wouldn't make Kate get better any faster. The reason we treat strep with antibiotics is to prevent heart complications from developing later; they won't shorten the illness.

"Are you refusing to see her? Do you know how much my co-pay will be if you make me take her to an ER? Why can't you just do your job?"

My anger flared, and I was helpless to stop it. All I could do was swallow it and try to keep my voice even, switching from healer to customer service representative. But I could detect the edge in my own voice, too. We went around in circles until I finally declared that the conversation was over.

It was a very long weekend. I went home after Sunday morning's telethon and answered calls from the comfort of my couch. The weather calmed later that afternoon, and I returned to the office to see patients I had deferred during the storm. I stuck around for a late-night C-section, grabbing a slice of pizza for dinner, and crawled home to bed about midnight, tossing and turning in between the smattering of pager calls that generally came in between 2 and 4 AM. I woke the girls for school just before I left the house at seven o'clock; Randy would get them to the bus. I made morning rounds in the nursery, eyeballed a patient in the ER whom the staff had a question about, and eventually made my way back to the office in time to start the day's appointments.

So I sat for a few minutes, dazed, that "morning after" as I tried to push my brain into a higher gear. It would be obvious to anyone looking at my desk that doctors often fly solo on weekends, without clerical help. A confusing pile of messages and half-written notes, milk curdling in abandoned cups of coffee, prescription pads used for scribbling, all testified to what a doctor is reduced to without a support system.

I was awakened from the daze by a call from Shirley, the nurse in Wickford. She thought I should know about the fuss Mrs. B had been making about the strep test, complaining to all within earshot of her shabby treatment and of Kate's missing class on account of my shameful disregard for patients. I closed my eyes as she filled me in, and rubbed at my forehead, wondering just how many hours a day I wasted on this kind of nonsense. I had been as conscientious and reasonable as I knew how. I did no harm. But this was the least of Mrs. B's concerns. She wasn't looking for smart or conscientious. She was looking for accommodating. And I had fallen short. As it turned out, the strep test was negative, but this happy news only added to the general level of Mrs. B's dissatisfaction: To her it meant she had been put through all this cost and inconvenience "for nothing."

The nurse who was working with me that day, Barbara, signaled to me that my first patient was in a room, and she handed me a note. It was from Molly's school—she had just thrown up. I thanked Shirley for dealing with my mess and hung up just as Bob Maltz walked in.

"Sounds like you had a fun weekend," he smirked.

"Just getting nickel-and-dimed." The frustration that eked out of our pores after a weekend on call was understood; little explanation was required. "Molly's throwing up," I said, waving the note in the air. The conflict of having a sick child at home when we were charged with attending to the army of sick children in our waiting room likewise needed little elaboration.

"Oh no, poor Molly. Can I help?"

Bob agreed to see my nine o'clock patient, and Barbara tackled a few of my more urgent phone calls while I made arrangements for our babysitter, Christine, to run to Molly's rescue. A quick call to the school nurse put me in touch with the patient herself.

"Hi, sweetie, I hear you don't feel so well."

"Are you coming to get me?" Her usual boisterous voice was hushed.

"Christine is, honey. She'll be there very soon."

"I threw up all over my pink dress."

"That's okay, hon. Christine will get you clean clothes. She'll take good care of you."

"When will you be home?"

Molly is a doctor's child. She didn't ask *Why can't you come?* or argue with the plan. She knew that unless she was bleeding—a lot—she would take a ticket and wait like everyone else. Molly seemed to accept this as the way things were. I was the one suffering.

"I am going to put everyone in the office to work rearranging my schedule, baby, so I can get home as soon as possible. Okay? And I'm going to call Daddy, too, because I know he'll want to come home as fast as he can tonight to see how you are doing."

"Okay, Mom. Can I watch TV when I get home?"

Patient reassured, I thought ruefully. How smoothly I could discharge my own daughter.

Barbara stuck her head back in as soon as I hung up. I never heard Barbara mutter an unkind word about anyone, and she was not about to start now. But I could tell by her frown that she was worried about upsetting me.

"The nine o'clock in room one, Mrs. K, is a little upset," she started, pained to be the bearer of unsettling news. "She saw that you are here and she wants to wait for you rather than see Bob. It's someone you know from Jamestown."

Oh boy. Kathy K. She was a nice woman, with a healthy family, but was pretty high-maintenance.

"Fine." At this point I just wanted to get through the morning. My head was starting to throb. It was now nine fifteen. "Is the nine twenty in a room?"

"Well, that's the problem. It's Mrs. P. She got here half an hour early with Jake, and she said she doesn't want to be kept waiting. So I wasn't sure if you wanted to see her before the nine o'clock. I think Mrs. K will be willing to wait if she knows she's seeing you."

I was pretty sure she'd wait, too, but I was also pretty sure that this would give her permission to stretch our encounter well past the twenty-minute block. We'd be weighing the benefits of naps versus no naps till the sheep came home.

"Okay," I started, gathering my strength. "Let me see Jake, then I'll see the family from Jamestown. See if you can block out the first open sick visit, since I'm sure I'll be way behind by then."

Donna, one of our brave receptionists, rounded the corner at that moment. She had the uncanny ability to be polite in the face of unforgivable rudeness and remain calm at the center of a typhoon, which is what had made the incident with Megan Smith's mother seem inexplicable. Donna was all business this hectic Monday morning, and she promptly squashed my plan.

"Your sick visits are already booked up, Maggie. And Timmy L's mom just called. He seems to be breathing a little heavier than usual."

Timmy was born with a very complicated heart defect. He had made a remarkable recovery from open-heart surgery but was still on several heart medications and needed close monitoring. It occurred to me in a flash of cynicism that, of all the patients I was going to see that day, Timmy might be the only one who actually required a doctor's attention.

"Give him the first sick visit and push all the rest back." The pounding in my head had localized to a quarter-sized area on my left temple, and I suddenly became aware of how thirsty I was.

"So move the last one to the end of your day?" Donna wanted to be clear she was extending my schedule.

"I guess," I said, shaking my head in resignation. I glanced over at the picture of Molly I kept on my desk. It had been less than fifteen minutes since I'd promised her I would shorten my day. I knew where these worried parents were coming from. I would have felt less anxious if I'd had a few minutes to catch one of my partners' ears about Molly and her vomiting. The part of my pulsating brain that stored doctor expertise was pretty confident she had a harmless bug. But the mother in me, like the mothers of most of my patients, worried.

What if the school nurse missed a fever? (Molly tended to hold her mouth open when she had a thermometer lodged under her tongue. That could make her measured temperature look lower than it was.) What if she was getting another urinary tract infection? What if this was strep? What if she was really sick and I just dismissed her with "reassurance" so that I could get back to discussing some other child's potty training?

There was no point in thinking about it. I moved into the hall and by the time I grabbed the next patient's chart off the wall, Molly was tucked away into her own little compartment in my brain.

Timmy L came in, looking a little paler than usual, and his breathing was a little more rapid. Listening to his lungs, I heard the crackles of fluid that had accumulated there. His liver was a finger's breadth larger than the last time I measured it, and I suspected his heart muscle was getting a little overloaded; blood wasn't pushing through his system as effectively as it should. I got his cardiologist on the phone, and we adjusted his medications. His mother, a Rock of Gibraltar who calmly did whatever needed to get done for her son, made sure she understood the directions and promised to call back in four hours with an update. By the time I waved them off, I was an hour behind.

This was the reality of office scheduling. You usually couldn't leave blank spaces in your schedule to allow for unexpected situations like Timmy's. Doctors over the last decade have had to see more and more patients every day just to keep their income stable.

So schedules need to get filled up. When the hospital calls or a sick child needs extra attention, the doctor runs around like crazy trying to be in several places at once, and all the other patients just wait or get rescheduled. Nobody wins.

"Here's Dr. Kozel," proclaimed Mrs. P to Jake, avoiding eye contact as I walked in the room, turning her back to me as she spoke to Jake. "Now hop up on the table like a good boy, Jake. We don't want this to go any later than it already has." I absorbed the comment the way I absorbed many such comments before it, acting as if I did not hear the hostility, moving right to the purpose of the visit. It was not just efficiency that moved me forward. I couldn't wait to get out of the room, to escape from Mrs. P.

When I got home that afternoon I cradled Molly in my lap, taking comfort in her cool forehead, her chatter, the way she squirmed out of my hold to run after Caitlin. Something else was squirming away from me as well. As hard as I was working to deny it, the very essence of what it meant to be a doctor—the wonder, the skill, the healing relationships—seemed to be slipping through my fingers. More and more I was falling short of parents' expectations, and the changing shape of my pediatric practice was falling short of mine.

TWENTY-NINE

Calling Dr. Pez

O ne of the most worrisome roles for me as a pediatrician was that of Pez dispenser, especially when it involved treating mood disorders.

There are many serious conditions in childhood that require expert evaluation and treatment from someone other than a pediatrician. Many of these conditions, like depression and anxiety disorders, involve a child's mental health. The number of patients whom pediatricians are called upon to evaluate and treat for serious mental and behavioral problems has been growing steadily, as insurance coverage has greatly limited the availability of outpatient psychiatrists and psychologists to young patients. A recent estimate by the AAP predicts that the number of pediatric visits for mental health issues will continue to grow to the point that it will make up 30 to 40 percent of a general pediatrician's practice.[16] In my very typical pediatric residency, I spent four weeks out of a three-year training program on the child psychiatry service and another four weeks on behavioral pediatrics, which is a specialty that addresses problems such as extremely oppositional behavior or learning challenges like ADHD. In comparison, I spent six months, and a good deal of additional nights on call, in the neonatal intensive care unit taking care of sick and premature infants. By the time I went out into practice, I could intubate a twenty-six-week premie in my sleep, but I knew very little about evaluating or treating, say, depression in an adolescent.

Health insurance reimbursements and a lack of informed public
v, however, *not* pediatric training programs, determine what
ιtrician is expected to do. So I found it especially alarming
rivate practice I was expected not just to screen for, but to
ιd prescribe medications for serious conditions like anxi-
·ession, with little recourse to mental health specialists.

Minor anxiety disorders were very common in my practice, starting in middle school and peaking in adolescence. The chief complaints of light-headedness or numbness in hands and feet, would point doctor and patient down the right path even as the child denied ever being worried or nervous. The situation is unlikely to be life threatening and is appropriate for a pediatric office. As I spoke casually about the physiological effects of hyperventilation, and how it produced their symptoms, or how talk therapy moved the symptoms out of the brain and the chest, into the light of day, I could see the relief wash over them. They believed me that they were not going crazy, that they were going to be okay. The biggest danger in adolescents is the use of alcohol or drugs to self-medicate for anxiety, and that was more difficult to uncover, especially in a primary care doctor's office, where time is at a premium.

Of course not all anxiety is that minor, and children can develop phobias, compulsions, and obsessions that severely limit their ability to go to school and carry on the other work of childhood and adolescence. For patients who can pay a psychologist's fees out of pocket, the prognosis is generally quite good. For those who can't, the symptoms may have to progress in a clearly destructive way before they will qualify for care.

Depression is a whole different story. Depressed adolescents worry me. They are good at hiding it, even from themselves. One of the tragedies of childhood depression is that more than half the patients do not get diagnosed until adulthood. Access to mental health professionals and insurance coverage for mental illness have been totally inadequate to the scope of the problem.

The depressed children and adolescents do not come in seeking help and are sometimes angry just to be sitting in the pediatrician's office. Fifteen-year-old Marissa was a perfect example. Mildly overweight, sullen expression, stringy hair falling in her eyes, she sat slumped against the wall.

"*I* don't know why I'm here. Go ask my mother. *She's* the one who made me come." Her tone is more petulant than defiant.

Marissa was not really asking me to get information from her mother. She was asking me to go out to the waiting room and tell her mother to go to hell. I pulled up a chair, gave Marissa an encouraging smile—which I wasn't sure she saw since she had so far avoided any eye contact—and began.

"I think it would be better if *you* could tell me what's been going on."

My preliminary fact finding revealed how stupid Mom was, how lame Stepdad was, what a waste of time school was, and what jerks all the rest of the kids were. Marissa grew slightly more animated as we talked, shrugging or waving her hand dismissively now and then. I slowly teased out more details—who was fighting at home, who was drinking, what substances Marissa herself used, her sexual experiences, just who her friends were, what she liked to do in her free time. We slowly achieved mutual eye contact, exchanged facial expressions.

"Your mom is worried that you are depressed, Marissa."

"That's because she's crazy." Marissa looked away from me again.

"Do you ever feel sad?"

Marissa looked down at the floor with great concentration and grew completely still, almost frozen, trying to will herself not to cry. Silent streams of tears rolling down her cheeks finally betrayed her. I handed her a box of tissues and she pulled one out, waving it like the flag of surrender that it was.

"I just don't know what to do," she whispered.

You're not the only one. Ironic me.

Marissa needed help; I nailed down that much. But how much help? How urgently? Had she just hit a rough patch in her transition through adolescence? Was there a genetic tendency toward a serious mood disorder? Was she hiding a devastating event, like rape, that triggered this? And the three most important questions:

Is she likely to hurt herself?

Is she likely to hurt herself?

Is she likely to hurt herself?

Once we worked through an anticlimactic medical history and physical exam, we called Mom in to join us. By this time I had three other patients already waiting in rooms, I knew, and more waiting out in the reception area. Mom had been keeping a lot bottled up, and I could tell she really wanted airtime, but I had to wrap this up somehow. I cut her off as artfully as I could and asked her what *I* needed to know: Had Marissa ever spoken of suicide, even vaguely? Were there any firearms in the house? (Even unloaded and locked away, the presence of a gun in the house greatly increases the risk of teenage suicide.) I explained that we needed to set Marissa up with a therapist. I knew Mom's next question before she asked it.

"Will insurance cover that?"

I skirted answering; all three of us were worried enough already. I advised her to check with her insurance company and see which therapists it would cover and for how many visits. I knew the list the insurance company would provide was very different from the list of therapists we recommended. None of the ones we personally knew and had confidence in accepted private insurance; the reimbursement was too spotty and too small. So Marissa and her parents would have to weigh everything in the balance and go with what they could afford. I hoped they wouldn't just give up and try their luck with herbal teas.

Before they left, I made them both swear that if Marissa had any thoughts about suicide or hurting herself, or showed any risky behavior, they would contact me. That seemed as airtight a plan as when I told my daughters, "And if there's any drinking at that party, I want you to call me."

I didn't refer Marissa to a psychiatrist. Although there were a limited number of inpatient psychiatry beds for emergency situations, there were no child psychiatrists in Rhode Island who would see outpatients at the time, and few adult psychiatrists who would treat adolescents. More health care economics. Outpatient psychiatrists in our state mostly get reimbursed for fifteen-minute "med" visits, where they get to prescribe meds and then check in briefly with the patient now and then to make sure the meds are working okay. If it doesn't involve a pill, the visit isn't covered.

Psychologists are an important resource, but they cannot prescribe drugs. I had the privilege of working with some excellent psychologists, skilled professionals to whom I could entrust my patients. The problems arose when those skilled professionals concluded that the patient would benefit from medication, like an antidepressant. That is when they referred the patient back to me, the Pez dispenser.

It's not just that I had very little psychiatric training in my pediatric residency. Selective serotonin reuptake inhibitors, or SSRIs—that major class of antidepressants that are now the mainstay of managing depression and other mood disorders—were then but a twinkle in a drug researcher's eye. What I learned about Prozac, Zoloft, and all the others I learned by reading articles largely based on data provided by the drug companies that manufacture them, and by going to conferences that were often sponsored by these same drug companies. Because primary care doctors are often the only medical professionals in this situation who will get paid for prescribing these powerful medications to children, we scramble to teach ourselves what we can about dosing, efficacy, and adverse effects. Correspondence school for depression.

By 2003, an estimated 10.8 million patients between the ages of two and seventeen were being treated with an SSRI drug in the United States.[17] That number has since decreased by about 20 percent amid a controversy as to whether these medications can actually increase suicide risk,[18] but many physicians and patients have come to rely on them, especially in this day and age when insurance companies are unlikely to pay for "talk" therapy. Complicating the clinical appropriateness of who treats mood disorders, and how, is the fact that SSRIs represent a multibillion-dollar business for the pharmaceutical industry, with hundreds of millions of dollars spent annually on direct marketing of the drugs to both physicians and patients. New versions of the expensive drugs are released just as fast as the old standbys, like Prozac, go generic. How many of us who watch the nightly news could hum the sound track to Cymbalta ads without thinking?

The AAP, recognizing the role that pediatricians have had to take on, has again jumped in, providing diagnostic screening tools for our patients, publishing guidelines for referral of high-risk patients. "Tool kits." How-to manuals, essentially.[19]

All in all, a TV repair person has more formal education about TVs than I had for depression. A survey of primary care physicians in 2004 revealed that only 8 percent of pediatricians felt that they had adequate training in the prescribing of antidepressants, 16 percent felt comfortable prescribing them, but 72 percent actually did prescribe them. [20] So what I had going for me in my practice is what pediatricians in general had going for them: I was smart, and motivated, and I knew how to use resources. Still, it felt like a gamble. Once again, it was driven not by medical decision making, but by our system of health care coverage—businessmen in the boardrooms of health insurance companies creating health care policy that shapes practice methods, while those in pharmaceutical companies use marketing to create both supply and demand for expensive drugs.

So when I sat down to write in Marissa's chart, my antennae and my anxiety were up. I carefully documented every crucial question and answer that arose in that exam room. My notes showed that I took it seriously: I explored the relevant issues, made a reasonable determination that Marissa was not a suicide risk, and made a referral to a mental health professional. I gave clear guidelines for follow-up.

Subtext: If anything bad happens, it is not my fault.

When the therapist that Marissa's family chose wrote a letter to me three weeks later, recommending a trial of antidepressants, I went back and reviewed relevant articles. Then I reviewed the *PDR* (*Physicians' Desk Reference*) for correct drug dosages and adverse effects to watch for. I kept reminding myself that these drugs, despite some well-publicized examples to the contrary, seemed to do more good than harm in preventing suicide. But I wouldn't lose the feeling that I was flying by the seat of my pants.

What choice did I have? Marissa probably did need the antidepressants. If I didn't prescribe them, who would? At least in this case, the therapist was one I had recommended; I had some confidence that what she was asking me to dispense was appropriate. If Marissa's family had chosen a therapist whom their insurance covered but I didn't know, then I would have been flying blind, practicing medicine by the keeping-my-fingers-crossed method.

It made me worry for my patients and for myself, professionally. I resented it. I resented that the psychologist could not call up her partnering (hah!) psychiatrist to evaluate Marissa for meds. I resented that I was the Pez dispenser for other people's clinical decisions. Having to shape my practice around what insurance companies covered rather than what I felt competent to do was emblematic of the growing discrepancy between who I was, professionally, and what was expected of me. In no other area of my clinical practice would I have taken on therapies that I was not comfortable with. Compromising my own professional standards, however, was not—is not—the biggest issue. Clinical decision making shaped by profit is.

THIRTY

Spoonfuls of Sugar

Throughout my medical career, people often gushed at me how I must love children to have gone into pediatrics, like I was some kind of medical Mary Poppins. I would generally respond in some vague, satisfactory way: "Oh yeah, kids are great." But my little secret was that I didn't "love" other people's kids any more than obstetricians "love" pregnant women, or orthopedists "love" clumsy skiers. It's what we do that we love. I like kids a lot, but making a seriously ill child better, or spotting an illness long before it becomes dangerous and preventing it from doing harm, and working to make sure that each child's essential needs were being met—that is what I loved about pediatrics. And that is what we should all want our pediatricians to love. My practice, however, like most private pediatric practices, gradually drifted from what I had learned in specialty training into the realm of child rearing.

My days in private practice went by in a blur, especially if I had been on call the night before. As blood pounded through my fatigue-addled brain, I strained to listen to unedited accounts of bowel patterns, creative descriptions of the color of nose drippings, complaints of dinner table misbehavior. I wished I could hire a grandmother as an assistant.

"Mabel, could you step into room two? Mom says Jenny will only eat vegetables if they have chocolate syrup on them."

Parents have always needed reassurance. But unlike our parents, we live in a world rife with experts, with an expectation that we should be getting expert advice on every detail of child rearing. Even if an older generation is around to guide us, we are unlikely to have complete confidence in them. And just keeping a copy of the latest version of Dr. Spock on the nightstand seems not nearly enough.

When bookstores carry 101 different titles on how to toilet-train your children, how to get them to sleep through the night, and how to orchestrate their toddler years to maximize their chances of getting into Harvard, parents feel that there is much at stake with every little day-to-day decision they make. When experts are interviewed on the morning talk shows about the best way to handle a child's first day of school, it can, rather than feeling helpful, leave a parent overly worried about the magnitude of the issue and handling it "the wrong way." Parents lose confidence in their own inexpert ability to make basic child-rearing decisions. And baby boomers in particular seem to have little faith in children's natural resiliency; one false move and your child is ruined for life.

Common sense has in some ways become as obsolete as the slide rule. Pediatricians have had to step up to the plate, offering the advice that parents crave on everything from developmental toys to night-lights. It's as if the role of accountants had shifted from figuring out taxes to teaching clients how to balance a checkbook. That's an important skill to teach, but not quite what a CPA is designed for. When I was a pediatric resident, I spent little time on the ordinary concerns of normal child rearing—or learning how to dispense common sense. But common sense became the bread and butter of well-child visits. The hardest parts of my day frequently involved getting parents to swallow it in the allotted time.

"Hannah will only eat sweets, Dr. Kozel. I feel terrible about it. But look at her. She's so thin. She has to eat something."

So thin. Sadly, that's how most American parents today would describe children at their healthy weight. This was the flip side of little Robby's chubbiness—the primal urge to fatten our children up.

"Healthy children look skinny to us, Mrs. D. They're supposed to. Look at her growth curve. She's growing steadily at the 25th percent. That's good. If you can't see an eight-year-old's ribs, that's when you worry."

"She looks thin to me," Mrs. D insists. "So what do you suggest I do?" There is a subtle annoyance to her voice. Clearly, I am determined to be difficult. I am not going to offer something as simple as vitamins, or a drink supplement, so now it's my problem to fix this.

I take my hundredth deep breath of the day and begin. Information is power.

"Well, first off, it helps to keep in mind that we eat primarily to fuel our bodies, not for pleasure. Hannah needs to learn this. We all need to be reminded of that now and again. You only offer Hannah what you, the adult, think she needs to eat to be healthy. That's your job. Her job is to eat it or not."

"But she's not going to, Doctor . . . I guess I'll just keep making sure she gets her vitamins."

"The kids on vitamins in my practice, Mrs. D, are the ones with the worst eating habits. Vitamins give us a false sense of security. If they are popping that pill, we don't feel nearly as resolved to stick with our own choices for what they should eat."

"So I let her starve?"

"I've never seen healthy kids let themselves starve, Mrs. D. You just offer her a nice variety of healthy foods—what the family eats—and your job is done."

"How about juice?"

"Juice is just sugar water." Judging by the look on her face, Mrs. D is starting to wonder now if I'm even a real doctor.

"I only buy 100 percent juice, Doctor."

"Which means it's mostly made up of water and fruit sugar, unless you're giving her some pretty pulpy stuff," I say evenly, trying so hard not to pontificate, not to lose her. But juice is one of the biggest culprits in our children's malnutrition. It is important to be clear. "Fructose is just a different form of sugar. And it's a great appetite suppressant. A glass of juice here and there and Hannah will be happy to skip a meal."

"So what do I give her to drink?"

"Water. Three cups of skim milk a day."

"She won't drink water and will only drink a little milk if it has chocolate syrup in it."

"I have never seen healthy children let themselves die of thirst, Mrs. D. Not when there's plenty of water around."

Mrs. D will remain unconvinced. I know that. And I will strive to maintain a tone that is helpful, not finger wagging or judgmental, because I want her eventually to consider what I have said. It will be better for Hannah in the long run to get weaned off her sugar addiction, and to grow up with a healthy attitude toward eating. And it will be more satisfying for Mrs. D to know she is providing her daughter with what she needs. But the odds against that happening are overwhelming. Mrs. D has lost confidence in her own abilities to make decisions for Hannah. She is desperately trying to gather cues from Hannah's behaviors and reactions as to what her daughter needs. She is telling her native intelligence to "shush" and ignoring her experience of reality, as well as an avalanche of media revelations—that American children are suffering in epidemic proportions from obesity, not undernourishment, and that she, indeed, has never heard of children starving themselves because the food they were being served didn't have a high enough sugar content. Mrs. D is also forgetting that she, herself, would have never expected her own parents to tailor the family meals to what their child demanded. Common sense and confidence, that's what I was dispensing these days.

Mrs. D also has to contend with an adversary that her parents did not: the constant onslaught of marketing to children. Hannah is being force-fed a steady diet of enticements that are directly at odds with healthy nutrition every time she turns on the TV, listens to the radio, or passes the soda machine on the way to class. Our society's allegiance to unfettered advertising has in many ways made it enormously difficult for parents to do their job.

Culture and marketing are not the only challenges to parents and pediatricians. Anyone who watches *Dateline* on TV has more things to worry about than they can possibly handle. Will vaccinations give my child autism? Is he tired because of Lyme disease? Is she refusing to sleep in her own bed because she was sexually abused at day care? We have no bloody civil war outside our doors, no bombs dropping on our neighborhoods, no epidemic contagions ravaging our youngest loved ones—those are presently for other parts of the world. Instead, we have the perils of our imagination, fueled by an overpowering media that values sensation more than informative discussion, leaving us in constant fear of the catastrophe waiting to slip in under our door.

So genuinely worried parents rush in to see the doctor at the first signs of low-grade fever, or call the pediatrician at midnight because a child is coughing in her sleep.

"Is the coughing keeping her awake?"

"No, I only woke her up now to give her cough medicine."

It's midnight. She woke the child up. I let that one pass for the time being.

"Does she look like she's working hard to breathe? Making extra effort?"

"No, Doctor, in fact I think she's fallen back to sleep. I'm just worried it's something serious."

Who can blame her? And where else could she have turned?

When parents called because of fevers or rashes or coughs and I had to sort it out over the phone, I almost always asked, "How does she look to you?"

"What do you mean?" was the most frequent reply.

"Is she calm, happy, paying attention to what's on TV? Willing to eat?" The parent on the other end of the phone would so often be surprised that this was important information—a person didn't need to go to medical school to answer those kinds of questions.

Actually, a person didn't need to go to medical school for a lot of the services I provided to my patients—maybe most of them. The types of things we talked about were the things that all parents of healthy children should know about: Is their diet varied enough? Are they drinking too much juice? Are they falling asleep with a bottle in their mouths, putting them at risk for cavities? Such topics are best discussed in an unrushed setting, with a caring, knowledgeable person who can tailor the discussion to the parent's needs. But unfortunately, in this great age of information, a visit to the pediatrician's office is often the only way a parent can be offered this basic knowledge. I would repeat myself so much over the course of the day on these matters, I sometimes worried I was repeating it to the same parent. And where did I get my information about everything from pacifier use to choice of laundry detergent? Often from the same child care books I recommended for my patients.

My college roommate, Nancy, on the other hand, got her certification as a pediatric nurse practitioner after graduating with me from Fairfield University, and she learned an awful lot about well-child care and minor pediatric illness in the process. Her daily patient load, in a rural office practice, looked remarkably like mine, and her therapeutic interventions were similar. The biggest difference in how we spent our days was that she had more time per visit and her day was defined by her office schedule. She didn't take after-hours or weekend call or have any hospital responsibilities. The biggest difference at the end of the day was our paychecks; my time was a lot more expensive. The irony here is that an office model that had fewer available doctors could offer basic health care that was more in-depth and less hurried than what frequently happened in my wealthier but physician-heavy setting.

The longer I practiced general outpatient pediatrics, the more irrational and inefficient our delivery system appeared to me. The lessons I had learned in the navy were only reinforced during my years in private practice: Nurse practitioners and nurses are the logical choice for delivering most pediatric health maintenance and preventive care. This is what they are trained to do. This is what they are passionate about doing. And since their paths of training mean they are so much less expensive to utilize, they can take more time with patients. An hour-long visit with a nurse practitioner, regardless of how high-quality it is, will be nowhere near as expensive as a much shorter, and often harried, visit with a physician. In a specialty where patient education and reassurance are critical commodities, nonphysician practitioners can simply do a better job, less expensively.

With a health care system that is careening toward insolvency, it does not make sense to overtrain pediatricians and then underpay them because what they are actually doing doesn't hold much medical value. It does not make sense to invest huge amounts of time and money into training pediatricians to manage complex illness, then pay them the lowest salaries of any specialty because they spend their time chatting about bedtime rituals.

The road to rational health care reform is paved with logic. Pediatricians, in addition to being able to diagnose and treat pediatric illness, should be specifically trained in their residency programs to coordinate and supervise a team of other health care providers in the screening and education of healthy patients. The pediatrician remains ultimately responsible for all the patients cared for by the team, with appropriate protections from a predatory legal system. The experts are then in perfect position to keep the team current with the latest research, to provide professional education to them (as well as to learn from them), to closely monitor the level of care for good practice standards, and to watch for any red flags. Pediatricians could also coordinate services with the community, particularly schools. We would need fewer pediatricians per busy office, and they could put more time into the direct patient interactions that called upon their unique expertise. The more expensive level of care would thereby be directed to where it was most needed.

With such options for making pediatric care more affordable and more effective, the United States has few excuses not to offer universal health care to our children. This is not some crazy, abstract ideal. We only need to look to our military health care to understand what it might mean for the rest of us. This concept of team approach is also well described in recent pediatric literature,[21] but as long as our system of paying for health care is not aligned with such an approach, it cannot happen.

What would that team approach mean for a practice like Narragansett Bay Pediatrics? It would look different, and that notion makes me wince; it is the only kind of private practice I have ever known, and change is hard. But if I get past that, and think about the most cost-effective and medically sound approach that could be funded by universal coverage, then I would see that practice as perhaps having two or three well-paid pediatricians instead of six. In a single-payer system, they could be paid much as hospitalists are: reimbursements for patient visits, supplemented by a salary for their role as health team coordinators. They would be responsible for a team of nurse practitioners and nurses who would supply the first tier of health care and would have ready access to mental health professionals, nutritionists, and so forth. The end result would be more comprehensive care, for less money.

But this was not my reality and still is nowhere close to reality for most pediatric medicine. Having half as many doctors in my practice in our current third-party payer system would have meant half the income, with the job of paying all those nurses coming out of the doctors' pockets. It is hard to get insurance companies to pay the cost of something as crucial as having a nurse administer vaccines; they are certainly not going to pay to have a nurse discuss bicycle helmets. Their solution is to just have the doctor add it to the list of things she is already doing in that visit for a flat rate. If the doctor wants a nurse to do it, the doctor can pay for that service herself. Most doctors will not find this a viable option.

So our third-party reimbursement system meant that there was little effective division of labor on my routine well-baby checks. It was mildly satisfying to note a skin tag or birthmark; these were generally of little consequence to the child, but the chart would at least reflect that I was paying attention, in case they should turn out to be part of a larger picture later. My typical plan for such trivial abnormalities, scribbled hastily in the chart, was "observe." I might offer cream for diaper rash, or shampoo for cradle cap. I cannot discount the discussions that occurred in those exam rooms. It did matter what the child ate and drank, when he took his first steps, if he was developing language appropriately. But I felt more and more like Dr. Poppins in these conversations.

"It's important to read to Luke." (Source: *Parenting* magazine.)

"Try offering the strained vegetables before the applesauce." (Source: Maryellen, the nurse manager.)

This often was the level of expertise I was left to provide, pulling lines and lines of fuzzy child care advice out of a bottomless carpetbag, dispensing spoonfuls of sugar while the nurses, charting growth patterns and giving immunizations, went about the business of delivering health care.

THIRTY-ONE

Night Vision

To allow Randy some sleep, I was dozing on the bed in the guest room. The house was still, but the noise in my head would not stop: beeping from my pager, real and dreamed, disjointed fragments of conversations with parents, someone calling urgently, "Dr. Kozel!"

I jolted to full wakefulness and tried to focus.

Did I just give a medication order over the phone? Did I dream it?

I lay back down and tried not to think about the woman back at the hospital whose labor was progressing so slowly. If I allowed my thoughts to pull me there, I would lie awake and agitated, waiting for the phone to ring.

I was exhausted. This was a matter of routine for me. I had seen patients in the office until almost ten o'clock earlier that evening— or had it become, technically, yesterday? There was a respiratory virus making its way through the day care centers and schools in the area. Many of the children were running fevers and coughing through gobs of mucus; a few were developing ear infections. Most of these children were perfectly safe, even if their parents were frantic, but I sent a few of the more ill-appearing patients for tests, to rule out pneumonia or other complications.

As the evening wore on, the waiting time for the patients became longer and longer, and so not only was I dealing with illness and worry, but I had to trudge through children's fatigue and parents' impatience as well. I worked hard to maintain an interested, alert expression as I heard the hundredth description of fever, crankiness, and cough. I listened with concerned nods to how high the temperature was and how juicy the cough sounded. I tried to keep fatigue and tension out of my voice as I explained over and over again the nature of the illness, what to watch out for, simple measures to take.

"Tanvi is tolerating this illness very well, Mrs. Bhatt. The first twenty-four hours are the worst, and then you should see her gradually get better over the next three or four days. The fever is helping her fight the infection. It's not dangerous, so you don't have to keep using medicine unless the fever is making her very uncomfortable. Give her lots of fluids . . ."

The fact that I was dispatching them home in the evening without any cures took a variable amount of time to sink in with parents, just as it did during the day. It was rarely met with appreciation; a tidal wave of advertising coupled with a drugstore on every corner has conditioned many of us to believe that we can purchase a remedy for anything. When skeptical parents challenged me, I swallowed my frustration and kept searching my brain for the words that would convince, reassure.

"Believe me, Mrs. Bhatt, that cold medicine won't do anything but keep Tanvi awake—and suppress her appetite."

"Well, what *am* I supposed to do?" asked this tired, frustrated mother who put in an eight-hour day at work, just spent the entire evening in a pediatrician's noisy, germ-filled waiting room, was growing certain she would get no sleep tonight, and had to get up and go to work again tomorrow—if day care even took her child.

"Keep the room cool, elevate her head, let her sip . . ." I'd lost her. She headed to the checkout window to pay her fifteen-dollar co-pay "for nothing." Like many patients, she would never have come into the office in the first place if she hadn't thought I could do better than letting things "run their natural course."

Then, with an office full of patients still waiting to be seen, I was called away to the hospital's labor and delivery ward for a potential emergency. There, a healthy newborn shrieked the sound of false alarm in greeting to me—good news to be sure—but by the time I raced back to the office, I was hopelessly behind schedule.

I finally walked through my own front door a little before 11 PM. My daughters, having spent most of the evening alone—again—were now asleep: It was a school night. I could see from their halfhearted attempts at cleaning the kitchen that they had again cooked boxed macaroni and cheese for dinner. Randy, who had come home from the hospital around nine after seeing all his patients, was asleep on the couch. I stood stupidly in the kitchen for several minutes, trying to decide if I should eat or just go to bed.

And then the phone rang. I uselessly wailed "Nooooo . . ." out loud; only labor and delivery called directly rather than using the pager system. I felt defeated, almost tearful as I picked up the phone. It took several seconds before I could focus on the clinical situation—the obstetricians needed me to come back in to stand by for a C-section. I gulped down a Diet Coke and a few cookies. As I drove back over the distance I had just covered, staring like a zombie at the lines on the road, I thought to myself, as I had many times before, *I can't keep doing this.*

I was in the hospital for less than an hour and in quick succession changed into scrubs, dried off a screaming baby, congratulated the parents, and changed clothes again. I would be seeing them again in a few hours when I made my morning rounds. On the ride home, sometime after midnight, my mind drifted involuntarily to pointless calculations:

How many more years can I keep this up?

How many years till my youngest is out of college? Can I last that long?

If this is what it feels like at forty-six, what will it feel like at fifty-six?

I needed to be careful; this was like counting sheep. Some night I might fall asleep behind the wheel, lost in this kind of reverie.

I made it home safely and crawled between the sheets of the guest room bed. My pager went off five or six more times. Wakefulness and sleep blurred. This is the kind of sleep a pediatrician on call comes to expect. With any luck, the next electronic intrusion would be my alarm clock; it was set to go off in two and a half hours, the start of my "next" workday.

So now, in the 3 AM darkness, eyes willfully shut, I tried to distract myself from the din in my head. I tried to remind myself of the good things I'd accomplished that day. I could at least claim to have reassured some worried parents and, by being scrupulous, prevented their children from taking a lot of unnecessary medications. *First, do no harm.* I have always felt that Hippocrates set the bar a bit low. Perhaps his oath was a product of a night on call.

———

Randy and I both provided after-hours call coverage as part of our practices, and when our children were young, our professional effectiveness was directly related to the quality and scope of our child care.

Christine Chase, our own Mary Poppins, walked into our lives shortly after we moved to Rhode Island, carrying her six-month-old son, Dylan, in her arms. Over the ensuing decade we frequently joked that Christine would remain our babysitter until the girls went off to college, but by the time Caitlin was entering eighth grade, it was clear we were on a shorter timetable. Fourteen-year-old Caitlin seemed perfectly capable of managing for herself and keeping her eleven-year-old sister out of trouble until Randy and I got home. In fact, by that time Christine had started calling Caitlin when she needed a babysitter for Dylan.

As a parting gift, we bought Christine a framed watercolor of two small girls and a boy playing in the sand at the shore. Caitlin, Molly, and I drove over to her little house one evening after work so she could show us where she had hung the painting. I self-consciously swallowed back tears as I turned from the pastel-colored scene and walked out her door. My daughters' childhoods were slipping into memory, dissolving into that dream like space that beckons and grieves us at the same time. Two lovely girls, almost as tall as me, climbed into the car for the ride home. Oblivious to any sense of passing, they immediately began to fight over the radio.

"Caitlin, you are so annoying. Why do you always get to pick the stations?"

"Because you have no taste in music, dumbhead. Who listens to Eminem?"

"Oh yeah, like it's so cool to be obsessed with Sum 41. Don't you ever get sick of them?"

"At least I listen to music," Caitlin says to me. "Her radio stations make me want to shoot myself."

"Cait-lin," I threw in disapprovingly.

"Mom, have you ever heard the 'music' she listens to?" Caitlin asked, using air quotes for emphasis. "You would freak!"

"Mah-ah-am," from Molly, the number of syllables indicating her frustration, "why should she always get to work the radio?"

I smiled through the bickering. I loved every precious moment of their company. It mattered little to me what the drama on stage was; I enjoyed just being on the same stage, having a few lines in the script.

"Caitlin's in the front seat, Molly. She works the radio. Tomorrow you can pick the station—as long as I don't have to listen to the nasty details of gangsters' sex lives."

"Okay, that was awkward, Mom."

"Really, Mom. Who says that?"

At that very moment a Talking Heads song filled the car, and we laid aside our differences.

The world was moving she was right there with it,
And she was.
The world was moving she was floating above it,
And she was

We were all singing, heads bobbing. The girls moved their arms and torsos with a natural rhythm, their bodies at one with the music even as they were strapped down by seat belts. They backed up the instrumentals, mouthing the bass guitar.

"Bomp, babomp," in exaggerated deep voices.

"Bomp, babomp."

Feeling a certain obligation to keep my hands on the wheel and my eyes on the road, my dancing was confined to hunching and twisting my shoulders. Caitlin and Molly teased me about my stiff, deliberate movements and took turns imitating my jerky style until we were all crying with laughter. I shrieked at them to stop.

"I can't drive like this!"

I knew they would reenact the moves for Randy when we got home; there was no more recurrent a family joke than how terrible a dancer I was. Randy howled and joined the mimicry, the three of them gyrating mercilessly around the kitchen, me laughing so hard at my own expense that I was unable to mount any kind of respectable defense. I loved these girls. I loved these moments. I felt like it was day five of an enchanted week of sea, sand, and sky in the

Caribbean. I didn't want to think about the letting-go that was only a few years away.

Ten years into my practice at Narragansett Bay Pediatrics, my dancing may not have had much rhythm, but my workweek did. We had six doctors at the practice by then, a deliberate attempt to balance income and quality of life. None of us was seeing as many patients as some of our wealthier colleagues in town. We were splitting our pie into smaller pieces, but we had a little more time off. I was generally on call five or six nights a month. It would go as high as ten when any of the other doctors were away at conferences or on vacation, but then I would have respites, too. The beat went on. I was on call Wednesday, exhausted as I worked through Thursday, counted on a migraine Friday. But if I didn't have Friday-night call, I had the day off to recuperate. That was my cycle. Most weekends that I was on call—which meant a forty-eight hour stretch—I would not be on the following Wednesday, which was good because it would take me that long just to feel right again.

Randy was on call every third weekend, which meant, as it did for me, that his beeper was going off twenty-four hours a day, and he spent a good deal of time shuttling back and forth between home and the hospital. There was always one weekend a month, sometimes two, that we had off together. We looked forward to these like they were vacations. Of course, they were filled with yard chores and soccer games and laundry, just like any other weekend, and it took a conscious effort not to feel a bit deflated by Sunday night when our precious shared weekend hadn't quite felt like a trip to Paris.

Academic work revitalized me, however. When I sat in medical conferences, I felt the same excitement I had as a medical student. Whether it was new research, clinical material, or public health issues, I swallowed it all whole. I craved the intellectual drama that had pulled me into medicine to begin with. I sopped up the latest research on neurodevelopment in Washington, DC, and discussed sexually transmitted infections in Boston. An update on Lyme disease at Yale reinforced my practice methods and excited me with the details of new research. When I wasn't on the road, I was taking

THIRTY-TWO

A Ride through the Desert

When Caitlin was in seventh grade, she transferred to Lincoln School in Providence, and she loved it. Transferring to the all-girls Quaker school moved her into a culture of learning unlike anything she had imagined, and for Caitlin, born with an insatiable intellect, a whole new world had opened up—which left us with a dilemma. What about Molly? One private school tuition was a pinch. Two seemed impossible. But how could we not offer to Molly what we had to her older sister? I wondered if I could somehow increase my hours at work. Convincing ourselves we would "come up with something," we went through the motions of having Molly apply to Lincoln for seventh grade two years after her sister did.

At about this time, Aunt Dorothy, heading toward her eighty-fifth birthday, was in failing health and, although doggedly independent, was finding it harder to live on her own in Point Lookout. Her sixty-year-old house had more ailments than she did, and most of her friends were long gone. We moved her into senior housing on Jamestown, and she soon set up housekeeping with her frilly curtains and matching appliance covers. It was good to have her nearby, after so many years of too-infrequent visits, but it was also time consuming, getting her to all her doctor's appointments, worrying over her late-night calls about alarming blood sugar levels, sorting out the shameful mountain of paperwork that shadows health care for the elderly. My stress level had been turned up a full notch.

In February 2001, I took Molly with me to an infectious disease conference in Scottsdale, Arizona. The conference was wonderful, and I was pleased to realize my own expertise on tickborne illnesses. A case of fever, muscle aches, rash, and a distinctively abnormal white blood cell count was presented to our group of a hundred or so pediatricians, and I confidently blurted out, "I'd consider ehrlichiosis and test for that."

"No," chuckled the moderator good-naturedly. "You expect the monocytes to be affected with that." I felt the burn of embarrassment in front of all these strangers, but I knew I was right. So did the infectious disease specialist who stepped in and took the mike.

"Actually, that's an excellent thought. The type of ehrlichiosis that we are seeing on the East Coast characteristically attacks the granulocytes, not the monocytes, and would present very much like this case." A lot of heads turned and looked at me. That was fun. It was too bad, though, that I was enjoying medicine the most these days when I was in a dark, air-conditioned auditorium looking at slides.

One afternoon we took a bus ride out to the desert on a trip organized for the conference attendees. The easygoing chatter quickly turned to call coverage—no surprise for a group of pediatricians. What did surprise me was that every one of the dozen or so doctors on that bus, except for me, had found a way to avoid getting up in the middle of the night except in rare circumstances. Most of them practiced somewhere near a teaching hospital, so house staff—residents and interns—attended deliveries and admitted patients, notifying the private docs by phone, sometimes not till the next morning. Many of these pediatricians also had phone triage services, organized by their local hospitals, where nurses and nurse practitioners fielded the night and weekend phone calls, forwarding on only a few to the pediatrician. When I mentioned that I still covered deliveries and the ER at night, all heads turned to me for the second time that day. "You're kidding!" said one pediatrician about my age. "God luv ya!"

Continuity of care is generally considered to be a linchpin of quality primary medical care. Over the last decade or so, physician practice and pediatric on-call coverage have been scrutinized for practice trends and their effect on continuity of care. More and more community pediatricians have elected not to attend deliveries, see newborns in the hospital, or consult on patients who presented to the ER; hospital staff handle these. Also, larger hospitals have been providing those phone triage services for after-hour calls. As after-hours care, especially for minor illness, has grown more demanding and less likely to be reimbursed, pediatricians everywhere have looked for ways to balance professional commitment with quality of life. For those of us working at a distance from teaching hospitals, that meant sharing call with larger and larger numbers of doctors, taking on insanely busy call nights in exchange for having fewer of them.

I spent the rest of that bus ride looking out the window, counting the saguaro cacti as they marched by like prisoners with their hands up. I wondered what my life would feel like if I weren't carrying a call schedule. After all, the most frustrating of days were easier to handle if I wasn't sleep-deprived. Would I get more enthusiastic about explaining when to introduce solid foods? Would I be more patient with parents who came in with three pages of written questions? Would I stop constantly counting the days till I had some time off? And then stop counting the hours till I had to go back?

I worked out of a small community hospital that would never supply the level of coverage these other pediatricians had. I had never considered that when I'd eagerly jumped into my practice at Narragansett Bay. Even if I had, it might not have influenced my choice; one of the main reasons I had jumped from Wood River to private practice had been so that I could provide call coverage to my patients if they urgently needed me. I also wasn't so tired back then. To change my practice style now, not only would I have to leave my patients, but our entire family would have to move to a very different kind of community, somewhere much more densely populated, with a larger teaching hospital. Randy would have to move his practice, too.

One thing was clear. There was not going to be any easy solution.

THIRTY-THREE

An Open Door

A few weeks after my return from Arizona I was back in the office
on my regular schedule, having survived "payback" call for the
time I had been away. Caitlin's science teacher had asked if I might
make a presentation at their school, and I had offered to give a talk
on Lyme disease—always a juicy topic in our neck of the woods.
In between patients, and still on an academic high from Arizona,
I gathered up reference texts and journal articles, contacted a
University of Rhode Island researcher to borrow some teaching
slides, and set to work.

A few days before my presentation, I took Molly up to Lincoln for a
visit. She had been accepted for the following year and was spending
the day with her future classmates. The head of the middle school,
Cathy Capo, chatted with me about some of the school's science
teachers. "We have quite an interesting group," she said proudly.
She told me about the veterinarian who now taught biology and
physical science, and about the physicist who had left a university
position to teach at Lincoln when her second daughter enrolled.

"If you are on faculty, one daughter gets tuition remission, you
know," Cathy mentioned.

"Wouldn't that be great," I answered casually before I ran back to
my car, now in a rush to get to the office in time for the day's first
appointment.

Somewhere between Providence and Narragansett, as I hurried
to meet my first appointment of the day, I started to do the math. I
realized that with Molly's tuition covered, the school wouldn't have
to pay me very much for the two pieces to add up to close to what I
was earning in my practice. Even more significantly, breaking even
in that way would also include coming home every night knowing
that when I went to bed I would stay in bed until my alarm clock

went off, that when I left work on Friday I wouldn't be back until Monday. It would mean summers off, too. These were luxuries I'd never dared let myself think about before. And I would have time with my daughters. I had no misconceptions about becoming their new best friend, but the idea that I could communicate with them in ways that did not entail leaving long detailed notes—

Remember, Dad and I are both working tonight. Denise said she would pick you up at the bus stop. Call me when you get home. Bring a snack for after school. Your soccer uniform is in the dryer. I am leaving the money for your field trip. Good luck at the Science Fair!!!!

—that I could eat dinner with them, go to their soccer games, hear their voices, laugh at their jokes, seemed to be too good to be possible.

I felt guilty even thinking about what it would be like, as if I was fantasizing about running away with another man. But that's all it was, just fantasy. Nobody left a medical practice at the peak of a career to teach high school. Even if I could no longer see the invisible strings that held me to medicine, they must still be there— the nobility of purpose, the impact I could have on patients' lives, the respect for my expertise. It was too painful, too disappointing to consider that those strings had frayed over the years, that the productive, trusting doctor–patient relationships that I counted on to sustain me through all the headaches of modern practice seemed fewer and farther between.

I couldn't get the wild idea of leaving the practice out of my head, though. I began to picture what it would be like to commute with my girls, instead of dropping them off at a bus stop in the morning dark and not seeing them again until the darkness had returned. I pictured teaching science to high school girls, burying myself in textbooks again, playing in the lab. I pictured not being sleep-deprived. I pictured a rhythm in my work that resonated with all the other parts of my life, rather than the dissonance that currently described my days and weeks.

I gave my talk on Lyme disease to a group of seniors and Sarah Fogarty, head of the Science Department. The girls asked lots of questions and clamored to tell me their own stories.

"So, my aunt was really sick," began a tall dark-haired girl, waving her hands back and forth for emphasis, "and those doctors told her it was her pressure, and stress, and that she was overweight, but she finally figured out it was Lyme disease, and before they could treat it, she was dead." The last word was delivered with all the drama of a scary campfire story finale.

"Well, a lot of other things can get mistaken for Lyme disease," I started diplomatically, and we were off. I answered their questions; they laughed at my jokes. The presentation was met with rave reviews that genuinely seemed to exceed the requirements of politeness, and I had a blast.

"You're a natural teacher," Sarah Fogarty said kindly as she shook my hand good-bye.

As I passed by the school's front office, I ducked my head in on impulse. A few minutes later, as if in a dream, I was sitting across from Joan Countryman, the head of school, asking just what kind of salary and tuition benefits a science teacher could expect. Within a few days, Joan called me with an offer. Lincoln School needed a chemistry teacher for the following year.

THIRTY-FOUR

Just What the Doctor Ordered

I had always thought of a medical career as a predictable linear progression—four years of medical school leading up to more years of intensive clinical training, followed by the establishment of a medical practice that would span decades. But in a surprising way, twenty years after I had received my medical degree, I found I had come full circle from my naive student days.

By my senior year at Fairfield University, in the gray winter of 1976, I was in a holding pattern. I had sent out my carefully crafted medical school applications the previous summer, like so many polished messages in a bottle, and was helplessly, hopefully waiting for an answer.

The first hurdle on the road to medical school was to be granted an interview. Duke University's medical school utilized local alumnus interviews, and I was directed to Yale, half an hour up the road from Fairfield, to meet the Duke grad assigned to interview me. He was the director of what was then referred to as the "Infertility Clinic."

I borrowed a pink turtleneck sweater from my roommate, Nancy, and drove my battered Pontiac up I-95, in search of one medical school so that I could interview for another. My insides were trembling for this, my first interview, as I took a seat in the small office that belonged to Dr. Watson. He was a thin, deflated-looking man in his thirties, with short, neat hair and rimless glasses that suggested a well-circumscribed life.

We spent little time talking about me. Dr. Watson's opener was, "I'm not sure I should even be encouraging you to go into medicine."

Excuse me? I had come with no idea what I would be asked, or on what I would be judged. A depressed, prematurely burned-out doctor was not at all what I had been expecting.

He went on about the long hours, the paperwork, how little time he had for his family. I assumed he was referring to the pretty woman and two small children captured for him in a simple frame on his desk. Were they having problems?

"You will never see your kids," he sadly warned.

I felt awkward, at a loss for what to say. I was a college kid with big dreams and a borrowed sweater, trying very hard to act like a grown-up. I didn't know how to comfort him; I couldn't even grasp what was wrong.

My mind kept swirling around the conversation on the drive back to Fairfield. I was worried and disappointed. Had this been some kind of a test? Was I supposed to have jumped in with a convincing counter? Was there something about me that led him to feel utterly hopeless about the future of medicine? Later, I replayed the scene over and over again for Nancy, and we analyzed it to death. What never occurred to me was that the man might simply have had a point.

Twenty-five years later, when I was offered an opportunity to leave medicine, I was torn up by the choice. Being a doctor was my identity. Even as the reality of twenty-first-century medicine poked holes in that identity, it was still hard to walk away. Randy, fully aware of the financial risk, supported the idea right from the beginning. He, of all people, understood the toll that medical practice was taking on our lives. But I couldn't imagine what I would say to other people—especially my partners; I doubted even my close friends and relatives would understand. I had been there, in Dr. Watson's office, listening to the disillusionment of someone I thought had it all, and I had been unable to make any sense of it. Now I was the one on the other side of the framed picture, and I wasn't sure I could explain the yearning and disappointment any more clearly than he had. First I had to admit it to myself.

᠁ did I have to admit? I wanted my expertise to be seen as a ᠁ot something that thwarted parents' plans for what ᠁m the visit. I wanted to do what I was trained to do, ᠁e form of my clinical practice into whatever shape ᠁s decided it should have. I wanted to be paid for the

happy. But it was getting harder to keep them in mind, much less get satisfaction from them, because they were surrounded by walls of vines and brambles that blocked the view, and that would some-times scratch me, too, if I wasn't careful where I tread. If someone asked me about my work in the garden, my response would increas-ingly be about what was going on with all that overgrowth, not about the blossoms.

I ended up spending much of my time as a customer service repre-sentative: I reassured the worried well, and I worked to convince health care consumers that they were getting their money's worth. I adapted: I put most of my energies into delivering types of health care that would have been better delivered in another setting by different kinds of health care professionals, resigned to the reality that my practice model was shaped more and more each year by corporate or bureaucratic myopia rather than medical science. I was a one-woman convenience store: I worked impossible hours, so that even the most trivial of problems could get handled as if they were emergencies. I was a functionary: Parents needed that camp physi-cal form yesterday.

Most demoralizing of all, I was conscientious and much too often was disrespected for that, too, as I swam against a tide of parental expectations in my determination to avoid unnecessary tests and medications—to do no harm.

Could I have kept it up? Sure. I am nothing if not resilient. There are plenty of pediatricians and family practitioners and internists who are doing exactly that. Keeping it up. Would that have been the right decision for me? In the end I decided no, it would not. I needed to break out of the corner I was being painted into. I needed to reclaim the person I felt I was and reconsider how I could best use whatever gifts I had to share. A few years of teaching science, I decided, was just what the doctor should now order.

THIRTY-FIVE

Ripples of Grief

The first five phone calls were the hardest. I called each one of my partners one Sunday afternoon and confronted a mix of surprise, sadness, encouragement, and anger. The next day, back at work, I told the nursing and office staff I would be gone in six months. From that day on, the atmosphere in the office was changed for me. My colleagues wished me well; that was clear. But a step like this was unsettling for everyone, challenging everyone's assumptions, not just mine. I imagined that each of my partners must have been running their own mental balance sheet in response:

How satisfied am I with this life? What parts would I gladly walk away from if I could?

Why do I keep doing what I do? What aspects of it do I love? What would it take to make me leave?

The balance would have tipped a little differently in each doctor's case. How it leaned had a lot to do with who in the ensuing weeks treated me with warmth, who with civility, who sometimes got tears in their eyes, who pointed out the financial pitfalls, who disapprovingly asked when I was going to get around to letting the patients know.

My departure was set for the last week in August. I would go right from my practice to new-teacher orientation. This gave my partners a chance to break in my replacement, and it gave me an opportunity to earn a doctor's income as long as I could. In June, three months before my departure, I officially announced to my patients and the world that I was leaving medicine. I immediately felt a huge weight lifted from me, and I realized how eager I was to start my new life.

People's reactions were not always what I expected. Parents of my complicated special-needs patients and those of my patients with chronic illness expressed the sadness most openly. I explained to each of them what arrangements I had made for their follow-up care, but the feelings went deeper than pragmatic concerns, for them and for me. If I had moments of doubt over that summer, it accompanied those special partings.

Most of my other patients graciously said they would miss me, but curiosity was the predominant theme.

"Aren't you going to miss being a pediatrician?"

"How can you just give it all up after all that training?"

"So why did you decide to leave?"

They didn't ask me anything I hadn't asked myself many times, but I felt I had to construct my answers carefully. I wouldn't tell them how tired I was of explaining that most illnesses just run their course, why antibiotics were a bad idea more often than they were a good idea, and that so many of the travails of parenting—sleepless nights, teething, toilet training—were not medical problems at all. I wouldn't say that I was frustrated by all the parenting dilemmas that had been turned into pathology—temper tantrums, bed-wetting, not reading before kindergarten. I wouldn't tell them how hard it was to come up with interventions just so parents would feel like they were getting their time and money's worth.

I knew where my families were coming from, so I looked for truthful answers that they could relate to. I confessed I was tired, that it was getting harder and harder for me to recuperate from call nights. I pointed out that I had two teenage daughters at home who were spending way too many nights on their own. Parents could sympathize with this and would nod supportively in response.

The question I found most painful was the one I couldn't bring myself to answer honestly: "Will you still practice medicine?" The truth hurt. I would have loved to continue to practice—moonlight at Narragansett Bay or volunteer at a community clinic. But this would almost certainly be out of my reach. Doctors can't put a Band-Aid on someone without malpractice insurance, and malpractice insurance costs a lot of money. It seemed unlikely I would ever be able to practice occasionally or for only a fraction of the year and be able to afford the insurance premiums necessary to do so. Likewise, an employer would find it a prohibitive expense if I were not generating regular income for the practice. It was a bitter pill to swallow, but liability issues meant I might not be able to practice again.

What most surprised me was the reaction of doctors outside my practice when they heard the news. They would stop me in the hall at the hospital, in the office building, in the cafeteria—anywhere. "Is this really true?" they would ask. "Are you really going to teach?"

"I am," I'd say, nodding. I expected to see goodwill or skepticism or even derision. But more often than not, a sadness would shadow colleagues' faces, and they would start in with their own stories, as if I was the first person they had told, as if they assumed they were the only other one with such a story.

"I wish I could leave," said the surgeon who cornered me in the mailroom. "Medicine is nothing like it used to be. But what would I do? If I could live on a teacher's salary, I'd leave tomorrow. But I just can't."

"Man, if I could get out of this business, I would in a heartbeat," said an ENT specialist I brought my daughter to. "The malpractice situation is ridiculous, the patients are ungrateful. Why do I do this? I should have time to spend with my kids."

"That would be so great. I would love to just walk away from this," my eye doctor said as I sat there in his office, waiting for my exam. He looked sadly off in the distance for a long moment before he put on his doctor face and turned the conversation to my vision.

When I had my first appointment with a new gynecologist, she looked at my chart and exclaimed, "Oh my God, you're that pediatrician who left to become a teacher!" I knew what was going to follow; over the next ten minutes, sitting in my paper gown on the exam table, I listened to her frustrations and regrets, an echo of my own story.

It went on and on. At first, I would come home and tell Randy, "You wouldn't believe how Tom responded," or "You should have seen how sad Walt looked. I thought he was going to cry." But after a while I hardly mentioned it.

"How did Caitlin's orthopedic visit go?" Randy asked after her annual scoliosis check.

"The usual," I answered, shaking my head. "We spent the first few minutes talking about me and the next ten minutes talking about him and how miserable he was, and then we managed to fit in a few minutes about Caitlin."

I was startled by the discovery that there was an epidemic of sad, disillusioned, depressed doctors out there. Nobody talked about it, at least not until they found someone they knew would understand. They brought me their sad stories in lowered voices and averted eyes, in exam rooms, and lines at the grocery stores, and at parent–teacher conferences. They still do.

THIRTY-SIX

The Long Good-Bye

The summer before I started teaching, with one foot still in my medical practice and the other pointed toward an uncertain future, I spent every spare moment studying chemistry texts. I retaught myself electron configurations on the drive to Molly's camp in New Hampshire that July and was up to acid–base chemistry by the time we picked her up in August. Sitting at the kitchen table after dinner, I doggedly tackled every homework problem I came across, hammering away at my calculator, completely absorbed in the luxury of solving specific problems with distinctly correct answers. I still felt the tug of invisible strings, pulling me back to my practice, but I steadily grew more confident about my decision.

Marian, my brother Brian's wife, came down from New Hampshire one weekend in early August to fetch Aunt Dorothy for a visit. Two days after their arrival back at Brian's home in Nashua, Aunt Dorothy ended up in the intensive care unit at the local hospital, deathly ill with pneumonia. What I thought was going to be a one-week break from looking after Aunt Dorothy that summer turned into a twice-weekly commute to Nashua to sit by her withering body, listening to the sighs of her ventilator, stroking the loose skin of her quiet hand. My brother John and sister Helen made pilgrimages, too, as Brian and Marian adjusted to a constant stream of sad, overnight guests.

As the summer waned, I grew nervous about my last day of work. Sentimentality always made me uncomfortable. I dreaded saying good-bye to everyone; I didn't know what to say, how to respond to their kind wishes. Randy, my most stalwart supporter through everything, announced a plan to help me navigate the exit. He and Caitlin and Molly were going to drive over to Narragansett to pick me up after work and take me out for a nice dinner.

As I wrapped up the last hour's worth of patients on that last day, awkwardly accepting their thank-yous and good-byes, Maryellen, the nurse manager, pulled me aside. "There's a call for you," she said with concern. "It's about Aunt Dorothy." I loved the way Maryellen referred to her. Not your aunt Dorothy, just Aunt Dorothy, like it was personal for her, too.

I picked up the phone and heard the voice of the ICU doctor on the other end of the line. He kindly reiterated to me what he had been telling me all week. Aunt Dorothy wasn't getting any better, and she wasn't going to. She had been on the ventilator, unresponsive, for three weeks, and it was time to let her go. I knew he was right, but I didn't want to say good-bye. Aunt Dorothy was the only one who had really mothered my siblings and me, and I loved her.

"We'd like to gradually remove her from the ventilator. She's probably not going to breathe on her own. We think you should be here."

"When are you going to do this?" I asked, wincing back tears.

"We should do this today. There's no reason to prolong it."

No reason, except my brain was about to explode. How was I going to pull the plug on my medical career and watch Aunt Dorothy die all in the same day? But I just could not put Aunt Dorothy on a back burner.

I hung up the phone and turned to Bob and Maryellen. "They're taking her off the ventilator. I have to drive up there as soon as I finish here," I explained in a quivering voice. More people crowded into my office, and uncomfortable looks began darting back and forth.

Meg finally spoke up. "The thing is, we were having a surprise party for you tonight at the beach club. We've been planning it for weeks—the catering, everything. I don't think they'll let us reschedule."

This latest revelation had to wait on line for a few seconds before it could be processed. "That's why Randy's coming over?" I asked, finally putting it all together.

"Yep," said Meg, sadly. "It was his job to get you there."

I closed my eyes against the crushing pain of loss that suddenly filled my chest, and slumped in my chair, holding my head in my hands. "I can't be there," I said. It was all I could manage.

"We know," Maryellen said softly. "You need to be with Aunt Dorothy."

They gave me a few minutes to collect myself, which I did by packing the previous fifteen minutes up into a little corner of my brain, like a jack-in-the-box. I only had to hang on to my sanity for another half hour.

I went through the motions of seeing the last two patients and then Maryellen popped her head in the room again.

"Mae is here with her parents."

I glanced at the schedule with alarm. "She's not on the schedule."

"No, they just stopped by to say good-bye. They said they'd wait."

Mae. Ten years earlier, my first morning on call for the practice, we had met in the ER, a sick little girl and her worried parents. I had been so eager to set out in the morning darkness to see her, was so engrossed in her care. Now I just wanted to escape out the back door.

Mae and her family were waiting for me at the front desk. Her father, speaking formally to me in his thick Korean accent, thanked me for seeing them. He wanted me to know how grateful they were for all I had done for them. "You are a wonderful doctor, Dr. Kozel," he said, "but now your family needs you, and it is time to be with them. You are doing the right thing. We wanted to say this to you."

Mae, just a few inches shorter than me now, slight in her frame, bright eyes dominating a beautiful, sweet face, beamed at me the whole time her father was speaking. "Thank you for everything, Dr. Kozel," she said shyly in her hushed, breathless voice.

"We will never forget you," said her father.

That was the moment my heart broke.

I managed to get out the back door and to my car and pointed my way north. The jack-in-the-box sprang loose, and I began to sob, wiping away my tears like a windshield wiper in a downpour, trying to keep a visual hold on the road. I cried all the way to New Hampshire. I cried for Aunt Dorothy, and the sweetness of Mae, and the fear of failure in my new life. But mostly, at that moment, I cried for the doctor who saved Casper, who had held a beating heart in her hand with reverence and love, who had felt the power of science and the nobility of medicine, and who, for a while at least, got to be everything that a doctor can be.

Epilogue

She was glad about it . . . no doubt about it
She isn't sure what she's done
No time to think about what to tell them
No time to think about what she's done
And she was

—Talking Heads

The word *doctor* comes from the Latin word *doctus,* or "teacher." This was first pointed out to us in medical school, as a way of underscoring the physician's role in educating the patient. But that was a time in my life when such philosophical connections were unlikely to grab my attention, and I filed this etymological nicety away in the same place I stored sayings like *There's no I in* team.

As a young doctor, I had cared a lot about some connections: how a headache could be related to prostaglandin levels, why Lyme disease could be traced back to how many acorns fell off a tree in a given season, or how knee pain could be caused by flat feet. But when it came to my place in the universe, or even in the course of my own life, I was a pragmatist at heart and devoted little time to reflection. I was most comfortable measuring my daily life in tasks accomplished rather than fulfillment found: *I saw thirty patients today. I started that baby's IV. I read this week's* New England Journal of Medicine.

Twenty years into my career, faced with the complicated decision to shift my *doctus* gears, I had to bring my constantly humming engine to a halt. I idled at a crossroad just long enough to consider who I was and what was important to me. What astonished me were not the answers themselves, but that I had never before considered the questions completely worthy of my time.

———

Lincoln School sits high on a broad expanse of grass on the east side of Providence. At seven forty-five every morning, droves of breathless, squealing girls in plaid jumpers and kilts converge on the long, three-storied yellow building, jackets unzipped, wisps of unruly hair caught in their mouths as they giggle and greet one another. The groggy upper-school girls, with their kilts hiked up well above their knees and mountains of books slung in nylon packs across their backs, step through and around the younger ones or lag behind, like ponies oblivious to a stampede of Scottish terriers. I start each day now blending into this herd as they converge on the red front doors of the Quaker school, trying not to sound too startlingly cheerful as I greet sleepy students, making my way through the noisy throng up to my lab in the science wing. Tossing my books and computer down on a lab bench, I scan the room, taking in the previous day's scrawling on the board, the haphazard piles of lab reports, the various experiments in progress. I find sticky notes everywhere—*Dr. Kozel, Lisa and I stopped by to see you but you weren't here. We don't know how to do problem four.*—signed with hearts or happy faces. I look around the room the same way I look around my house when I get home in the evening. It is full of things that matter to me. It is good to be here.

Chemistry always came readily to me, an endless series of puzzles just begging to be solved. Now I get to teach this subject to classrooms full of bright, lively teenage girls, and I can hardly contain my excitement or my animation. I scrawl formulas over the board, make silly jokes, buzz shamelessly around the room depicting a heated gas molecule.

"Dr. Kozel, the juniors told us you could imitate a mole. Do it, please. Pleeeease."

I have been teaching the class about the mathematics of chemistry, and the basis for its counting system, the "mole." But who can pass up the chance to imitate a goofy-looking mammalian? I scrunch up my nose and buck my teeth and curl my hands up like claws, and they laugh so loud I have to close the door so as not to disturb Mrs. Fogarty's biology class next door.

"What was it like being a pediatrician, Dr. K?"

They love listening to my stories. And why not? It's that or balancing equations. I know what they're doing, but I have also discovered that I love to tell stories.

"You met your husband over a cadaver? No way! Tell us about it!"

"Well, we oughta learn a little something about the periodic table, don't you think?"

"Pleeeeease!"

So off I go, at least for a little while, floating around the room, laughing, performing, having the time of my life, even as I segue into the subject at hand:

"And speaking of that exciting 'period' of my life . . ."

"Ughhhhhh!" they groan.

Then off I go in a different direction, coaxing their brains to switch on new pathways, enthusing about the reactivity of sodium, posing now on the left side of the large laminated periodic table, now on the right, arms swaying between the metals and the nonmetals, full of puns and silly jokes, encouraged by their giggles and wisecracks. I get them to see science, to feel the connections that stirred me when I was their age.

When I told Caitlin, who was entering ninth grade, that I was leaving my practice to teach at her school, her exact words were: "You are going to ruin my life." Molly, on the other hand, about to start Lincoln in the seventh grade, was delighted. Not requiring quite as much personal space at that point in her life, she could see the benefits of rides to school and having her own personal ATM machine upstairs in the chemistry lab.

Caitlin was in my class three years in a row, squeezing as many science courses into her high school years as she possibly could, sitting in the back by the window, doodling and writing silly limericks, not making eye contact. We had a tacit agreement: I never called on her; she did well enough to earn straight A's. As time went on she'd drop off some of her artistry on my desk after class, smirking to herself. There was one of a fairy draped elegantly in a periodic table, complete with elements listed in their proper order. I laughed in amazement as her exiting classmates and I pored over the intricate drawing. It wasn't until she was halfway down the hall that I came to my senses.

"Caitlin," I called after her, "when exactly did you do this?"

"During class. It keeps me from falling asleep when you're droning on," she added, her mouth partly open in a half smile.

The girls behind me gasped in mock horror.

"We feel so sorry for you, Dr. K. How did someone as nice as you end up with such an awful daughter?" said her close friend Ashley, shaking her head in a show of mock disapproval.

"I know, Ashley. I only wish she could be more like you."

"We all do," added Drew, sympathetically.

We were enjoying ourselves, as was Caitlin. I grabbed some thumbtacks and posted the chemistry fairy prominently on the bulletin board out in the hall, like a finger painting from kindergarten. We were well into the world's longest-running game of "she who laughs last."

I rarely had a moment alone in the chemistry lab. Even last period on Friday, when my schedule looked empty and I was secretly hoping that all adolescent thoughts in the building had turned to boys and parties and what to wear that was not green plaid, students would drift into my room.

"Dr. Kozel, can I make up that flame tests lab?"

I looked up from the pile of papers I thought I was going to grade that period. Sarah's freckled face looked hopefully at me.

"Uh, you mean now?"

"Unless you're busy . . ." She smiled sweetly.

"Okay," I said, unwilling to stand between our field hockey goalie and the beauty of science. "Let me just set it up. Mary, what's up? You didn't miss the lab." Mary, tall and shy, was hanging back in the doorway.

"I know, I just couldn't figure out the calculations from last week's lab. I was wondering if you could go over them with me?"

I looked around for the electrolyte solutions Sarah would need as we talked. "All right," I conceded. Mary's dad grounded her if she got less than a B. "I just have to get Sarah started."

I turned to get out the Bunsen burners only to find Erika and

Leslie, two of my Advanced Placement students, entering from the other door at the front of the room. "Hey girls," I said, wondering what the chances were that this was a social visit.

"Dr. Kozel, we're really having trouble with that last homework problem."

"You'll have to take a ticket. There are a couple of inquiring minds ahead of you." Surely they would have no heart for a delay at this hour on a Friday afternoon. They would turn right back around, head for the lounge in search of weekend plans.

"That's fine," they said agreeably, unslinging their bulging backpacks and settling in at a table.

I was still fumbling for equipment when I saw Caitlin slide in. "Hello, Dr. Kozel," she singsonged. She had gotten in the habit of using my room as a place to study when it was free, and she headed to her usual seat in the back, propping her feet up on an empty chair.

"Uh-oh, Dr. K, the slacker's here," remarked Sarah as she snapped on her goggles.

"Very funny, Sarah. Mom, when can we leave?"

"Ummmm, I got a little bit goin' on here, hon," I said, glancing around the room. Girls were multiplying in front of my eyes.

"Mom," she started slowly, as if talking to a dull child, "the only reason anyone is here is because they are sucking up." Chuckles bubbled up from around the room.

Mary was seated by the blackboard, chewing nervously on her pencil, staring at her lab report with a frown. I sat down next to her and helped her untangle the mess of numbers scratched randomly over her report sheet, imposing some order, adding labels, constructing tables. By the time we were done with the editing, she arrived at the answer herself.

I pushed myself up from the table just in time to see Alexa tumbling in, talking fast and looking worried. "Dr. K, I was just working on my lab report and I think I did the last procedure wrong! Was I supposed to weigh the crucible first?"

"Good one, Alexa," chuckled Caitlin, now settling in with her crumpled copy of *Macbeth*.

I handed Alexa the large plastic bottle of copper sulfate. "Gloves and goggles, " I warned her.

"Caitlin, are you going to Snow Ball?" asked Sarah.

"Focus, Sarah," was my parting shot as I walked over to the table where Leslie and Erika hunched over their books. They were working on a problem about bond energy, frustrated that they couldn't relate a certain wavelength of light to the number of molecules it would break down. Meanwhile, Molly charged into the room breathless; the sprint up the stairs under a forty-pound backpack had winded her.

"Mom . . . ," she started, then halted at the sight of the three-ring classroom.

"Did you calculate the energy required for one molecule, or the entire amount?" I asked, holding off Molly with the palm of my hand.

"Huh?" started Leslie, but I could almost predict the number of seconds that would pass before one of them exclaimed "Ohhh!" and resumed the scribbling and calculating.

The musical sound of breaking glassware brought my attention back to the lab benches. Alexa's begoggled face was turned to Sarah, who was staring dumbfounded at the shattered beaker as if this was her first experience with gravity. "I am soooo sorry," she began, but I cut her off.

"Everyone's entitled to break a beaker now and then," I reassured her. "If I don't have to order new glassware at the end of the year, we haven't done enough labs." I value caution in these girls, but it is risk I am interested in cultivating. Both girls visibly relaxed.

"You moron," laughed Caitlin from behind her book.

"Shut up," chuckled Sarah.

"Ah, that's the Quaker spirit," I added.

I reached for the dustpan and broom in the corner. This was not the first time that lab brought back memories of playgroup. "So what's up, Molly," I finally asked, sweeping shards of glass off the floor and counter as I spoke.

"Okay." Molly always announced her stories like this, as if she had just concluded something. "So, Breana's mom is picking her up at five thirty? And she wants to know if I can hang out with her? We were going to get something at Starbucks?"

My thirteen-year-old and I went back and forth about this, the end of each of her sentences drifting up to the ceiling as if attached to a helium balloon. I finished my negotiations with her in between helping Alexa transfer a hot sample off a burner and confirming one of Sarah's measurements.

Erika and Leslie were on the move again. "Thanks, Dr. Kozel. We got it. Have a nice weekend!" They waved good-bye. I glanced up at the clock. It was well after three.

This happens every day now and still takes me by surprise. I check the time when I get in every morning, and then, it seems, the next time I look up it is time to go. I am that absorbed in what I am doing. And that happy. My life is full of connections now: the pleasure I take in basic science and in being in the company of young people, the constant tickling of my intellect and the voice I can give to it, the rhythm of my work and the life I share with my daughters. I don't watch the clock or count the hours or tick off days till vacation. I am not waiting for anything.

I also relish any chance I get to share my pediatric knowledge. Many of my new colleagues have young families, and lots of health questions. They will often start off a conversation with "I hate to ask you this, but . . ." I smile immediately, knowing what's coming. And I happily delve into whatever the topic of concern is. The internal battle I waged against the changing tide of medicine is over.

At one point, at the height of post-9/11 terrorism fears, Joan Countryman, the head of school, asked if I would be interested in giving a talk to the faculty on bioterrorism—smallpox in particular. America's political leaders were publicly making all kinds of hare-brained suggestions for dealing with the possible threat, and I leapt at the chance to bring science into the discussion. I spent weeks compiling slides and gathering research. My presentation started with the history of vaccines—"Which comes from the Latin word for 'cow'!" offered the Latin teacher, Mr. Bagg, from the back row— and went on through the methods of transmission of smallpox and the flaws of a mass immunization program. It was a wonderful, energizing opportunity for me to blend clinical medicine and teaching.

———

My colleagues often ask me if I miss pediatrics. I generally answer in two ways. I get a lot more sleep now. But when I miss pediatrics—which I do very much—it's the medicine I practiced ten or fifteen years previously that I miss. I wish I could put my skills to use as a volunteer, but malpractice insurance remains, to date, an insurmountable obstacle to any form of practice for me.

I left pediatrics wondering if I would ever be able to answer the constant stream of questions from others about my decision. I knew I held the answers inside me, but they were all tangled up, like a string of discarded Christmas lights. One evening, driving home from school, the Providence skyline receding in my rearview mirror, Molly surprised me by lobbing a cannonball of a question from the backseat.

"Mom, are you sorry you went to med school?"

The question stunned me, and I babbled like Porky Pig for several seconds before I was finally able to stretch the sounds into a coherent sentence. "My God, Molly. No. Being a doctor was everything I wanted to be. It's who I am." I leaned intently toward the rearview mirror, catching her eyes. I felt this urgency to get it right, to make her understand. "If I had never gone to medical school, never understood what makes people sick or how to make them better, my life would have been—" I searched for the right word "—smaller. I would have gone through my entire life feeling that I had missed out on something I was meant to do."

I was surprised at the urgency in my voice, the burning need to make this clear. "Health care changed in a lot of ways; it started wearing me down," I continued, shaking my head at the road in front of me. "But I can love teaching now—I can love doing all sorts of things now—because for a big part of my life, I got to be a doctor." This was the moment of truth for me, but it was not until I said it out loud that I understood it. Medicine had challenged me, thrilled me, frightened me, and humbled me. But it had never disappointed me. It was the system we use to deliver health care, with its inefficiencies, misplaced incentives, and misguided use of resources, that distorted the doctor–patient relationship and exhausted me.

I sat back in my seat and played back my own words, astonished by their passion, and stunned by the clarity of their conviction. I would always feel ambivalence about leaving medicine, I knew, but never any about having entered it.

Now, when my eager students tell me they are thinking about medical school, I urge them on emphatically. These are bright, confident girls, and I have seen firsthand that their generation has what it takes to move our society forward. Too discerning for rhetoric, they will ask hard questions about the challenges in our society and demand intelligent answers. They have grown up in a complex world and are not expecting simple solutions. They will, in fact, expect to be part of the solution. Most important, these young women have been raised with a global view, and they have as much electricity flowing through their hearts as through their brains; they will not accept social injustice, and particularly inequitable health care, as an inevitable by-product of a free market. I have one enthusiastic word for these would-be physicians and pharmacists, policymakers, and poets: "Go!"

Acknowledgments

Many talented and generous people have left their mark on this book. I would first like to thank my editor, Jonathan Cobb, for the remarkable guidance he offered in the final shaping of this story. I also wish to thank the wonderful people at Chelsea Green Publishing, with a special note of gratitude to Emily Foote, for helping to make this book a reality.

My indebtedness reaches several years back, to the beginning of this project. I will always be grateful to Lauren Sarat, my writing instructor from Brown University, for teaching me the ways a writer pays attention, and I will never forget that Charles Capaldi treated me like a serious writing colleague long before I gave him much reason to.

I would like to acknowledge as well the E. E. Ford Foundation, for making it possible for me to participate in the Brown Writers' Symposium. I am also grateful to the many friends and colleagues who have studied this manuscript at various stages, for being so generous with their support and careful with their advice. And a special note of thanks goes to Liv Blumer, John Minahan, Nancy Cottrill, and Louise White, all of whom moved this project forward with their particular areas of expertise. Last, but not least, a million thanks to my editors-in-residence, Caitlin and Molly Kozel, for the endless grammar checks, gentle critiques, patient (mostly) tech support, and constant encouragement.

REFERENCES

1. *2003 Massachusetts Medical Society Physician Workforce Study.* July 2003. www.massmed .org/workforce.
2. *2009 Massachusetts Medical Society Physician Workforce Study.* July 2009. www.massmed .org/workforce.
3. athenahealth and Sermo. *2010 Physician Sentiment Index: Taking the Pulse of the Physician Community.* February 2010. www.athenahealth.com/sermo.php.
4. Task Force on Circumcision. "Circumcision Policy Statement." *Pediatrics* 103 (3): 686.
5. A. Hibbs and S. Lorch. "Metoclopramide for the Treatment of Gastroesophageal Reflux Disease in Infants: A Systematic Review." *Pediatrics* 118 (2): 746–752.
6. National Center for Health Statistics, CDC. *SIDS Rate and Sleep Position, 1988–2003.* www .cdc.gov/mmwr/preview/mmwrhtml/00017250.htm; Hiroshi Shiona, et al., "Sudden Infant Death Syndrome in Japan." *American Journal of Forensic Medicine and Pathology* 9 (1) (March 1998): 5–8.
7. Task Force on Infant Positioning and SIDS. "Positioning and Sudden Infant Death Syndrome (SIDS): Update." *Pediatrics* 98 (1996): 1216–1218.
8. Ronald T. Brown, et al. "Prevalence and Assessment of Attention-Deficit/ Hyperactivity Disorder in Primary Care Settings." *Pediatrics* 107 (3): e43.
9. Tara F. Bishop, et al. "Physicians' Views on Defensive Medicine: A National Survey." *Archives of Internal Medicine* 170 (12): 1081–1083.
10. PricewaterhouseCoopers Health Research Institute. "The Price of Excess: Identifying Waste in Healthcare Spending." 2008. www.pwc.com/us/en/healthcare/ publications/the-price-of-excess.jhtml.
11. Kaiser Family Foundation. "Trends in Health Care Costs and Spending." 2009. www.kkf.org/insurance/upload/7692_02.pdf.
12. Stephen M. Schwarz and Michael Freemark. "Obesity." *emedicine from WebMD* (2010). http://emedicine.medscape.com/article/985333-overview.
13. Centers for Disease Control and Prevention. "Overweight and Obesity." 2009. www.cdc.gov/obesity/causes/economics.html.
14. Julius B. Richmond. "Pediatrics and Society: Some Observations on the Sociology of Pediatric Education and Practice." *Pediatrics* (June 1959): 1175–1178.
15. Peter F. Belamarich, et al. "Drowning in a Sea of Advice: Pediatricians and American Academy of Pediatrics Policy Statements." *Pediatrics* 118 (4): e964–e978.
16. AAP Department of Community and Specialty Pediatrics. "Resources Help Primary Care Clinicians Address Mental Health Concerns." *AAP News* 31 (7): 34.
17. Laura K. Leslie, et al. "The Food and Drug Administration's Deliberations on Antidepressant Use in Pediatric Patients." *Pediatrics* 116 (1): 195–204.
18. Tanvir Singh, et al. "Decreased Use of Antidepressants in Youth After US Food and Drug Administration Black Box Warning." *Psychiatry* 6 (10): 30–34.
19. AAP Department of Community and Specialty Pediatrics, "Resources Help Primary Care Clinicians Address Mental Health Concerns." AAP News Vol. 31 No. 7 July 2010, p. 34
20. Jerry L. Rushton, et al. "Pediatrician and Family Physician Prescription of Selective Serotonin Reuptake Inhibitors." *Pediatrics* 105 (6): e82.
21. Tina L. Cheng. " Primary Care Pediatrics: 2004 and Beyond." *Pediatrics* 113 (6): 1802–1809.

About the Author

Dr. Maggie Kozel graduated from Georgetown University School of Medicine in 1980 and went on to specialize in pediatrics, completing her residency at the Bethesda Naval Hospital. She then served as a general medical officer on board the USS McKee and as a pediatrician at the US Naval Hospital in Yokosuka, Japan. When she returned from Japan, Dr. Kozel worked as a pediatrician in the active reserves at the US Naval Hospital in Bethesda. She also entered private practice first in Washington, DC, and then in Rhode Island. For ten years she was a pediatrician/partner at Narragansett Bay Pediatrics. Dr. Kozel, a Fellow of the American Academy of Pediatrics, left practice after seventeen years, and is currently teaching high school chemistry in the Providence area. She lives in Jamestown, RI, with her husband and daughters.

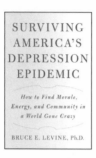
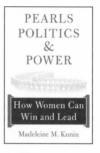

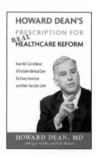